Thematic Structure in
Syntax

Linguistic Inquiry Monographs
Samuel Jay Keyser, general editor

Thematic Structure in Syntax

Edwin Williams

The MIT Press
Cambridge, Massachusetts
London, England

This book was set in Times Roman by Asco Trade Typesetting Ltd., Hong Kong, and was printed and bound in the United States of America.

Library of Congress Cataloging-in-Publication Data

Williams, Edwin.
  Thematic structure in syntax / Edwin Williams.
      p.   cm. — (Linguistic inquiry monographs ; 23)
  Includes bibliographical references and index.
  ISBN 0-262-23173-5. —ISBN 0-262-73106-1 (pbk.)
  1. Grammar, Comparative and general—Topic and comment.   2. Generative grammar.   I. Title.   II Series.
P291. W55   1994
415—dc20   93-33688
                                                                          CIP

Contents

Contents

Series Foreword

We are pleased to present this monograph as the twenty-third in the series *Linguistic Inquiry Monographs*. These monographs will present new and original research beyond the scope of the article, and we hope they will benefit our field by bringing to it perspectives that will stimulate further research and insight.

Originally published in limited edition, the *Linguistic Inquiry Monograph* series is now available on a much wider scale. This change is due to the great interest engendered by the series and the needs of a growing readership. The editors wish to thank the readers for their support and welcome suggestions about future directions the series might take.

Samuel Jay Keyser
for the Editorial Board

Acknowledgments

For the intellectual and spiritual wherewithal enabling the research and writing of this book, I would thank first the Department of Linguistics at the University of Massachusetts, where this work began, and where it was encouraged by everyone at every step.

Next, Henk van Riemsdijk, whose influence on me has been so great that it is hard to imagine what kind of linguist I would have become without it.

I am also grateful to the Program in Linguistics at Princeton University, which has provided me with a congenial and stimulating environment since 1990, and to Bob Freidin, who has brought it about. A sabbatical leave in the fall of 1991 made possible the early work on the ideas for the manuscript.

Conversations with—and objections from—Jane Grimshaw, Viviane Déprez, Bob Freidin, Maggie Browning, James Pustejovsky, Bill Hawkins, Lyn Frazier, Tom Roeper, and Jim Higginbotham were crucial to turns the work has taken.

For a close reading of an earlier draft, I owe Len Babby a close reading on his next book, but I will not be able to match what he has done for me.

I would like to thank Viviane Déprez for sharp critiques of a number of sections of this book.

Finally, I am grateful to Anne Mark for her expertise in bringing order and readability to the text.

Introduction

This book is an attempt to draw into a coherent whole a number of different ideas about the locality of theta role assignment. As I anticipated when I undertook the project, a number of problems have arisen that do not arise when the topics are treated separately. I have consequently been led to retheorize widely—the Empty Category Principle, the theory of linguistic scope, the binding theory, and weak crossover have all been reworked. I have also been forced to abandon several conclusions I had reached earlier; one, for example, concerns the relation of control to predication (see section 3.2), and another is the notion that *there* (and existentials in other languages as well) is a scope marker (see section 4.2 for a new idea). Other ideas have found new applications.

But the basic threads of earlier work remain the same. At the core are (1) an assumption about the relation of X-bar theory and theta theory that is encapsulated in the term "external argument": *the relation between the fact that a verb has a subject argument and the fact that the VP it projects is a one-place predicate is a consequence of the definition of "head"*; (2) the notion that *theta relations are strictly local, though chainable*; and (3) the notion, ultimately derived from morphology, that *the notion of "head" is relativized*, a notion of widespread applicability, having arisen first in my work on morphology proper (Williams 1982b and subsequent work, as well as chapter 2 of this book, explore its relevance to syntax, specifically its role in category determination (1982b: chap. 5) and in the analysis of raising constructions (1986a, forthcoming b, chap. 4)).

One overall theme will be to diminish the role of movement, and especially of constraints on movement, for these will be seen to duplicate independently needed constraints and mechanisms. As an example, consider affix hopping. This is a rule that relates two head positions. But is such a rule needed? I think not. Are there head-to-head relations? Perhaps not primitively, but only as a combination of two other relations: head-to sister [1], and head-to-phrase [2], as shown in (1).

(1)

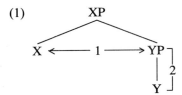

So, for example, faced with the fact that certain verbs select certain specific prepositions in their complements (*give-to*, for example), it might seem that we need to extend subcategorization from a head-to-phrase relation to a head-to-head relation. However, a head-to-phrase relation will do, if the phrase contains the "signature" of its head, as in (2).

(2)

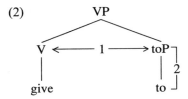

Of course, since *to* is a preposition, a *to*P is also a PP. The point here is that we already have the X-bar mechanism (the definition of head) to accomplish this without extending the range of subcategorization. To return to affix hopping: affix hopping is a head-to-head *movement*. Can the affix-hopping relation be reconstrued as a subcategorization relation? Yes, trivially. In general, all cases of head movement, NP-movement, and the context sensitivity known as subcategorization can be decomposed into a chain of relations of the sort illustrated in (1).

As this discussion suggests, another overall theme of the book is to explore the full explanatory role of the notion "head of a phrase." The mechanism of "feature percolation" I take to be nothing more than the consequence of this notion—a claim that has been an explicit basis of my work since Williams 1978a. In other words, there is no feature percolation that is not a direct consequence of the definition of head.

Another fundamental assumption is a strong version of the lexicalist hypothesis, one that says that with respect to syntax, a word has "top level" properties, but no internal structure. For example, a passive participle may lack the ability to assign a subject theta role, and syntax will know that it has this property; it may get this property from a rule of affixation, but syntax will not know that it got the property this way. In the same vein, rules of morphology do not apply after rules of syntax.

The lexicalist hypothesis has consequences for the theory of functional heads that is argued against in this book, though perhaps the consequences have been exaggerated. Under a strict version of the lexicalist hypothesis, such as the one outlined in Di Sciullo and Williams 1986, a verb cannot move to Infl to "get tense," because this implies that a rule of morphology (the one that creates tensed verb forms) applies after a syntactic rule (the movement from V to Infl), just the sort of interaction that is prohibited.

But it is important to bear in mind that for every theory in which an affix or feature is picked up in the course of derivation, there is a nearly indistinguishable theory in which the affix or feature is already there and is "checked" in the course of derivation. The real empirical difference must be determined either by examining the cases where a syntactic rule is sensitive to the morphological complexity of a word, not just to its having certain features, or by realizing that no such cases exist. This issue is significant for at least one sort of case discussed in section 5.1.2.1.

Although nominally this is a book about theta roles and the locality of theta role assignment, it has proved impossible to hold the rest of the theory still, and several general categories of linguistic theorizing have needed to be rethought.

1. Scope. The usual notion of scope is identified with the rule of quantifier raising (QR), but a more articulated notion is required to prosecute the ideas of chapters 4 and 5. Language has some sort of rule of wide scope assignment: a rule that assigns to an item X some phrase of arbitrary size containing X as the scope of X—call this QR. But QR, here called Quantified Argument Scope Assignment, is in fact relevant for only a portion of the scope phenomena that language exhibits. The rest are accounted for by rules of a different sort: the Head Scope Rule and the Adjunct Scope Rule of chapters 4 and 5 (also see Williams 1982b, 1984). Heads have scope over their projections, and adjuncts over their sisters. Quantified Argument Scope Assignment is in fact applicable only to *arguments*; it does not apply to predicates, a crucial ingredient of chapter 4.

2. The ECP. In chapter 4 the notion of relativized head is shown to give an account of the adjunct/argument distinction that the ECP requires; the distinction is able to relate the ECP to scope in a way unavailable to other theories because here the NP-movement constructions do not fall under the ECP: the ECP is reduced to conditions on scope.

3. X-bar theory. First, a new X-bar construct is shown to be necessary, the "bivalent" projections of chapter 1. Beyond that, the notion "head

of," the notion X-bar theory is about, is shown to be a relative, not an absolute, relation.

4. Binding theory. Binding theory is turned into an aspect of theta theory in chapter 6. In addition, the elimination of empty functional projections in chapter 5 leads to a reevaluation of what relational predicates the binding theory conditions are to be stated in terms of; "precedes" is shown to be a grammatical (and not, for example, a language-processing) predicate relevant for a range of phenomena, including weak crossover, superiority (argued to be a special case of weak crossover in any case), and the Path Containment Condition. The Weak Crossover Condition, formulated as the Leftness Condition, is shown to be a condition on referential dependence, not referential equality, and is shown to govern any sort of NP dependency, including quantifier-scope interactions.

I am encouraged by the wide spectrum from which these considerations must be drawn, though, for the more disparate phenomena that can be patched into the web of evidence, the more confidence I have that the proposed theory is on the right track.

The overall framework assumed in this book is the NP-Structure model of Van Riemsdijk and Williams 1981, but especially the reduced version of this model (Williams 1986b) in which there are only two levels of representation, NP-Structure and S-Structure. As I will argue in chapter 4, NP-Structure has A-movements already represented in it, so there is no D-Structure distinct from NP-Structure. And as I have argued in Williams 1986b, S-Structure has quantifier scope already coded in it, so there is no LF distinct from S-Structure. The first element of this reduction is explicitly argued for here. The second element, the elimination of LF, plays a direct role in only a small amount of the material in this book, and is mentioned here by way of full disclosure.

Chapter 1 outlines a theory of the clause—specifically, of the distribution of nominative Case and Tense. This theory is meant as an alternative to current affix-hopping/verb movement theories; it is also the only theory compatible with the notion of predication developed in chapter 2.

Chapter 2 is the heart of the book: it develops the formalism for the notion "external argument" that is used in the rest of the book. The formalism consists of (1) the locality of theta role assignment, and (2) the X-bar-theoretic mechanisms that allow the chaining together of local theta relations to give long-distance theta effects. One such long-distance effect is theta role assignment to the subject—the verb and the subject are not sufficiently proximate for the former to directly assign a theta role to the latter.

Chapter 3 reviews the issues surrounding the syntactic expression of the subject-predicate relationship. The standard account reduces all predication to the syntactic [NP XP]$_S$ relation, with NP = PRO for all but a small number of cases (tensed clauses). The problem with this theory is that it relies too heavily on the notion of control to establish the basic theta relations of a sentence, and I believe that there is no theory of control that can do what is needed. The chapter includes a study of "controlled" adjunct modifiers (*John died singing*) and concludes that one group of them does have the properties of control, but the rest have the properties of direct theta role assignment to their modifiee. But if the proper theory of "control" for these structures requires a subcomponent whose empirical effects match the effects of direct theta role assignment in the first place, then we gain nothing by substituting the theory of control for the theory of theta role assignment.

Chapter 4 extends the methodology of chapter 2 to include NP-movement. Just as the relation of verb to subject is achieved by chaining together theta relations, so the NP-movement relation is achieved by chaining together more primitive theta relations. It is demonstrated that no features of the NP-movement relation are explicated by the theory of movement, once the proper theta-theoretic concepts are deployed, and almost all of them must be deployed anyway. The behavior of expletives and idioms in NP-movement constructions is shown to require exactly the theta theory at hand.

Chapter 5 demonstrates that the supposed need for verb movement derives from a conflict that arises between surface position of elements on the one hand, and modification and "argument of" relations among elements on the other. Verb movement is facilitated through the proliferation of empty functional projections. Chapter 1 has already developed a theory of inflection without empty functional projections, thus removing the facilitation. And chapter 5 removes the conflict, by supplying a more adequate theory of modification.

Chapter 6 shows the intertwining of binding theory and theta theory. On the one hand, binding theory is shown to be a relation among theta roles; and on the other hand, the theta assignment relation is shown to be a binding relation. Hence, each theory contains the other. The two predicates of binding theory, th-command and precedence, are sorted out, and precedence is shown to be relevant to referential dependence, not referential equality.

Chapter 1
Juncture and Clause Structure

1.1 Preliminaries

To begin, I will examine a notion of clause structure that is entailed by the theory of predication, or theta role assignment to the subject, which is the subject of chapter 2; hence, this chapter will assume in rough form the consequences of the next. Clause structure will be viewed as an instance of a novel X-bar construct, the bivalent juncture. I will substantiate that this construct has other instances, and I will also try to place this notion of clause structure in a wider theory of syntactic juncture, or nexus, to borrow a term from Jespersen (1924) .

In that theory, the topic of section 1.3, one of the typological dimensions of the space of junctures is "theta" versus "nontheta." Theta theory is in part a theory of theta junctures: in a theta juncture, one element in the juncture is a theta role donor, and the other is a theta role recipient. So, in juncture (1a) *saw* gives to *Mary*, and in (1b) *left* gives to *John*.

(1) a. [saw Mary]$_{VP}$
    b. [John left]$_S$

Importantly, though, not all junctures are theta junctures. It will be useful to enumerate the ones that are not; the full discussion will take place in chapter 2.

The relation of *seems* to its infinitival complement is not a theta juncture; instead, it is what I have called *function composition* (see Williams 1981a, 1982b, Di Sciullo and Williams 1986, and section 2.4). Rather than assigning a theta role to its complement, it transmits its complement's theta role to its subject:

(2) John [seems sick$_i$]$_i$.

That is, [seems sick]$_i$ is a predicate by virtue of containing the predicate *sick*. See chapter 2 (and Williams 1985a,b) for a full account.

The relation of a relative clause to its head noun is also not a theta juncture; all theta roles are satisfied inside the relative clause itself:

(3) the man [who I saw t]

Saw assigns a theta role to trace (*t*), or to *who*, so the relative clause is closed, theta-theoretically speaking. The juncture is an adjunct juncture, which is only to say that the nonhead is not an argument of the head. A kind of predication does hold between *man* and *who I saw*, what Pustejovsky (1984) *called $\bar{A}$-predication*, but that predication is not based on theta role assignment. Similarly, there is a kind of predication, or at least some sort of relation, between *your friend* and the clauses that follow in the following cases:

(4) a. Your friend, I saw him at the shore.
    b. As for your friend, we are not going to the shore.

Whatever this relation is, it does not involve theta roles; rather, it involves a requirement that the clause be "about" the NP in some sense whose strength varies from construction to construction.

All these constructions, including the ones that do involve theta role assignment, share a central property, that of locality; they are all junctures, differently interpreted, and the locality derives from the fact that only junctures (i.e., immediate sisters of a common node) are liable to these interpretations. But I will reserve the terms *argument of*, *predicate*, and *predicated of* for the junctures that are based on theta roles.

1.2 The Basic Structure of the Clause

I have chosen to begin by discussing the basic structure of the clause, because this enables us to immediately confront the role of movement in explanation in a way that engages a wide range of recent proposals. The discussion is based on material that will be laid out more formally in chapter 2 but is made explicit enough here to get the argument going.

Recent and classical proposals explicate basic features of clause structure with movement. In particular, the verbal inflections are realized on the verb through a combination of affix hopping (Chomsky 1957 and numerous recent accounts) and verb movement (Emonds 1978, Pollock 1989).

Given the lexicalist hypothesis, we are immediately skeptical of these accounts, although, as remarked in the Introduction, the ease with which such accounts can be reworked with "feature checking" instead of "feature assigning" prevents us from drawing decisive conclusions about them.

The principal features of the Aux system of English are that (1) the form of the auxiliary verbs is determined from left to right, (2) the determination is absolutely local, (3) the subject is marked with nominative Case, and (4) the first verb is tensed. That is, in the sequence *might have been running*, *might* determines the form of *have*, *have* the form of *be*, and *been* the form of *run*; and *might* is tensed. For (1) and (2), the obvious device to use here is subcategorization, since subcategorization is absolutely local and (in English) operates from left to right. I will therefore concentrate on (3) and (4).

In this section I will present an alternative account of the distribution of Case and Tense, based on an elaboration of X-bar theory: specifically, I will propose that the construct we call a clause is akin to another construct, the coordinate structure.

Some simple and appealing assumptions about the structure of the clause, ones we will have good reason to accept in the course of this book, quickly lead to paradox.

First, there is the notion (Williams 1981c, Chomsky 1986) that S is headed, and that Tense (Williams 1981c) or Infl (Chomsky 1986) is the head of S, as in (5).

(5)

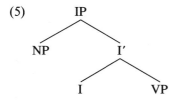

A compelling reason for this is the fact that complementizers select for the value of the Tense or inflectional element: *that* takes Tense, *for* takes *to*, and so on, suggesting that these elements are heads:

(6) *that*: _____ TenseP
    for: _____ toP

Second, there is the theory of the subject-predicate relation, which, I have proposed, involves the following ideas:

• The verb has a distinguished argument that is the "head" of its argument structure.

• The index of that head percolates to the maximal projection of the V.
• The resulting category, VP_i, is semantically a property defined by abstracting on argument i.
• The subject is assigned as the argument of VP_i under the usual sisterhood restriction on theta relations.
• "NP-movement" constructions arise not from movement but from an application of the notion "relativized head" (Williams 1982b, Di Sciullo and Williams 1986): when the head verb of a VP has no distinguished argument, the index of some unsaturated complement percolates its index to the VP:

(7) John was $[seen_0\ t_i]_{VP_i}$.

The 0 subscript in (7) indicates that the verb has no external argument. Other X_0s include Infl, *seems*, some adverb phrases, some instances of negation, modals, and many (but not all) Ps, as in (8).

(8) a.

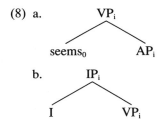

    b.

See chapters 2 and 3 for full elaboration.

Now, putting these two ideas together (in particular, structures (5) and (8b)) results in (9).

(9)

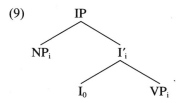

But this violates the definition of external argument; the index of argument i of V is external to VP, and is bound by I′ as in (8b), but it is then realized *internal* to the maximal projection of I; since it is represented on the head of IP (I′), it should be realized external to IP.

The problem is that we want I′ to be maximal for the purposes of the subject-predicate relation, but nonmaximal for the purposes of determining the category of S ($=$ IP) .

1.2.1   The Clause as a Coordinate Structure

There is another construction where a very similar nexus of requirements must be met: namely, coordinate structures, as in (10).

(10)

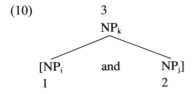

Here, NPs 1 and 2 are maximal projections, and yet they are both categorially related to NP 3, which dominates them both. We know that NPs 1 and 2 are maximal, because they have reference, and only maximal projections have (ordinary NP) reference. Furthermore, they can serve as binders,

(11) [[every boy]$_i$ and his$_i$ mother]

and only maximal projections can serve as binders. Coordinate structures are doubly headed, in that each of the conjuncts is categorially related to the whole conjunction, and doubly headed structures have the property that each of the heads by itself counts as maximal.

Now, we will borrow this double-headedness for the analysis of clauses and solve the problem we started with. Let us continue to suppose that S is the projection of Tense (or Infl, or anything equivalent), but let us also suppose that Tense is realized on both the subject and the predicate, as in (12).

(12)

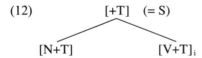

Now, we have a doubly headed structure, and each part will count as maximal. Hence, the definition of the external argument is satisfied, since [V + T] is maximal.

But what does it mean for an NP to be tensed? Suppose that nominative Case is simply the realization of Tense in the nominal category. There are other instances where the same feature is realized in two different categories, and where the morphological realizations differ considerably. For example, the feature [+plural] is realized in both the nominal and verbal categories in English, but the morphological manifestations are very different:

(13) $[N + \text{plural}] = N\hat{\ } s$
     $[V + \text{plural}] = V\hat{\ } 0$

So this should be no obstacle to our proposal. Nominative NPs are simply tensed NPs.

1.2.2 Bivalent Functors

Now, what is the nature of doubly headed structures?

I will first try to locate them in the space of possibilities already available, by identifying three grammatical oppositions.

First, there is the *functor/nonfunctor* distinction. I take a functor on X to be anything that combines with X without changing its theta structure. The functors then include *seems*, grammatical Case, certain but not all prepositions (the "grammatical" ones; see the discussion at the end of Williams 1989), and so on. These are the X_0s mentioned earlier. As (8a) illustrates, *seems* combines with an AP such as *sad* to form the VP *seems sad*. The external argument of *sad* is not used up in this combination, but is preserved; this is what makes *seems* a functor. This is an application of the notion "relativized head" of Williams (1982b) and Di Sciullo and Williams (1986): if the real, or "semantic," head is not marked for something, in this case the external argument index, then a nonhead can supply that marking. See chapter 2 for further discussion.

Second, there is the *head marking/governing* distinction. A functor on X may be realized on the head of X, or may govern X. Accusative Case in Latin versus accusative Case in Japanese differ in exactly this way: in Latin accusative Case is realized on the head of the object, whereas in Japanese accusative Case (the particle *o*) governs the object.

Finally, there is the *univalent/bivalent* distinction. This distinction can be illustrated with prepositions. Most prepositions are univalent; that is, they take one object. But there are some bivalent prepositions as well, for example, *from-to*:

(14) John played the banjo from Alabama to Louisiana.

From-to is not simply two prepositional phrases; rather, it is a single prepositional phrase with two parts. This can be seen in the following contrast, assuming that only a single prepositional phrase may be fronted:

(15) a. From Alabama to Louisiana John played the banjo.
     b. *To Mary for Bill I gave a book.

Furthermore, *from-to* means more than the sum of its parts—it desig-
nates a path by specifying its endpoints. In short, *from-to* is a thing in
itself, not simply *from* plus *to*.

But what kind of thing is it? It is a *bivalent* lexical item—that is, a
lexical item that has two parts, each of which projects a phrase. We may
represent the item as follows:

(16) [from_P, to_P]_P

By convention, each of the parts of this bivalent structure projects a
phrase, and then the combination of these two phrases is itself a phrase,
as in (17).

(17)

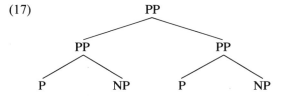

The phrase (like the lexical item (16) from which it is projected) is doubly
headed. The fact that the two parts are both Ps determines that the whole
will be a PP.

The projection of a complex lexical item [X, Y] can be defined as
follows:

(18) [X, Y]P → XP YP

[X, Y] is the (complex) lexical head of [X, Y]P and therefore determines
the category of [X, Y]P. For example, [from, to]P will be a prepositional
phrase, since both X and Y are prepositional. In the case of S, where
[Nom, Tense] is the head, we may regard this as defining a lexical category
of its own, since there is no independent reason to associate any of the
usual categorial features with Nom or Tense. Therefore, the category of
the phrase will also be [Nom, Tense]. Why is the clause composed of an
NP followed by a VP? Technically, the clause is simply "NomP TenseP,"
but on the assumption that NP is the only category that can project as
NomP and VP is the only category that can project as TenseP, the clause
will be "NP VP." If this is correct, it may be that the *for-to* infinitive ([for,
to]P) actually has PP VP structure.

Now, the structure in (17) is a sort of coordinate structure. In fact, I will
shortly propose that coordinate structures and structures like (17) are
both instances of bivalent structures. We can see some effects of the
"coordinate" status of (17) in the following contrast:

(19) a. *What did John go from A to?

     b. What did John go from the top of to the bottom of?

(19a) shows that the Coordinate Structure Constraint applies to such cases as (17), and (19b) shows that across-the-board (ATB) extraction is possible from such structures.

    Now, what about the structure of clauses? Suppose that Tense is not a simple functor, but a bivalent one:

(20) [Nom, Tense]

Then S is a projection of this item and will consist of two parts, one nominative and the other tensed. If Nom is defined only for Ns and Tense only for Vs, this determines that the two parts are NP and VP, respectively, as in (21).

(21)

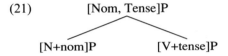

        [N+nom]P   [V+tense]P

What is the category of the whole? Since the two parts do not share features, the category of the whole is simply the projection of the functor itself, and so is [Nom, Tense]P.

    Thus, a clause is the projection of a head-marking bivalent functor, the one in (20). In fact, the clausal head is not always head-marking. [for, to], for example, is a bivalent governing functor, as in (22).

(22)

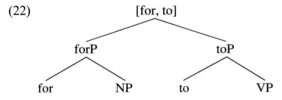

The diagram in (23) illustrates the space of possibilities.

(23)

	univalent	bivalent
governing	P PN	for NP to VP
head-marking	NP_{Case}	NP_{Nom} VP_{Tense}

The further dimension not illustrated here is the functor/nonfunctor distinction.

    (24) lists some bivalent functors.

(24)   Bivalent   Determines
        functors   category?   Head-marking?
    a. [Nom, Tense]   +   +
    b. [for, to]   +   −
    c. ['s, -ing]   +   −, +
    d. [from, to]   +   −
    e. [ablative, ablative]   +   +
    f. [0*, and]   −   −
    g. [0, and*]   −   −
    h. [et, et]   −   −
    i. [both, and]   −   −
    j. [either, or]   −   −
    k. [despite, -ing]   +   −, +
    l. [keep, from]   +   −, −

Case (24e) is the Latin ablative absolute construction. Cases (24f–j) are various types of coordination.

Case (24c) shows that the two parts of a bivalent item need not both be uniformly head-marking or not; the possessive is governing, and -*ing* is head-marking. This is an automatic consequence of the nature of each part. The affix '*s* exists independently of this structure, as does -*ing*, and their properties carry over to their role in the gerund. This is generally the case, though not necessarily.

Generally the two parts of a doubly headed structure are different, but often they are the same. In the Latin ablative absolute, for example, both parts of the clause structure are realized in the ablative. This means that the predicate of this structure must be an N or an A (or a participle), since only these can bear ablative; and this is indeed the case.

1.2.3 Coordination

In strict coordinate structures, there are several possibilities. In some, the two parts are marked identically, as in the Latin *et...et* 'both...and' coordination (24h). In others, they are marked differently (24i–j). And in the simple use of *and*, the marking appears on only one of the conjuncts, as in (25). The other is not marked, hence the *0* in (24f–g).

(25)

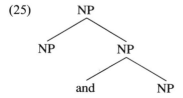

In the second column of (24), I have marked which of the bivalent structures determines the category of the whole structure. Basically, for the coordinate structures, the category of the whole is determined by the conjuncts, whereas for the rest of the structures, the category is determined by the function itself. The theory of projection must achieve this distinction at least, and if along the way it derives the law which says that two things that are conjoined must be of the same category, then that would be an encouraging bonus. Suppose that the complex conjunction is [0, and], as indicated above. Then (26) follows.

(26) [0, and]P = 0P andP

In other words, the coordinate structure consists of a projection of 0 followed by a projection of *and*. We will take "a projection of 0" to mean any phrase at all; one way to look at this is that the 0 head places no restrictions on what the phrase can be. We will take *and*P to be any phrase of the form in (27).

(27) [and XP]$_{andP}$

That is, the word *and* itself is a simple lexical item, like a preposition. What is the category of *and*P? If *and* has no category features, and we will assume that it does not, then the category of *and*P will be determined by the category of the complement of *and*, as is usually the case. Thus, *and*NP will be an NP, and so on.

In English *and*P barely exists as a phrase that occurs outside of a coordinate structure, but in many languages it functions as a comitative PP. And even in English it serves the following limited role:

(28) a.   John left. Oh, and Bill, too.
     b.   *John left. Oh, Bill and, too.

(28b) shows that *and* is prepositional, not postpositional; it is a construction one might expect in a language like Japanese, as pointed out by Ross (1967).

So, 0P can be any category at all, and *and*P will be the same category as the complement of *and*. What then will be the category of the two together?

(29) [0, and]P = 0P andP

Suppose we enforce the usual rule for determination of category: if the head ([0, and]) belongs to a category, then it determines the category of the phrase. In the special case where there are two heads, the phrase can have no determinate category unless the heads are categorially similar.

Hence, we might see the "Law of the Coordination of Likes" as arising from the need of the phrase to have a determinate category.

Conjuctions are not simply binary, they are *n*-ary. There are two ways to expand the representation of the conjunction we have discussed with the Kleene star:

(30) [0*, and]
     [0, and*]

This will give rise to the two kinds of conjunctions that are found, one where *and* separates all the conjuncts, and the other where *and* occurs only before the last:

(31) John, Bill, Danny, and Tom
     John and Bill and Danny and Tom

Since in the coordinate structures, the coordinate lexeme *itself* does not determine the category of the coordinate structure as a whole, we add a fourth dimension to our categorization of phrase types: the $\pm$-category-determining dimension. We will see reason in chapter 2 to associate "category-determining" with "category-bearing," so we may simply designate this as the "categorial" feature:

(32) $\pm$ governing
      $\pm$ functor
      $\pm$ bivalent
      $\pm$ categorial(-feature-bearing)

So, for example, [0, and] is a governing noncategorial bivalent functor.

Both the coordinate structure and the clause, then, are headed by bivalent functors. There is an important difference between the two, which the theory outlined here does not account for: namely, that one, but not the other, is subject to the Coordinate Structure Constraint.

In fact, both kinds of structures exhibit ATB extraction:

(33) a. Who did [pictures of t] [upset t]?
     b. Who did you [see t] and [imitate t]?

The mystery then is simply why ATB extraction is not enforced for clauses, demanding that any extraction from VP be accompanied by an extraction from NP.

I think the answer lies in the semantic symmetry of pure coordination, versus the asymmetry of the subject-predicate nexus. In the purest case, the two terms of a coordinate structure can be exchanged with no loss of meaning; this is certainly not true for the NP and VP of a clause:

(34) a. Ten is two times five and half of twenty.
      b. Ten is half of twenty and two times five.

In fact, many uses of coordination are not perfectly symmetric; for example, in (35) it is strongly implied that the activity denoted by the second VP follows in time the activity denoted by the first VP.

(35) John went to New York and bought a painting. ≠
     John bought the painting and went to New York.

Hence, these cannot be exchanged, at least not without changing the meaning. Interestingly, it is only the symmetric cases that fully require ATB extraction:

(36) a. *What is ten two times five and half of t?
      b. What did John go to New York and buy?

And, intriguingly, when the coordination is asymmetric, it is only the last conjunct that permits extraction:

(37) *What city did Hinkley go to t and buy a gun?

The picture that emerges, then, is this: ATB extraction is allowed for any bivalent structure (or more generally, for any juncture). However, it is enforced (the Coordinate Structure Constraint) for those structures that are semantically symmetric. The clause is neither categorially nor semantically symmetric. We will see in chapter 6 that the asymmetry of the clause is a binding asymmetry; in an extended sense of the term, the subject is the "antecedent" of the verb phrase.

I have emphasized the parallelism between the structure of the clause and the compound PP construction, but there is one notable difference between the two: the *from*P of a compound [fromP toP] construction cannot be moved away from the *to*P, whereas the subject of a clause can be *wh*-moved away from its predicate.

At first glance, it would appear that the *from*P can in fact be moved away:

(38) From which city did John go to Cairo?

But this example shows nothing, since we already know that the *from*P and the *to*P can each occur independently of the other, and (38) could be derived from a source where each occurred, but not as a double-PP unit.

There are, however, idiomatic uses of the [fromP toP] unit for which there are no corresponding uses of the *from*P or the *to*P by itself. One such case is time-interval specification:

(39) a.   John was there from Monday to the following Thursday.
　　 b.   *John was there to Thursday.
　　 c.   John was there till Thursday.

Given this, the following example shows that the *from*P cannot be moved away from the *to*P:

(40) *From which day do you want to be there to the following
　　　　Thursday?

This example is greatly improved if *till* is substituted for *to*; but this makes precisely the relevant point, since (39c) shows that *till*, unlike *to*, can be used separately from *from*.

　　We are left, then, with the puzzle of why the subject can be moved away from the VP. What is the difference between [PP PP]$_{PP}$ and [NP VP]$_{+Nom, +Tense}$ that would allow movement in one case but not the other? A plausible candidate is that the two members of the former structure are categorially identical, whereas in the latter structure they are not; perhaps movement cannot move one of two categorially identical conjuncts.

1.2.4   Agreement

The mechanism of bivalent projection coordinates the occurrence of Nom on the subject with the occurrence of Tense on the VP. However, it says nothing about agreement between the two; and properly so, if agreement is in fact an independent phenomenon.

　　In the first place, agreement does not occur in other bivalent structures —for example, coordinations—even when they are perfectly symmetric: obviously, one can coordinate a plural with a singular, or a feminine with a plural. The Cases must agree, but this is because Case is like a category feature, and the whole coordinate structure must bear a Case.

　　In the second place, agreement is found in a much wider class of environments than just the clausal nexus. For example, it occurs in the juncture between prenominal modifier and head noun of an NP; and it occurs in the construction shown in (41).

(41)

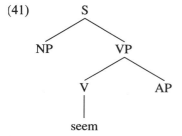

In many languages, agreement holds between NP and AP. Since AP and NP are not in the clausal nexus, the mechanics of the clausal nexus cannot be responsible for agreement directly.

Rather, agreement can be explicated in terms of the notion "head." Recall that the external argument is the "head" of its argument structure. Given this, and assuming, as usual, that the features assigned to a form are also assigned to its head, it follows that the Case and agreement features of an NP will be realized on its external argument, as in (42).

(42)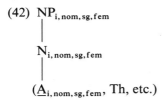

Now, through the mechanics of predication, the external argument of the AP in (38) will wind up linked to the external argument of the subject NP, as in (43).

(43)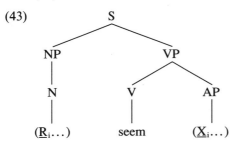

Agreement then comes down to the following:

(44) If X is linked to Y, then X agrees with Y.

This means that agreement is really a feature of anaphoric relations, and not of the subject-predicate relation, except insofar as it is itself an anaphoric relation. There is some evidence that the agreement found in anaphoric relations is the same phenomenon as subject-predicate agreement. For example, subject-predicate agreement respects the "arbitrary" plurality of such items as *pants* and *scissors*; but this is respected by anaphoric agreement as well:

(45) a. Scissors won't cut themselves.

b. The pants are scorched because I wore them to Bill's party.

Clearly, though, (44) is too strong for anaphoric agreement. In particular, an object pronoun does not agree with its subject antecedent in Case. Here we may assume that the object's Case is independently specified (by its position), and revise (44) to read as follows:

(46) If X is linked to Y, then X agrees with Y in features not
     independently specified for X.

In fact, in some instances of predication the Case of the predicate is independently specified and does not agree with that of the subject. An example is the instrumental Case found on predicate nominals in Russian, which do not then agree with their nominative subjects. This is an "inherent" Case, and a special meaning is attached to it, namely, that the predicate does not denote a permanent quality of the individual the subject refers to. When no inherent Case is assigned, the predicate agrees with the subject, and a different semantics holds. Thus, agreement is not an essential feature of the subject-predicate relation.

1.3 A Classification of Junctures

What is the range of junctures in language? We have already seen some different types. Some junctures involve a theta relation, and others do not. Some junctures are doubly headed (bivalent), some are lexically headed, and some are phrasally headed.

These properties are independent of each other; for example, some lexical junctures are thematic (ordinary transitive VPs) and others are not (the juncture of *seems* and its infinitival complement). In fact, as (47) indicates, these properties may be fully independent of each other, in that all possibilities are realized.

(47) a. bivalent   + thematic   subject-predicate
     b. bivalent   − thematic   expletive subject with predicate
     c. phrasal   + thematic   controlled adjunct
     d. phrasal   − thematic   noncontrolled adjunct
     e. lexical   + thematic   verb object
     f. lexical   − thematic   *seems* complement

Although I have used the usual notation for features here, I do not mean these to be syntactic features that appear in syntactic descriptions. Rather, I use the features as a convenient means of displaying the types of junctures. Some are straightforward; others require some discussion.

The subject-predicate relation (case (47a)) has just been discussed in section 1.2.2. The expletive subject construction (case (47b)) is bivalent, since (as (48) illustrates) Tense and Nominative are expressed, but no theta role is transmitted.

(48)   [Nom, Tense]

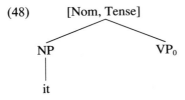

An ordinary adjunct construction is an instance of a nonlexical nonthematic nonbivalent construction (case (47d)). It is nonbivalent, because one of the members, the nonhead, has no expression in the character of the whole:

(49) John [[left]$_{VP_i}$ yesterday]$_{VP_i}$.

There are also adjunct constructions that do involve a theta relation; these are the controlled adjuncts (case (47c)), and their structure is as shown in (50).

(50) a.   VP$_i$

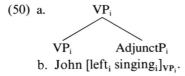

b. John [left$_i$ singing$_i$]$_{VP_i}$.

The correctness of this structure is discussed at length in section 3.2. The external theta argument of the adjunct is bound by the external argument index of the top VP and consequently forms a complex predicate with the embedded VP.

A lexical nonbivalent thematic juncture (case (47e)) is of course the complement juncture: a verb and its object, for example.

A lexical nonbivalent nonthematic juncture (case (47f)) is the juncture between a raising verb and its infinitival complement, shown in (51).

(51)   VP$_i$

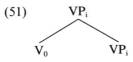

This juncture is the subject of extensive discussion in section 4.2.1. The verb in this case does not assign a theta role, but instead transmits the theta role of the complement VP to the top node, by the mechanism of the definition of "relativized head."

As this survey indicates, theta theory intersects with, but does not reduce to, X-bar theory. If theta role assignment were removed from the theory, all of the X-bar constructs would remain as they are, since they all have nonthematic instantiations.

1.4 Restrictive Modification

The adjunct junctures admit a further dimension: restrictive versus nonrestrictive. The nominal adjuncts are familiar: restrictive and nonrestrictive modifiers occur before and after the head noun; after the head noun the nonrestrictives are distinguished from the restrictives in being set off by an intonational pause, whereas before the head noun no such pause distinguishes the two types:

(52) the philosophical Greeks

(53) a. The Greeks, as philosophical as Bob, ...
     b. The Greeks as philosophical as Bob ...

(52) is ambiguous, whereas neither of the examples in (53) is.

Apparently, exactly the same distinctions are made in the verbal system. Certain sentence adverbs appear to be strictly nonrestrictive, in that they are not part of the main utterance, but are a side comment on it. For example, the adverb *frankly* cannot be the focus of negation:

(54) ??John didn't frankly leave.

Furthermore, when it appears in posthead position, it must be set off intonationally, just like a nonrestrictive adjective:

(55) John didn't leave, frankly.

Probably is similarly nonrestrictive in its patterning:

(56) a. ??No one probably left.
     b.   John left, probably.

That it is not part of the main assertion of the sentence is shown by the fact that it cannot be negated:

(57) a. John didn't probably leave.
     b. John probably didn't leave.

(57a) does not mean 'It is not probable that John left', even though this is a sensible thing to say.

Recently can be either restrictive or not restrictive. Consequently, it can appear intonationally united with the clause, or not:

(58) a. John left recently.

    b. John left, recently.

Furthermore, when it appears preverbally, it can be either negated or questioned:

(59) a. John didn't recently leave.

    b. Did John recently leave?

Cleverly in its so-called sentential reading is simply a "nonrestrictive" adverb. Thus, it cannot be negated, and when it appears at the end of the sentence, it must be intonationally separate:

(60) a. The box was cleverly placed over the second hole.

    b. The box was placed over the second hole, cleverly.

Cleverly is not subject-oriented; rather, it is agent-oriented, and it need not c-command the subject position.

Chapter 2
Theta Role Assignment and Predication

2.1 Preliminaries

Theta theory is the linguist's development of the intuitive logical notion "argument of"—the relation of *John* and *Mary* to *loves* in *John loves Mary*.

2.2 Properties of Theta Roles and Relations

The notion "argument" has an intuitively clear content, though the boundaries of the concept and its correct characterization are not only not agreed upon, but seldom discussed. *Love* is intuitively a two-place relation, taking two arguments, and *give* is a three-place relation, taking three; but is *cut* a two-place relation, which can be modified by *with a knife*, or is it a three-place relation with an optional instrumental argument? For that matter, is *love* a two-place relation that can be modified by a time adverbial, or is it a three- (or more) place relation with an optionally specified time element? These are difficult questions to answer in the abstract, though theory can force choices in particular cases.

For example, what can we make of the difference between (1a) and (1b)?

(1) a. *Where did you wonder [why John danced t]?
    b. Who did you wonder why John liked t?

What is the difference between *where* and *who* that gives rise to this contrast? A possible answer is that *where* is not an argument of the embedded verb, and that *who* is. Difficult and vague questions are always sharpened and sometimes answered by considering how the subtheories within which they arise interact with other subtheories. See section 2.5 for discussion.

Since verbs apparently differ in the number of arguments they require, some means of indicating this must be devised. The simplest means would be to assign each lexical item a digit that represented its "adicity"; however, the evidence for further structure will become apparent as we proceed. A somewhat more delicate question is how the arguments are distinguished from each other. We have already used such terms as *Patient*, *Goal*, and *Dative*, but their use was incidental, and their role in the theory remains to be determined. The arguments must be distinguished—*John recommended Bill to Mary* does not mean the same as *John recommended Mary to Bill*. Clearly, some sort of "realization conditions" distinguish the arguments from one another. But the core of theta theory can be explicated without the descriptive content that these labels such as *Patient* come with; all that is required is a number of distinguishable items in a list (a, b, c, d, . . .).

At a minimum, we might consider that each argument of each verb was annotated with respect to its realization conditions; for example, the *b* argument of *recommend* is annotated as "NP"; the *c* argument of *recommend* is annotated as "PP" headed by *to*; and so on. This is obviously the worst case, failing to acknowledge the redundancies that hold (e.g., Goals are always realized by *to* in English), and so some room for improvement, or perhaps even insight, remains. But for the discussion to follow, this is essentially what we will assume: that there are a number of distinguishable arguments, $A_1 \ldots A_n$, for each verb. This is "bare" theta theory.

2.2.1 Obligatoriness and Locality
Although we speak of a noun phrase as "having a theta role," it is important to realize that "argument of" is a relation, specifically a relation between a verb and a noun phrase, and it is this relation that the theory characterizes, not the property of "having a theta role." Three features of the relation stand out. First, it is *obligatory* in two senses. Second, it is *unique*, again in two senses. And third, it is structurally *local*—indeed, very local.

2.2.1.1 Obligatoriness and Uniqueness   Two senses of obligatoriness are relevant here. First, an NP in a sentence must be an "argument of" some verb. There are obvious exceptions to this: vocatives, for example. There are also more subtle exceptions, such as the "subjects" of pseudocleft constructions or the topics of certain topicalization structures:

(2) a. What John saw was Bill.
   b. As for fish, Bill likes mackerel.
       (cf. Japanese *wa* construction)

The topic in (2b) is not the argument of any verb, but it clearly fills a function in the sentence—it is the topic of the following comment. This obligatoriness probably reduces to a requirement of "full interpretation": every NP must have some business being in the sentence in the first place, and being an argument of a verb is one type of business.

The other obligatory aspect of the "argument of" relation is that at least in certain circumstances, there must be an NP to fill a certain "argument of" relation. As mentioned earlier, verbs take multiple arguments and some of these arguments are obligatorily specified:

(3) a. John tried.
   b. *John attempted.

It is not clear what the difference between (3a) and (3b) amounts to (I will outline a couple of alternatives below). But in one case there is no choice—namely, the case of the subject argument:

(4) *(*It) hit Bill.

The subject argument must be specified. Although the subject is sometimes inaudible, as in "pro-drop" languages, we will nevertheless assume that it is always present in S-Structure (see chapter 6 for further details).

The nonsubject arguments present a different picture. The two possibilities are (1) that nonsubject arguments are just like subject arguments, in that they are always obligatorily present, only sometimes inaudibly so, or (2) that they are simply optionally specified. Both possibilities have been investigated. The first was explored by Rizzi (1982), in a study of differences between English and Italian such as the following:

(5) a. *A serious doctor always visits — nude.
   b.   Un dottore serio visita — nudi.
       (Rizzi 1982:(14a))

Italian, but not English, seems to permit a direct object controller to be missing, although both languages permit direct objects in general to be missing, as idiosyncratically specified by particular verbs. Rizzi proposes that the direct object is always present, but that in Italian, unlike English, the direct object can be realized as "small pro," the same empty category that is used for missing subjects in pro-drop languages.

The opposing idea (developed somewhat in Williams, forthcoming a), is that these arguments are simply optional. The issue is complex, because there are some signal differences between missing subjects and objects, which makes an extension of a theory of the one to the other not straightforward. First, the interpretation is different: missing objects are interpreted as generic in some sense, whereas missing subjects are generally, though not always, interpreted as definite. Second, a missing object must be directly an argument of the matrix verb, and not the "subject" of a small clause, but there is no corresponding thematic restriction on missing subjects. I leave the issue open, but for concreteness we will assume that these arguments are optional, and that verbs idiosyncratically specify whether their arguments are obligatory or not.

We are left, then, with a lopsided "Theta Criterion," which includes at least the following requirements:

(6) Every NP must obtain some sort of interpretation in the sentence, and bearing an "argument of" relation to some verb is one way to do this.

The "subject argument" of every verb must be assigned to some NP.

Like obligatoriness, uniqueness has two senses. The standard Theta Criterion stipulates that the relation between NPs and verbal arguments must be one-to-one, a condition that could fail in two ways: there could be a many-to-one relation between NPs and arguments, or a one-to-many relation. For the moment, we will accept the standard stipulation. However, in chapter 6 we will consider abandoning the stipulation—in effect, we will accept the notion that NPs and arguments can stand in a many-to-one relation, and we will derive the fact that arguments and NPs are not related many-to-one from the binding theory.

The uniqueness component blocks such standard impossibilities as (7), where a single NP is assigned two theta roles.

(7) *John recommended Bill$_i$.
        (A, Th$_i$, Goal$_i$)

But an immediate sort of counterexample to uniqueness—the part of it that we will ultimately accept—is the following:

(8) John arrived sad.

Here, *John* receives a theta role from both *arrive* and *sad*. (8) differs from (7) in that in (8) *John* receives theta roles from two separate predicates

that have nothing to do with each other, whereas in (7) the two theta roles
are assigned by the same predicate. But it is not enough to bar coarguments of the same predicate from assigning a theta role; we also want to
bar *seem*, or any verb like *seem*, from assigning a theta role to a "raised"
NP:

(9) John$_i$ 'verbed' to leave
        (A$_i$)   (A$_i$)

That is, raising predicates assign no argument to their subject position.
The difference between (8) and (9) is that in (8) the two predicates have
nothing to do with each other, whereas in (9) the second predicate is an
argument of the first. Using this distinction, we can define the domain of
the Theta Criterion in the following way:

(10) *Argument complex*
     An argument complex consists of a verb (or any other predicate),
     its arguments, its arguments' arguments, and so forth.
     (Williams 1983:(44))

We can then restrict the Theta Criterion to this domain:

(11) *The Restricted Theta Criterion* (restricted to argument complexes)
     In an argument complex, each phrase is assigned only one theta
     role.
     (Williams 1983:(45))

Of course, there is another sort of answer to this question: one might
posit that in (8) there is a PRO subject:

(12) John arrived PRO sad.

If this is the correct structure, then *John* is not assigned two theta roles;
rather, *John* and PRO are assigned one apiece, and *John* controls PRO. I
have not adopted this solution, and will delay full discussion of the issue
until chapter 3.

2.2.1.2 Locality   The structural locality of the "argument of" relation is
the tightest of all grammatical relations. It is essentially as tight as it can
get—that is, immediate sister nodes may enter in the relation, and nothing
else. The reason for this locality, I believe, is that theta theory is a component of the general theory of "juncture." So, for example, although there
is a close parallel between Case marking and the "argument of" relation,
there is no analogue of "exceptional Case marking" in the theta system;

that is, there is no verb that can assign a theta role to the subject of an embedded clause, as in (13).

(13) *V [NP VP]ₛ
     |__|

The exact formulation of this locality depends on certain independent decisions about grammatical structure. We will examine some alternatives here, beginning with the nonsubject arguments.

Many verbs take more than one nonsubject argument; *give*, for example, takes a Theme and a Patient argument (*John gave the money to Mary*). In one possible structure, these two arguments are both sisters of the verb:

(14) [give [the money]ₙₚ [to Mary]ₚₚ]ᵥₚ

If this is the correct structure, the narrowest possible structural relation, strict sisterhood, can be imposed on the "argument of" relation. However, if one holds that phrase structure is strictly binary-branching, then the VP must have the structure shown in (15).

(15)

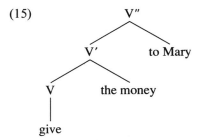

In such a structure, the first argument is a sister of the verb, but the second is not. Here, the notion of locality must be somewhat looser. Although sisterhood is not required, some other relation nearly as tight must be imposed. A likely candidate is *m-command*: a verb and its arguments must be dominated by all the same maximal projections (VP in (15)). Higginbotham (1985) has introduced a notation and rule that capture just such a relation. In his conception, the verb's argument structure is passed up the X-bar projection. At any level, the "argument of" relation can hold between the projection at that level and one of its sisters. This gives exactly the effect of m-command, since as (16) illustrates, every non-head in the projection is the sister of one of the projections of the lexical head.

(16)

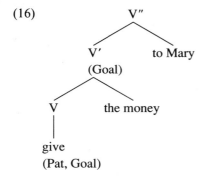

Either assumption—strict sisterhood or binary branching—will suffice for the discussion that follows in this chapter. We will assume strict sisterhood, since this is what we will need in chapter 4.

A different sort of challenge to locality comes from a closer consideration of the prepositional phrase *to Mary* in (16): if *Mary* is the argument of the verb *give* in (14) (or in (16)), then we have a case of an argument that is not a sister to (a projection of) the verb. On the other hand, if *to Mary* is the argument of the verb, then no such problem arises. But is there any reason to consider one or the other of these the argument of the verb? Clearly, at this point we would prefer to consider the PP the argument, just to preserve the notion of locality. In fact, some important generalizations are at stake, and sorting out the possibilities is a delicate matter we will take up in chapter 6.

2.2.2 Directionality

A lexical head with theta roles to assign assigns them only in a particular direction, left or right. In a given language the direction is determined by its setting of the theta directionality parameter, a parameter first isolated by Travis (1984).

I will not discuss directionality at this point; I note it because of the importance it will have in later sections. In particular, theta directionality holds not only for the assignment of theta roles, but also for the set of functor relations, to be discussed in section 2.4, relations that do not involve theta role assignment. And importantly, the theta directionality parameter does not hold for theta roles assigned across a nonlexical juncture. For example, the direction of the English subject-predicate relation is right to left, whereas lexical theta role assignment in English takes place from left to right. Likewise, the theta directionality parameter does not determine functor-argument relations where the functor is nonlexical; for

Table 2.1
Theta relations for English

	Lexical	Phrasal
Functor	L-R	nondirectional
Theta role assigner	L-R	nondirectional

example, in English an adverb phrase can occur on either side of the element it modifies. What emerges is a four-way classification of the relations governed by theta theory (see table 2.1); the theta directionality parameter holds only for the lexical cases.

We will return to the phrasal-versus-lexical issue after we look at the nature of the functor relations.

2.2.3   The External Argument

The subject argument has a special status. It is not a sister of the verb, but a sister of the maximal projection of the verb. For this reason, we may call this argument the *external argument* of the verb: it is located external to the maximal projection of the verb, whereas the other arguments are internal to the maximal projection of the verb. Underlining is used to indicate this argument in the list of a verb's arguments:

(17) give ($\underline{A}$, B, C)

The external argument has a further distinction: there can be only one external argument, whereas there can be an indeterminate number of internal arguments.

The argument structure of the verb is thus bipartite: the external argument on the one hand, and the internal arguments on the other. We will see reason to distinguish the external argument as the "head" of the argument structure.

The NP realizing the external argument of the verb is not "local" to the verb, since it is outside its maximal projection. However, there is still a locality restriction: the external argument of the verb must be a sister of the maximal projection of the verb. Thus, for example, a verb cannot take as its subject the object of a higher clause, since this condition would not be met.

The locality restriction on the external argument can be rationalized by viewing the external argument as bearing the same relation to the maximal projection of the verb that the internal arguments bear to the verb itself. This means that the maximal projection of the verb bears a theta role, and that theta role is assigned to the external argument. So the maximal projection of the verb is a predicate, in fact a one-place predicate. The theta role it assigns is the external theta role of the verb that is its head.

One way to implement this idea—that the VP is a one-place predicate based on the external argument of its head verb—is to assign to the VP an operator that binds an argument of the head V, like a lambda operator. Since there can be no more than one such operator (there is never more than one argument outside the VP), this should be a nonrecursive operator. If we assume that every maximal projection can have exactly one index—the referential index of referential expressions—we may use this index as the operator, as shown in (18).

(18)

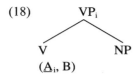

The coindexation of the VP and the $\underline{A}$ argument of the V indicates that the VP is a one-place predicate by virtue of binding the $\underline{A}$ role of the head verb, with the result that an NP, the subject, can now bear the "argument of" relation to it.

The theory just outlined is a theory of the "subject of" relation. It proposes that the "subject of" relation has two components: first, there is the binding of the external argument of the head by the index on the projection of the head; and second, there is the ordinary "argument of" relation holding between the projection of the predicate and an NP. The second relation is already familiar; the first, however, requires further specification.

In fact, the first relation can be seen as a derivative of the notion of head in X-bar theory. The binding of the external argument of the verb by the maximal projection is simply the (X-bar) projection of the index of the external argument, as shown in (19).

(19)

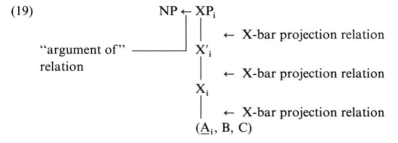

In fact, we may explain why it is the index of the external argument that percolates if we assume further that the argument structure itself has an X-bar structure with a head and nonhead component, with the external argument in head position and the rest of the arguments as nonhead. Since X-bar projection is "local" in that it relates only immediate constituents in a tree, the "subject of" relation, though it appears nonlocal, is actually composed of linking relations each of which is as local as any relation can be: the "argument of" relation, and the X-bar projection relation.

Any major category, not just V, can project a predicative expression, as the following absolutive constructions indicate:

(20) a. With John happy, . . .
     b. With John a judge, . . .
     c. With John in the Netherlands, . . .

In particular, note that a noun like *judge* must have at least one argument, an external argument, which ultimately is assigned to *John* in (20b). Since this argument is not one of the usual verbal arguments (Agent, Theme, etc.), it is designated $\underline{R}$. *Judge* is therefore represented as in (21a) and the projected NP as in (21b).

(21) a. judge
        $(\underline{R}_i)$
     b. $[a \; judge]_{NP_i}$

Hence, every category has a potential external argument. What happens to the external argument when a lexical item does not project a one-place predicate, as in the "normal" referential use of nouns? Why do such cases not violate the Theta Criterion, since the external argument is apparently unassigned? This issue can be clarified by comparing the two possible uses of the same NP, one predicative and the other referential. A noun like *father* has two arguments, the parent argument and the child argument ("*x* is the father of *y*"), and is clearly asymmetric:

(22) father
     $(\underline{P}, C)$

The parent argument ($\underline{P}$) is the external argument, since in *John is a father* the NP *John* is described as a parent, not a child. Now, when *father* is used referentially, the reference is to the parent end of the parent-child relation, just as in the predicative use. Clearly, then, the external argument, which defines the predicative use, is involved in the referential use of the projected phrase as well. This is what we would expect if the syntax of the two uses is identical: in both cases the external argument of the head is bound by the dominating maximal projection.

So, in saying *I saw a father*, one is saying that one has seen an individual on the parent end of the parent-child relationship. In logic, this might be expressed as follows:

(23) for some x, I saw x and father $(\underline{x}, y)$

In other words, the external argument of the head noun is *bound* to an argument of the verb. In our X-bar notation, we will indicate this by coindexation as in (24).

(24)

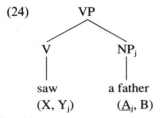

Here, the j index of the $\underline{A}$ argument of *father* ascends to the top of the NP by X-bar theory; the NP is coindexed with the Y argument of *saw*; and thereby the external argument of *father* winds up coindexed with the Y argument of *saw*. This conclusion plays an important role in chapter 6, where I will argue that binding conditions hold among theta roles, not among NPs. Here in (24) we can see that the theta role assignment relation is actually a binding relation between an argument of the verb and the external argument of the head of the NP.

Significantly, the internal structure of a predicative NP is identical to the internal structure of a referential NP—form is autonomous from use. In fact, the difference between referential and predicative will turn out in chapter 4 to be more subtle than is generally thought; some apparent arguments will behave theta-theoretically like predicative NPs (see section 4.2.2.2).

Sentences as well as NPs can be the arguments of predicates; this means that sentences must have external arguments. Where do they come from? Clearly, the external argument of the V of the sentence cannot be the external argument of the sentence, since that argument is used up by the subject. If we accept the notion that Comp is the head of S (Emonds 1985, Williams 1981c), then we would expect Comp to be the source of the external argument. Comp then is a sort of "nominalizer," that is, theta sugar that allows a clause to function as an NP would function:

(25) think   that S
     (...A$_i$) (<u>R</u>$_i$)

There is some evidence that this is the correct view. Raising is blocked uniformly across heads that assign external arguments; thus, it occurs only with the handful of predicates that do not (*seems*, etc., in English). But there are no known instances of raising across a complementizer. In later sections we will see that this is because the complementizer has an external argument.

The scheme just outlined is one means of achieving the locality of theta role assignment. There are some related proposals that differ in details.

The first concerns the notion "external argument." In the conception adopted here, externality is absolute—an argument either is or is not external. In the work of some authors, notably Grimshaw (1990) and Higginbotham (1986), the notion "external" is relative. In their conception, the arguments form a hierarchy, and any given argument is "more external" or "less external" than another. The entire argument structure is inherited at each X-bar level, with saturation occurring under a sisterhood condition. ((26) is based on Higginbotham's notation, where the asterisk indicates saturation.)

(26)

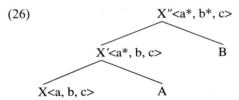

Of course, in Grimshaw's and Higginbotham's conception, there is still a "most external" argument, and it coincides with the external argument in the sense defined here. Differences between theories arise in the definition of forms with no external argument, to be discussed in the next section. Another difference is that in principle the Grimshaw-Higginbotham theories permit more than one external argument: if the argument structure of the head is inherited by the maximal projection with more than one unsaturated argument, then that phrase is not a one-place property.

A somewhat different theory of the subject argument is the *VP-internal subject hypothesis*. Under this hypothesis, the subject argument is generated internal to the VP in D-Structure. It is then moved, either obligatorily or optionally, depending on the theory and on the construction, to the VP-external subject position, the Spec of IP. For now, it is enough to note that the attractiveness of such a theory derives from the notion that all theta role assignment is VP-internal, and hence uniform. However, I believe that this uniformity is an illusion, as I will argue in chapter 3.

2.3 Predication

The relation between the VP and the subject, illustrated in (27), is simply another case of theta role assignment.

(27) John [left]$_{VP_i}$.
$\quad\quad$ ($\underline{A}_i$)

In this case the argument to be assigned is the external argument of the head of the VP, which has been passed up, through the X-bar mechanism of inheritance, to the top of the VP. Since this relation is an instance of theta role assignment, the notion of locality that it involves is sisterhood.

This mechanism of external argument assignment is an implementation of the notion that the VP is a one-place predicate, an implementation that capitalizes on the "inheritance" mechanisms of X-bar theory. In Williams 1977 a somewhat different characterization of the notion was suggested: specifically, that the status of the VP as a one-place predicate derived from its receiving an interpretation with an explicit lambda operator in LF. In the theory described here, there is no LF, and there is no explicit lambda. In the present conception of the propertyhood of the VP, the lambda is "implicit"—it lies in the relation of the verb's external argument to the index on the VP, that is, the "vertical binding" of the external argument. The explicit lambda of Williams 1977 played two roles that will now be taken over by that binding.

First, the explicit lambda served to capture the sloppy identity of subject-bound anaphors and pronouns. This role is now filled by the vertical binding of a reflexive or pronoun to the VP, by the percolated index of the external argument:

(28) John [saw himself$_i$]$_{VP_i}$.
$\quad\quad$ ($\underline{A}_i$, Th$_i$)

Here, the reflexive is bound in the first place to the containing VP, and only secondarily bound by the subject, via predication. I will develop the full analysis along these lines in section 3.1.2.

Second, the explicit lambda was intended to give object quantifiers the possibility of VP scope:

(29) John saw everybody $\Rightarrow$ John λx ($\forall y$ (x saw y))

But this role can be filled simply by allowing QR to use VP as a landing site and giving a rule of interpretation for Qs adjoined to VP:

(30) a. [everybody [VP$_i$]]$_{VP_i}$
     b. $[[\forall x \; VP]]^g = \{u : VP^n_x (u) = 1,$ for all $n\}$

Here, *everybody* is adjoined to VP, indicating that VP is the scope of NP, in the classical notation for indicating scope. The adjoined NP does not satisfy the external argument of VP, since it is not external to the maximal projection, which is the containing VP. (30b) is a rule for interpreting such a structure, in the framework of Dowty, Wall, and Peters (1981). The quantifier has VP scope, and the VP has the same external argument that it would have without the quantifier adjoined.

In sum, then, neither of the motivations for the explicit lambda holds in the context of the present proposals.

2.3.1 Instances of Predication
To begin, let us consider some of the different instances of predication:

Clause	John left.
Adjunct modifier	Sad, John left.
Causative complement	I made John sad.
Consider complement	I consider John sad.
Absolutive	With John sad, we left.
Raising complement	John seems sad.
Noun modifier	the sad man

It is somewhat contentious on my part to list these all as cases of predication. According to some theorists, notably Chomsky (1981) and Stowell (1983), there is really only one instance of predication, namely, the clause. All others reduce to this. For example, some theorists claim that the adjunct modifier case is not really a direct predication of *sad* applied to *John*; rather, *sad* is a part of a small clause structure with a PRO subject. The relation of *John* to *sad* is then broken down into two parts: *sad* is applied to PRO as an instance of clausal predication (the only kind of predication there need be in this scheme) and then *John* controls PRO. In chapter 3 I will explicitly argue that this is incorrect, but here I simply point out that views diverge.

A simple indication of the locality of predication is the behavior of adjunct modifiers of the object. When the object is direct, the modification is possible, but when the object is in a prepositional phrase, it is not:

(31) a.   John ate the meat raw.
     b.   *John ate at the meat raw.

The prepositional phrase prevents *the meat* from being a sister to *raw*, so predication cannot hold. Thus, predication seems to have the same locality as theta role assignment by a lexical head: sisterhood. This should not be surprising, since in effect the VP has a theta role to assign still.

The relation of the subject to the verb then consists of two parts. The first part is the relation of the V, which has the external argument, to the VP. This part is given by X-bar theory, in that projections of V inherit the index of the external argument of V. The second part of the relation is predication—but this is simply another instance of theta role assignment. Thus, the relation of the V to the subject, which looks special and nonlocal, is in fact completely local and not really special, since the two parts that make it up—X-bar theory and theta role assignment—exist independently.

But there is one special thing about predication that distinguishes it from theta role assignment: it is not governed by the theta directionality parameter. Languages differ in whether the object precedes or follows the V, and this, at least in part, is due to this parameter, which determines the direction of theta role assignment by lexical heads. However, the direction of predication is not directly related to the setting of this parameter. Although there are many VO languages, like English, there are few (if any) VP-S languages, that is, languages in which the subject basically follows the VP. This alone shows that predication is not subject to the theta directionality parameter, but it leaves unexplained what the directionality conditions are on predication. In general, clausal predication is NP VP, regardless of the theta directionality parameter, but some languages (e.g., Hungarian) lack external subjects in D-Structure, and in that case the subject follows V in the VP (see chapter 4).

Clausal predication is just one instance of predication. Adjunct predication, which is subject to the very tight locality restrictions of theta role assignment in general, permits "backward" predication, as in (32).

(32) Sad, John left.

And as illustrated in (33), in languages like English and French an AP can precede or follow the noun it modifies, depending on a variety of factors, including meaning, and including a restriction that a prehead modifier must itself be head-final. Presumably these other factors are independent of restrictions on predication in general.

(33) a. the proud man
    b. the man proud of his children
    c. the present board
    d. the board present

In these languages the directionality of *lexical* theta role assignment is independent of the directionality of what we might call *phrasal* theta role assignment.

But in a language like Japanese, not only is the theta directionality parameter set to OV, and clausal predication is naturally NP VP, but all other predication is of the form modifiee-modifier. In other words, the theta directionality parameter is generalized in this language to cover all relations, not just theta role assignment by a lexical head, so that all heads are final, no matter what the relation. Perhaps there is a master parameter, independent of theta role assignment, the setting of which automatically throws the theta directionality parameter. Japanese has set the master parameter, but English has not.

2.3.2 What Assigns, What Receives
The common assumption is that theta role assignment works according to a "valency" mechanism: there are theta role donors (V, A, P) and theta role receivers (N), and the donors and receivers must match up in a certain way. This assumption is warranted in general, but special questions arise in the case of copular constructions with two NPs. We have already assumed that NPs could be used predicatively or referentially. Here, we will reconsider the question, and supply arguments. Second, we will consider the relation between the predicative and the referential use.

First we must address the possibility that there is no such thing as a predicative NP, and that all NPs are quantified terms; for example, a sentence like (34a) would have the representation given in (34b), where the postcopular NP is a referential quantified NP.

(34) a. John is a man.
    b. $\exists x(\text{man }(x))\,(\text{John is }x)$

In such a theory, NPs could always be seen as theta role receivers, or at least, never as donors.

I think that there is conclusive evidence that this view is wrong, and that predicative NPs cannot be assimilated to referential NPs. Similar arguments apply to PP; only VP and AP appear to be "pure" categories with only one semantic function.

First, there is the fact that predicative NPs cannot be extracted long-distance:

(35) a. *How big a man does Bill wonder whether John became?
     b. How many books did Bill bring?

We will defer discussion of this contrast until we consider the ECP in section 2.5; essentially, since predicative NPs are not arguments, they are not assigned scope, and therefore cannot be long-moved (out of a *wh*-island), since long movement entails long scope assignment. In this, predicative NPs pattern like other items with no scope, such as adjuncts, and unlike referential NPs in A-position.

A second argument is based on the following contrast:

(36) a. *His$_i$ town's mayor is a friend of mine$_i$.
     b. His$_i$ town's mayor executed a friend of mine$_i$.

Of course, (36a) is a Weak Crossover violation. But I contend that it is far worse than a Weak Crossover violation; it is, for example, much worse than (36b), which is also a Weak Crossover violation. Why would (36a) be so much worse? I believe that the difference is this: in (36a) the NP *a friend of mine* is not referential, and so cannot be the antecedent of a pronoun, whereas in (36b) it is, and can be. To put it differently, in (36a) the NP is not quantified and so cannot bind the pronoun in the subject, whereas in (36b) it is. (36a) exemplifies a "specificational" use of the copula, in the sense of Higgins (1972); see the discussion surrounding examples (38)–(40) for more analysis.

Another piece of evidence that predicative NPs are not the same as quantified argument NPs can be inferred from the following contrast (Higginbotham 1983):

(37) a. *John$_i$ is [his$_i$ cook].
     b. John$_i$ likes his$_i$ cook.

We will defer discussion of this contrast until chapter 3, where we will be able to make sense of it in terms of the theory developed there. Crucially, the difference turns on a special role that predicative expressions play in the binding theory.

These arguments establish that there are predicative NPs; now we turn to the question of what distinguishes a predicative NP from a nonpredicative one. First, of course, there is the fact that a predicative NP is a theta role donor. Second, there is the fact (established in a couple of the arguments just given) that predicative NPs do not have scope. Beyond this, can we say that predicative NPs are distinguished by any formal properties?

I think that the answer is no; that is, predicative NPs have the same range of forms as referential NPs. For example, it seems clear that there are both definite and indefinite predicative NPs (the postcopular NPs in (38a–b):

(38) a.   John is a mayor.
     b.   John is the mayor.
     c.   *John is a man who fathered Bill.
     d.   I consider John the mayor.
     e.   I consider the mayor John.

If these are both predicative NPs, and predicative NPs are not quantified, then the determiners clearly serve some function other than quantifying. The definite determiner, in both predicative and referential uses, signals that there is an obvious function that will pick out what fits the description; and the indefinite determiner signals that there is no obvious function. Note the anomaly of the indefinite determiner in (38c)—clearly, since the description itself provides the function for picking out the unique satisfier of the description, the use of *a* is anomalous.

Thus, this signaling of an obvious function (or the absence of such a function) for picking out something that fits a description must be dissociated from quantification, since it occurs in predicative nominals as well as in quantified argument nominals.

(38d–e) bear on the question of whether definite NPs can be predicative. Importantly, these two differ in meaning. (38d) is straightforward, whereas (38e) is peculiar. This alone shows that the embedded clause is not an identity statement, since identity statements, if they are anything (and if they exist), are symmetric.

I think that examples like (38e) have a valid but obscure reading, one that arises just in case they contain a name whose bearer is known to exist, but is unknown—a better example is perhaps *I consider the mayor Batman*. The utterer of (38e) has a certain knowledge of the world, including knowledge of what entity is the mayor, but no certain knowledge of what entity the name *John* applies to. There are various ways of completing the utterer's knowledge to give a complete description of the world; in some of these, the mayor is the entity *John*, in others, not. In this sense, *John* is "nonrigid," whereas *the mayor* is "rigid."

Hence, there is really no difference between (38d) and (38e), except that it is more difficult to construe a proper name as less rigid than a definite description.

I think this distinction is fundamental to the difference between subject and predicate in general. The subject is more concretely and directly known than the predicate; that is, the subject is more rigid than the predicate.

These considerations do not extend to copular clauses:

(39) a. Helen is the mayor.
    b. The mayor is Helen.
    c. The fireman is the postman.

rigid	rigid	ID
rigid	nonrigid	PRED
nonrigid	rigid	SPEC
nonrigid	nonrigid	ID (higher order)

In (39b) we are not forced to construe the name as nonrigid—(39a) and (39b) are in fact synonymous. It seems to me at this point an irreducible fact that copular sentences allow the precopular NP to be less rigid than the postcopular NP. The (b) example is what Higgins (1972) calls "specificational": the postcopular NP "specifies" the identity of the referent of the precopular NP. The question then arises, What is the theta structure of these cases? Which NP is donor and which receiver? We should probably take the more rigid as the receiver, and the less rigid as the donor.

A copular sentence with two definite descriptions is actually four ways ambiguous, as (39c) shows. In the rigid-rigid case we have an identity statement, on a par with 'John and Bill are the same person'. In the rigid-nonrigid case we know who the fireman is, and we assert that the postman is that person. In the nonrigid-rigid case the reverse is true. Finally, in the last case we have an equation of two nonrigid descriptions, and the sentence says, 'Whoever is the fireman is always the same person as whoever is the postman'.

The copula can be used to specify roles in a play or movie. The role is intrinsically less rigid than the actor, so (40a) is a predicational sentence, but (40b) is a specificational sentence.

(40) a. Olivier will be Hamlet.
    b. Hamlet will be Olivier.
    c. Jerry Lewis will be himself (in the movie).

(40c) is particularly revealing of the nature of specificational sentences: it can only be understood as parallel to (40a), not as parallel to (40b). In other words, in a specificational sentence the precopular NP cannot bind the postcopular NP.

The account of this fact depends on results established in chapter 6 about the nature of theta role assignment; there it is shown that the predicate is *dependent* on the subject in a binding-theoretic sense. Suppose this is so, and suppose further that in a specificational clause it is the precopular NP that is the predicate (it is after all the less rigid of the two NPs). Then the incorrect construal of (40c) would be contradictory— the precopular NP would depend on the postcopular NP with respect to theta role assignment, but the reverse dependence would hold for reflexive binding.

If this analysis is correct, it confirms the idea that the precopular NP is the predicate, or theta role donor, in a specificational construction.

2.4 Function Composition

The principle of Full Interpretation, or some such principle, insists that everything in a sentence belong there. For an NP direct object to belong in a sentence, it is enough that it be an argument of the adjacent verb; for the verb, it is enough that it have such an argument. Hence, the theta relations are at least one kind of licensing relation in syntax. But there are relations that cannot be reduced to theta relations, despite sharing many fundamental properties with them. For example, an adverb bears some sort of relation to the sentence in which it appears. However, the relation of an adverb to the verb or VP that it modifies cannot be a theta relation. For example, consider (41).

(41) John [slowly [arrested Bill]].

Arrested Bill has one argument, the external argument of *arrested*. This argument cannot be involved in the modification of the VP by *slowly* in this example, for if it were, then that argument would be used up, and *John* could not be assigned it. Besides, such an involvement of the argument would get the meaning wrong as well. Thus, *slowly* must bear some other kind of relation to *arrested Bill*. It will be the purpose of this section to outline the properties of that relation. I will refer to this relation as the *functor* relation and will distinguish it, as I have just done, from the theta relation.

First, we need some idea of the range of this relation. The following is a list of relations in syntax that seem to be neutral with respect to theta roles—that is, the relation neither provides, nor uses up, theta roles:

1. Adverbs
2. Negation, auxiliaries
3. Adjectives modifying N
4. Complementizers (relation to IP)
5. Infl
6. Certain Ps (nonsemantic, "grammatical" Ps) (chapter 5)
7. Raising predicates

Each of these items takes an argument, or modifiee. The relation of the item to the modifiee is structurally identical to the theta relation: that is, absolute locality is required. For example, Neg is sister to what it negates; an adjective in an NP modifies its sister; and so on. In addition, for a significant set of cases (2,4,5,6,7) directionality is the same as the directionality of a theta-assigning head, which depends on the setting of the theta directionality parameter for the language in question. For these reasons, we will want to subsume this relation under theta theory.

On the other hand, we also want to distinguish this relation from theta relations, for the reason given above: this relation is "transparent" to theta relations in that for a given functor f, the object, shown in (42),

(42) [f X]

has exactly the same potentiality for theta relations that X had. For example, *slowly arrest Bill* has one external argument, just as *arrest Bill* does.

Clearly, the functor relation is a semantic relation, akin to the theta relation. However, rather than filling theta roles, a functor maps theta assigners into theta assigners. And, as in the case of theta role assignment, the relations are both asymmetric: one item is the functional element, and the other is its argument.

We will assume, then, that theta theory encompasses at least two relations, the theta assignment relation and the functor relation. Both relations are governed by strict locality. When the function element of either relation is lexical, then the theta directionality parameter holds.

2.4.1 Raising and Relativized Head
In this section I develop the notion "relativized head," a notion introduced in Williams 1982b and developed for morphology in Di Sciullo and Williams 1986. This notion is the point of contact between X-bar theory and theta theory, and, theta theory aside, is one of the basic organizing principles of grammar, if I am correct.

Consider the predicate *seems* in the case where it takes a predicate adjective complement:

(43) John seems sick.

Patently, *John* is the subject of *sick*, and also the subject of *seems sick*. At the same time, *seems* bears some relation to *sick*. How is all this possible? *Sick* is an AP with one theta role to assign. *Seems*, we will assume, has no theta role to assign. This will give the structure in (44).

(44)

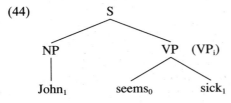

The locality of theta role assignment could be maintained in the face of this example only if the external argument index *1* on the AP could get up to the dominating VP (as indicated in parentheses); then it could be assigned to *John* under strict locality.

The fact that *seems* has no external argument itself makes this possible, if we adopt a somewhat novel view of headship. Under the usual view, a head and its projected phrase must agree on all features. Suppose, instead, that we were to adopt a more "relativized" view.

Suppose first that there is an "absolute" head. Then, "head with respect to F" is defined as follows:

(45) X is the head with respect to F of Y if X is marked for a value of F, and either X is the absolute head of Y, or the absolute head of Y is not marked for F.

This provides a sort of unification that always succeeds, for in cases of conflict the head wins. This definition gives the usual results for most cases; for example, the VP in (46) is a VP because the absolute head, V, is marked for category features ($[+V]$), so the category features of the non-head ($[+N]$) do not affect the categoriality of the projection.

(46) $[V\ NP]_{VP}$

However, in certain cases the relativized notion of head will give different results from the standard nonrelativized notion. For example, in (47) we may speak of $[+a]$ as the "absolute" head, but of $[-a, +b]$ as the "b" head.

(47)   [+a, +b]

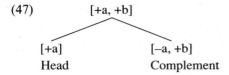

          [+a]   [−a, +b]
          Head   Complement

Given this convention, there must be some means of identifying the (absolute) head in the first place, since feature matching is no guide, being calculated on the basis of an already given identification of the absolute head. In morphology, at least in the languages under consideration in this book, the head is always the rightmost element, even when a suffix; the suffix -*ion*, for example, is a (bound) noun, which combines with a stem to form a noun. Although both French and English are left-headed in the syntax, we will see in chapter 5 that French differs from English in having left-headed compounds, or at least left-headed constructions at the X^0 level. The absolute head in syntax is determined semantically: one of the two elements will be a lexical item that takes the other as a complement.

The first case in point is (44). Ordinarily, the external argument of the head is transmitted up to the dominating phrase. However, when the head does not have an external argument, then the opportunity arises for the nonhead to pass up its external argument, and this is exactly what is needed to get the right result for (44).

The relation of *seems* to the AP in (44) is still in question. It is clearly not theta role assignment; if it were, then the external argument of the AP would be "used up" by this relation, which it clearly is not. Instead, it is passed up. This is the nature of what we have called the "functor" relation: it maps theta assigners into theta assigners with the same theta potentiality.

The notion of relativized head applies only to the complement relation, not to the adjunction relation. To see why, consider the following example:

(48) *John was [[raining]$_{VP_0}$ [singing]$_{VP_1}$]$_{VP_1}$.

Here, the head is *raining* and the nonhead *singing*. *Raining* lacks an external argument and so is not the head with respect to the external argument. But if the notion of head was relativized here, then the fact that the adjunct does have an external argument should render this example grammatical, since that external argument could become the external argument of the matrix VP and ultimately be assigned to *John*. But the fact that it is not means that the notion of relativized head does not apply in adjunction structures.

This is the second difference between adjunction structures and complement structures; the first was that the theta directionality parameter does not apply to adjuncts. I will later attempt to develop a theory that unites these two differences.

Using the notion of relativized head, the interaction of functors, theta role assigners, and theta role receivers reduces to a fairly simple X-bar calculus. Let us review the particulars of this notion. A lexical item with an external argument projects the index of that argument to the maximal projection. A lexical item with no external argument (e.g., *seems*) projects no index. A nonhead sister of *seems* may then project its index; under the notion of relativized head, *seems* is not the "head with respect to external argument" in that case. All functors (a number of which will be reviewed in what follows) obey these rules.

The analysis and theory just exposed have an important consequence for the typology of NP positions: the $A/\overline{A}$ distinction is eliminated. This issue will be addressed fully in chapter 4, but is worth mentioning here.

The analysis of (44), repeated here, establishes a nonlocal relation of theta role assignment by chaining together local relations.

(44)

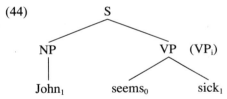

The nonlocal relation is the relation between *John* and *sick*; it is established by chaining together two relations: *sick* to VP_i, and VP_i to *John*. Importantly, both of these relations are theta relations. *John* in particular is in a theta position, because that position is assigned a theta role by the VP. Consequently, for this example, we have no need for a typology of NP positions that includes a position that is an A-position but is not a theta position. In chapter 4 we will see how to extend this analysis to all cases of raising and passive; the theory of NP-movement and NP-trace will be shown to reduce to the chaining of theta relations. The upshot is that we may eliminate the difference between A-position and theta position; every theta position is an A-position, and only theta positions are A-positions. Given this, we should eliminate the term *A-position* entirely from the theory. A position is either a theta position, like the subject position of (44), in which case it receives a theta role, or it is not a theta position, in which case it does not. Examples of nontheta positions are the Spec of CP position and the subject position of a VP that does not have an external argument, as in (49).

(49) It seems that George has eaten it.

The principal use of the notion of A-position is in delimiting the domain of the binding theory, but in the context of the current theory, we could use the notion of theta position just as well. In fact, though, in chapter 6 I will suggest that the binding theory is not about syntactic positions at all, but about theta roles.

2.4.2   Functional Categories and Relativized Head

The notion of relativized head is not just useful for determining theta roles—it applies completely generally. Whenever a lexical category is not fully specified, the nonhead categories will determine the properties of the whole. For example, the English negation word *not* (of constituent negation) is a lexical item not specified for category. As a consequence, *not* can head a category of any sort, depending on the nature of the nonhead:

(50) a. John is [not happy]$_{AP}$.
       b. John could [not go]$_{VP}$.
       c. John is [not a doctor]$_{NP}$.
       d. John is [not in the pantry]$_{PP}$.

In chapter 3 I will argue extensively for the constituency and labeling illustrated here; for now, it is enough to figure out how it could come about, if it is correct. Suppose that *not* is a lexical item that takes a single XP complement, and suppose that *not* itself is unspecified for category; then projections of *not* will be of the category of the complement of *not*.

Note that the nonhead in these cases determines not only the category of the projection, but also its theta potential—*not happy*, for example, is a one-place predicate, a property it clearly inherits from *happy*, not from *not*. But again, this is expected, if *not* is not marked for external argument—if it is, in our terminology, a functor.

One of the arguments that *not* is a head of a projection in these constructions, and not a satellite of the phrase that follows, is that *not* appears strictly on the left—in English lexical heads uniformly take their complements on the right.

Adverbs are similar to *not* in being theta-neutral; that is, adding an adverb to a category does not alter its status in theta theory. However, adverbs behave quite differently from *not* in that they can appear either to the left or to the right of what they modify. Why is *not* different from adverbs in this respect? Or, to ask an easier question, what is this difference in the first place?

It appears that it would not be appropriate to analyze adverbs as heads that take what they modify as complements. But if not, why not? What is the difference between *not* and adverbs?

The difference is this: *not* itself *is* a functor, whereas an adverb *projects* a functor. That is, *not* is a lexical item that takes a *not*P internal complement, the thing it modifies. An adverb, on the other hand, does not take its modifiee AdvP internally, but instead takes it externally ((51a), not (51b)).

(51) a. [[quickly]$_{AdvP}$ [run]]$_{VP}$
     b. *[quickly [run]$_{VP}$]$_{AdvP}$

The difference between *not* and adverbs is then the difference we have seen between external and internal theta roles, though in this case we are dealing with functor arguments, not theta roles—*not* takes an internal functor argument, whereas adverbs take external functor arguments. Which is just another way to say that it is the adverb *phrase* that modifies, but the *word not* that modifies. Using *f* to indicate the functor argument, we might represent this as follows:

(52) a. not (f)
     b. quickly (f)

As noted earlier, the theta directionality parameter governs only lexical theta relations, not phrasal theta relations. Hence, an adverb can appear on either side of its modifiee for the same reason that an AP can appear on either side of its modifiee, or that a predicate XP can appear on either side of its modifiee: namely, all else being equal, theta theory does not determine a choice of direction ((53f–g) are the sole cases of lexical theta relations):

(53) a. John arrived tired.
     b. Tired, John arrived.
     c. The men sick of peanuts are here.
     d. Quickly the men dispersed.
     e. The men dispersed quickly.
     f. John ate beans.
     g. *John beans ate.

This is not to say that nothing governs the NP VP order in a sentence. As studies of subject-postposing languages have shown, many factors do play a role; I note only that the theta directionality parameter does not.

I suspect that it is the fact that adverbs project functors that ultimately explains why they take no internal complements, but I have not devised a theory with this consequence.

It is not universal that adverbs do not take internal modifiees, or complements. We might restrict the generalization even in English to -*ly* adverbs, since *not* does take an internal complement. In French (V. Déprez, personal communication), sentential adverbs can take internal complements:

(54) a. [Probablement [que Pierre est parti]].
          probably   that Pierre has left
      b. *Que Pierre est probablement parti.

The complement here is a *que* clause, as shown by the presence of *que*, but the example is a matrix utterance. The *que* clause is not itself a matrix clause, since it is embedded in the AdvP. The "matrix" here is an AdvP, but semantically it is propositional, since *probablement* maps propositions to propositions. Such a construction cannot itself appear in the position of an embedded S, since it is categorially an AdvP. (54b) shows that the construction is impossible except where the modifiee is in the theta role assignment configuration with the adverb. Thus, French has a systematic ambiguity in its sentential adverbs. In one use, they *project* functors, just like English adverbs; but in the other use, they *are* functors (like English *not*).

2.4.3 Nominalization and Function Composition

In the standard view of raising, what is required from the standpoint of theta theory is that the target of movement be a nontheta position. The requirement of the theory espoused here is slightly different: it is that the matrix predicate not have an external theta role. This corresponds to the fundamental difference between the two mechanisms used for raising constructions in the two theories: movement versus X-bar percolation.

In the ordinary clausal cases of raising, it is difficult to discriminate these two views, for whenever the subject is a nontheta position, the verb has no external argument.

In NPs, however, the situation is different. If we assume that an N always has an external argument, the argument that permits the NP projected from the N to be used either predicatively or referentially, then it follows that we will not find raising in NPs, since raising requires that the governing predicate not have an external argument of its own. This is abundantly borne out, as shown in (55).

(55)

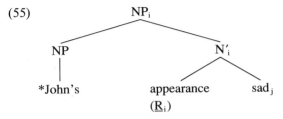

Here, the $\underline{R}$ external argument of *appearance* is inherited, blocking the inheritance of the *j* argument of *sad*; hence, the external theta role of *sad* goes unassigned, and the phrase is ungrammatical. This strongly supports the notion that what raising requires is that the matrix predicate not have an external argument, not that the target position for raising be a non-theta position, for in NPs the Spec of NP is a nontheta position, and raising still cannot take place. We thus find a direct way to discriminate the usual view of raising from the view espoused here. See Williams 1982b for further discussion of this argument.

2.4.4 Satisfaction versus Composition

Thus far we have characterized the difference between theta role satisfaction and function composition along traditional lines: referential NPs are theta role recipients, and predicates are donors; the relation between a verb and a predicate and between a verb and a referential NP follows from this. In chapter 4 I will argue for an analysis of existential sentences in which one aspect of the traditional picture must be changed. I will propose, and argue there, that theta-theoretically speaking, the existential NP of an existential sentence is a predicative NP, and that the expletive subject is its subject. This will have as a consequence that in a sentence like French (56)

(56) Il est arrivé   trois personnes.
     it has arrived three persons

il is the subject of *trois personnes*. But it also means that the relation between *arrivé* and *trois personnes* is one of function composition, as illustrated in (57).

(57)

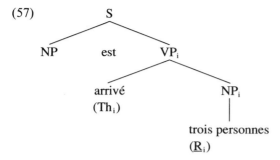

Here the theta role Theme of *arrivé* is assigned to NP_i. Next, it is "verti-cally" bound by VP_i, and then VP_i is predicated of the subject, and the expletive in subject position satisfies the i theta role. Importantly, the i theta role is not satisfied by the assignment to NP_i; if it were, then it could not be vertically bound by VP_i. Rather, the theta role simply *passes through* the NP.

NP_i in (57) is acting like a predicative NP, but it occupies the position normally occupied by a referential NP (an argument position of *arrivé*). We must theoretically disentangle the notion of referentiality from the notion of theta role satisfaction. In (57) the theta role Theme is ultimately satisfied, just not at the level where it is assigned to *trois personnes*. An NP can satisfy a theta role, but it need not—it can pass on the need for a theta role to a higher constituent, just as a predicative NP does. There is no reason to force any particular NP in any particular position to take one or the other of these options, because the situation will generally dictate what must be done in order for the Theta Criterion to be satisfied. In this example the NP could be taken to satisfy the Theme theta role, but then this sentence would violate the Theta Criterion, since *il*, a thematically active element, would be assigned no theta role.

Of course, a referential theta role can be passed up from an NP just assigned it only when the verb has no external argument of its own, for if it did have one, the notion of relativized head would insist that the verb's external argument be passed up.

I will resume this discussion in chapter 4 and give arguments for this analysis. The point here is that it is neither desirable nor necessary to determine that particular syntactic positions will be predicative or referen-tial. The Theta Criterion by itself, coupled with the notion of relativized head, will sort all the cases out correctly, including cases like (57), which might at first seem counterintuitive.

2.5 Extraction and Adjuncts: The Scopal ECP

The well-known difference in extractability between adjuncts and arguments is I think determined by their essential nature. In this section I will
sketch a version of the ECP phenomena that is suggested by and compatible with the theta theory of this book. (I of course can do this in only a
preliminary way; see Williams, in preparation, for further argumentation
and analysis.) In short, the difference is this: an argument bears two relations to the sentence in which it appears, a theta relation and a scope
relation, whereas an adjunct bears only one relation.

In sections 2.5.1 and 2.5.2 I will outline the relation between the ECP
and scope, proposing a restatement of the ECP in terms of scope (the
Scopal ECP). In sections 2.5.3 and 2.5.4 I will then sketch the role of the
notion of relativized head in characterizing the relevant notion of scope.

In order to reduce the ECP to the principles for assigning scope, it is
necessary to restrict the range of explanations in which the ECP plays a
role. In particular, the SECP will play no role in explaining Superiority
effects, bounds on NP-movement, or the supposed inability of adjuncts to
remain in situ. On the other hand, it may play a role in determining the
Head Movement Constraint (Travis 1984).

I will first consider replacing the head government condition with an
articulation of argument and adjunct scope (sections 2.5.1, 2.5.2). I will
then consider what might replace the antecedent government relation
(section 2.5.3).

2.5.1 Scope and Long Extraction

Classically, the ECP is a condition on movement, applying by extension
to the Quantifier Scope Assignment Rule construed as a movement rule.
In this section I will suggest a reversal in the usual relation between scope
and this condition on movement: rather than being a condition that applies equally to movement and to scope, the ECP is a condition on movement stated in terms of scope. To put it informally, the ECP says that a
phrase can move as high as it can be assigned scope.

I will begin with two substantive proposals about linguistic scope.

In Williams 1986b I suggested that the scope of an NP is marked in
S-Structure by indexing a phrase containing that NP as the scope of the
NP:

(58) John [saw everyone$_i$]$_{\text{VP};i}$.

Here, VP is marked as the scope of *everyone*. The *:i* index on the dominating S serves as a lambda abstractor and, as such, marks a scope.

I argued in Williams 1986b that this representation of scope is superior to the one derived by QR. One argument was based on the following contrast:

(59) John knows how to do something, but I don't remember

    a. what$_i$ [...t$_i$...]$_{S:i}$.

    b. *what$_i$ he knows how$_j$ [...t$_i$...t$_j$...]$_{S:j}$.

If variables free in a deletion site are ungrammatical, then (59b) is ruled out, but (59a) is good, because the variable is bound by the lambda abstractor on S, which is included in the deletion site.

This scope-marking index is independent of the external argument of the NP. The external argument of the direct object will be satisfied, by theta role assignment, within the VP. However, the scope index, *:i*, can be realized on higher nodes; in fact, it can potentially be realized on any arbitrarily high containing node.

The second proposal concerns the typology of linguistic scope. In chapters 4 and 5 I will defend the notion that there are three sorts of linguistic scope, namely, head scope, adjunct scope, and quantified argument scope:

(60) a. *Head scope*

        John doesn't think that anyone is there.

        Projection

        Adjunct scope

        John never thinks that anyone is there.

        Sister (or projection of sister)

        Quantified argument scope

        John thinks that no one was there.

        Some containing phrase

    b. Someone thinks that Bill always lies.

Only the last of these involves assigning an arbitrarily large containing constituent as the scope of a phrase. The first two are quite limited: the Head Scope Rule assigns the projection of the head as scope of the head, and the Adjunct Scope Rule assigns the phrase adjoined-to as the scope. These relations are in fact probably better considered theta relations than scope relations. And, importantly, the Quantified Argument Scope Rule (QASR) applies only to arguments of verbs. So, for example, in (60b) *always* modifies *lies*, not *thinks*. Moreover, *always* cannot be construed by any stretch of the imagination to have scope over the matrix, giving (60b) an interpretation like 'Every time is such that someone or other thinks that Bill at that time lies'. (For more details, see section 4.1.1.)

The QASR can assign potentially infinite scope. Although the scopes of natural language quantifiers are limited, in some cases and situations severely so, I feel this is a result of the interaction of scope assignment with other features of grammar—for example, the Nested Scope Constraint of section 2.5.3 and the Leftness Condition discussed in chapter 6. For example, I believe the Leftness Condition explains the strong limits on wide scope universals, compared to the weak limits on wide scope existentials. See chapter 6 for more discussion.

One way to view the difference between adjuncts and arguments is this: an argument has both a theta relation (to some predicate) and a scope, whereas for an adjunct, there is no notion of scope apart from the theta-theoretic modification relation. From this difference between adjuncts and arguments follows the difference in long extractability.

Regarding the ECP, I will begin with the fact that an adjunct, as opposed to an argument, can be "moved long"; that is, it can be moved, for example, out of a *wh*-island.

For the moment, I will simply assume that only quantified NP arguments are assigned arbitrarily large scope ("long scope"), and see what relation this has to the ECP. (We will turn to an explanation for this assumption in section 2.5.2.)

Now, let us suppose that movement can be licensed by satisfying either of the following two conditions:

(61) *Scopal ECP* (SECP)
   a. Analogue of antecedent government (or subjacent movement)
      (to be discussed later)
   b. Analogue of lexical government
      The movement of the phrase and the scope assigned to the
      phrase coincide.

In having two parts, the SECP recalls the classical "disjunctive" ECP. For the moment we will concentrate on (61b); we will return to (61a) in section 2.5.3.

The SECP predicts that an argument can be moved out of a *wh*-island, because an argument can be assigned long scope by the QASR and hence be sanctioned by (61b). But an adjunct, which is not assigned long scope, can only be sanctioned by (61a) and so cannot escape weak islands.

This prediction is illustrated in (62) and (63).

(62) Who does John wonder when Bill bought t?

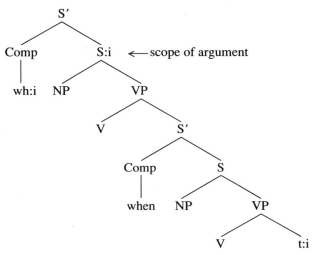

(63) *Where does John wonder [when Bill bought t]?

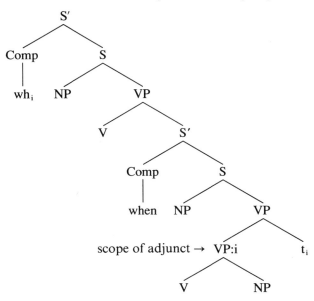

In (62) the argument is assigned the matrix S as its scope. This scope coincides with the movement, and so (62) is grammatical despite the fact that the movement is not subjacent. But in (63) the scope of the adjunct is restricted to the embedded VP. In addition, the movement in (63) is not subjacent, because the embedded Comp is filled. As a result, (63) cannot be sanctioned by either (a) or (b) of the SECP and so is ungrammatical.

Rule (61b) is probably not the most insightful way to state the restriction, because it sounds like an arbitrary stipulation that scope and position must match. We might instead see this arrangement as arising directly from scope assignment in the first place.

An argument in general is licensed by two relations to the sentence in which it appears: a scope relation (assigned by the QASR) and a theta relation (assigned under sisterhood). A displaced argument (as in (62)) is assigned a theta role (to its trace under sisterhood). The QASR cannot apply to a displaced NP, because it does not occupy an argument position; its scope is assigned by the Adjunct Scope Rule and hence is the sister of the displaced argument:

(64) $wh\text{-phrase}_{:i} [\ldots t_{:i} \ldots]_{S:i}$

An unmoved adjunct is assigned a relation to its sister, a relation of modification, assigned by what I have called the Adjunct Scope Rule. Unlike an argument, an adjunct bears no other relation to the sentence in which it occurs.

Now, how is a displaced adjunct licensed, as in (63)? It cannot be licensed by the Adjunct Scope Rule, since if that rule were to apply to it in its displaced position, it would simply reassign it scope (or a modification relation), and the adjunct would not be perceived to have moved in the first place.

Since it cannot be licensed by a scope rule, a displaced adjunct must be licensed by antecedent government. However, antecedent government of the adjunct is impossible in (63), so the example is ungrammatical.

Thus, a less stipulative formulation of (61b) would be simply this:

(65) An argument in displaced position can be licensed (with respect to scope) by the Adjunct Scope Rule.

It is probably incorrect to consider a displaced adjunct to bind a trace, since it enters into no theta relation apart from its scope relation. Its "trace" is its scope.

By limiting the QASR to NP arguments, we exclude nonarguments and non-NPs both from nonlocal scope and from long movement. Adjuncts are subject not to nonlocal scope assignment, but to the Adjunct Scope Rule; and as we have just seen, adjuncts are not subject to long movement.

There is some question whether non-NP arguments can move so as to escape weak islands. Although the literature on the topic expresses a mixed opinion, the following example seems to suggest not:

(66) *To whom did you wonder why John talked t?

Assuming that the judgment here is correct, we must conclude that argumental PPs cannot be assigned wide scope.

The SECP rationalizes the ECP in a certain way: if an item can be licensed in its displaced position by scope assignment, then that is sufficient; but otherwise, the antecedent government discipline must be observed.

Importantly, I am not claiming that movement and scope will always coincide; this will only be the case for long movement (i.e., for movement not licensed by (61a)). We can see this quite clearly in the case of adjuncts. An adverb undergoing short movement can escape its own scope even in its own clause:

(67) a. How slowly$_i$ will everyone [arrive]$_{VP;i}$?
b. Everyone will be slowly [arriving]$_{VP;i}$.

In (67a) *how slowly* can be understood in its VP-modifying sense, where it is strictly subordinate to *everyone*. Hence, these short movement cases show that it is impossible to reduce the constraints on short movement to constraints on scope, or constraints on scope to constraints on movement —in (67b), where the adverb has not moved, scope is confined to the VP. Since adverbs can move subjacently to positions higher than their highest possible scope, it seems doubtful that limitations on the scope of adverbs could be derived from the laws of movement.

The sort of rationale for the ECP just discussed is not available in a theory in which "NP-movement" constructions such as raising and passive fall under movement theory and are governed by the ECP. This is because in such theories, there can be no match between scope and movement: the surface position of an NP moved to subject position does not fix its scope, which can be much larger, as in the indicated interpretation of the following sentence:

(68) John believes that someone was arrested.
$\exists x$ (John believes that x was arrested)

But of course, in the theory of this book, the raising and passive relations are sanctioned entirely by theta theory, and theta theory governs the assignment of referential indices to theta roles. The ECP governs scope indices and so belongs to a separate system. See chapter 3 for discussion.

Another limitation of the SECP is that it does not derive the Superiority Condition, as Aoun, Hornstein, and Sportiche (1981) and others following them have suggested it should. I will suggest in chapter 6 that Superiority is actually a Weak Crossover violation, and is governed by the Leftness Condition that is proposed there.

But a benefit of the SECP is that it can derive Travis's (1984) Head Movement Constraint, which says that the head of a phrase cannot move any higher than the next highest head. A head is assigned scope by the Head Scope Rule: the scope of a head is the phrase it projects. But this means that a head can move no higher than to a position that is sister to its projection, by SECP(b). For example, in (69) YP is the scope of Y, so Y can move to X, but no higher; in position X, it marks its scope exactly.

(69)

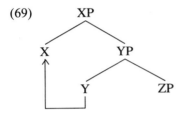

2.5.2 Scope Reconstruction

The term *scope reconstruction* refers to the notion that the scope of a quantified expression is determined by its D-Structure position. Scope reconstruction is incompatible with the view of scope presented here. In addition, it is incompatible with the position taken in Van Riemsdijk and Williams 1981 and Williams 1986b, where it was established that scope, being an $\overline{A}$-relation, is determined at S-Structure, whereas reconstructed structure pertains only to A-to-A relations, such as binding relations.

However, examples like the following have been taken to show that there *is* a process of "scope reconstruction":

(70)

How many books do they think you published t?

a. they think [you published [QUANT books]$_i$]$_{s:i}$ What is QUANT?
          └── scope of QUANT ──┘

b. [they think you published [QUANT books]$_i$]$_{s:i}$ What is QUANT?
          └──── scope of QUANT ────┘

(70) is ambiguous, the quantifier *how many* appearing to take either embedded or matrix scope.

Kroch (1989) cites an existential presupposition of a set of books for (69b), but not for (69a). The (69a) reading is the one derived by scope reconstruction. One mechanism for realizing scope reconstruction would be to derive an LF representation in which the *wh*-moved phrase was in its D-Structure position, and then to apply the scope rules to that representation.

In order to see what is reconstructed under such an analysis, we must distinguish two sorts of "quantifiers" in (70). What is invariant in (70) is the fact that the matrix S is a direct question, and that question is about a number, not about a set of books. So, the *wh* "feature" or operator has matrix scope in all cases. It is the structure [QUANT books] that is ambiguously assigned scope. [QUANT books], with QUANT = *how many*, can be assigned scope in exactly the same way as *every book*—in other words, we do not need to know the identity of the quantifier in order to know how to assign it scope.

The difference between the scope of *wh* and the scope of the phrase that bears it can be seen in the following example:

(71) Who knows when Bill left how?

Here, as always, *how* can have only adjunct scope: it modifies *left*. But *wh* can have as its scope either the embedded or matrix S, giving the well-known ambiguity of such examples.

Scope reconstruction is blocked by *wh*-islands (Longobardi 1985, Cinque 1990, Kroch 1989):

(72) a. How many books do they think they will publish t?
   b. How many books do they wonder whether they should publish t?
      (adapted from Kroch 1989)

      [QUANT books] (V (...))   a, b
      V ([QUANT books] (...))   a, *b

The fact that (72b) is not ambiguous is meant to show that scope reconstruction is blocked by weak islands.

There is some convincing evidence against such a rule or process of scope reconstruction, which I will present first; I will then return to the illusion of scope reconstruction in these examples.

Consider the specificational pseudocleft construction, which shows a variety of reconstruction effects—for example, Condition A binding:

(73) [What John likes t best] is himself.

This construction also appears to show scope reconstruction effects:

(74) What every boy saw was a friend/many friends of his.
     (every boy (a friend (...)))

Here, the indefinite *a friend of his* appears to be subordinated to *every boy* (there can be different friends for each boy), an effect that could be achieved by the scope reconstruction mechanism. But there is a peculiar and fatal gap in the scope reconstruction paradigm:

(75) What bothered a friend of mine is every article that appeared.
     *every article (a [different] friend (...)))

Here, the reading that is missing is the one in which *a friend of mine* is subordinate to *every article*—that is, where each article bothered a different friend of mine. This reading could be achieved under the scope reconstruction mechanism by putting the universal back in its D-Structure position, where it would naturally take scope over the indefinite, so it is a puzzle why that reading does not exist.

I think this sort of example suggests that there is no scope reconstruction. Two ways to revise the scope reconstruction theory would be (1) to restrict scope reconstruction to indefinites, or (2) to block scope reconstruction from applying in cases where the reconstructed position c-commands no other quantifiers. Apparently, a quantifier can be "reconstructed" if it is going to be *subordinated* to another quantifier, but not if it is going to be *superordinated* to another quantifier—a generalization that is at least unexpected, and in fact perhaps the opposite of what one would expect, since it would seem to be an antilocality effect.

Neither restriction provides a satisfactory explanation of the phenomenon, but I think each points to the problem with scope reconstruction: it is limited to placing indefinites in subordinate positions.

The first restriction is in fact empirically incomplete. Even an indefinite cannot be reconstructed to a position where it will have superordinate scope over another indefinite:

(76) What bothered three friends of mine was five articles.
     *15 articles (= 3 friends × 5 articles)
     (*cf.* Five articles bothered three friends of mine.)

This cannot have the "multiplicative" reading where each article bothered a different set of three friends; hence, scope reconstruction cannot apply so as to give *five articles* wide scope over *three friends*.

I think the answer to these puzzles lies in Lewis's (1975) and Heim's (1982) account of indefinites, and in Chierchia's (1992) account of quantified questions. Consider the following case:

(77) Every boy saw five friends.
   a. $\forall(\text{boy})x\ [\exists 5(\text{friends})y\ [x\text{ saw }y]]$
   b. $\forall(\text{boy})x\ [x\text{ saw }[f_x\ 5\text{ friends}]]$

Suppose indefinites are ambiguous. On the one hand, they can generate an existential quantifier, which takes scope, and which binds a variable ranging over individuals (or, in (77a), sets of five individuals).

But in addition to this reading, there is also one in which the indefinite does not generate its own quantifier and does not give rise to a quantifier ranging over individuals, but is rather construed as a function, a Skolem function, from its context to individuals (or, in (77b), to sets of five individuals). The context includes the quantifier whose scope it is in, and so it is dependent on the quantifier. In that reading, *five friends* has no scope. Rather, it is a referentially dependent NP, dependent on *every boy*. See chapter 6 for further discussion of this dependence in connection with Superiority, WCO, and Chierchia's (1992) analysis of quantifier-*wh* interactions.

Now in (74) we will suppose that the variable in the pseudocleft ranges over functions from context to friends rather than ranging over friends; and these functions are functions of the context of the variable, which includes the quantifier *every boy*. This gives the appearance of scope subordination but instead is unselective binding. In this interpretation, the clefted NP is given 0 scope and hence behaves just like any scopeless element: it must obey the antecedent government discipline and so cannot penetrate weak islands.

Any indefinite or definite is liable to this functional, context-dependent interpretation. The following paradigm illustrates the place of the *wh*-quantifier in the set of functionally interpreted expressions of language:

(78) a. Every doctor likes her hospital. (explicit function)
   b. Every doctor likes the hospital. (obvious function)
   c. Every doctor likes a hospital. (no obvious function)
   d. Every doctor likes what hospital? (unknown function)

In each of these cases the object NP is interpreted as a function from doctors to hospitals.

This functional interpretation is nothing other than unselective binding. In the case where the unselective binder is an NP, the unselective binding displays weak crossover effects.

(79) a. The hospital pleases every doctor.
   b. Every doctor likes the hospital.

(79b) but not (79a) permits an interpretation in which the identity of the hospital varies from doctor to doctor.

This shows that the unselective binding is by the A-position of the quantifier (and not by the $\overline{\text{A}}$-scope position of the quantifier, as suggested by Heim (1982)). (For further discussion, see chapter 6, Williams, in preparation, and Chierchia 1992.) If this is true, then it is not surprising that unselective binding shows reconstruction effects—reconstruction effects are limited to the A-system. $\overline{\text{A}}$-relations are not "fed" by reconstruction, as shown in Van Riemsdijk and Williams 1981 and Williams 1986b.

For a universal quantifier, there is no nonscopal interpretation and so no possibility of achieving this illusion of scope subordination; hence, (76) cannot receive any sort of interpretation in which the universal subordinates the existential.

Hence, we conclude that there is no scope reconstruction; rather, indefinites and definites are optionally construed as functionally dependent in the manner illustrated, giving the illusion of scope subordination.

Heim (1982) has suggested that indefinites are never quantificational, and that when they appear to be, they are instead being bound by an invisible existential operator. If her view is correct, then we must add that there is also no existential closure of indefinites under reconstruction. But the cases at hand suggest that the notion that indefinites are ambiguous is correct: if there were a rule of existential closure, why would it be unavailable after reconstruction?

We are now in a position to answer the question we began with: Why do weak islands block the phenomenon of "scope reconstruction"? Precisely because (1) long movement must be licensed by the scope assignment rule, and (2) the appearance of scope subordination in "scope reconstruction" cases is due to unselective binding, precisely the cases in which the indefinite does not generate its own scope.

Returning to adjuncts: I have argued that adjuncts do not have any notion of scope apart from a notion of what they modify. But adjuncts do participate in nonselective binding of the kind just discussed:

(80) How did every boy arrive t?

Here, the "scope" of *how* is the VP *arrive. How* itself is interpreted as a function from contexts to methods (of arrival)—that is, every boy arrived in a possibly different way. In this sense, adjuncts too show scope reconstruction. And of course, adjuncts will not show scope reconstruction into *wh*-islands:

(81) a. *How$_i$ does John wonder when every boy [arrived]$_{VP}$ t$_i$?
      b. *How$_i$ does John wonder when every boy [arrived]$_{VP:i}$?

The fact that even adjuncts show scope reconstruction effects is a further argument that scope reconstruction is not a matter of constructing a new scope, since adjuncts do not have the relevant notion of scope in any case. It is perhaps wrong to think of a moved adjunct as binding a trace (see (81a)), as in the case of a moved argument; rather, the trace of a moved adjunct *is* its scope (see (81b)).

2.5.3 Antecedent Government

So far I have suggested that head government be replaced by an articulation of the natures of adjunct and argument scope. In this section I will speculate on the nature of the antecedent government condition and will suggest that this condition as well can be understood as the interaction of conditions on scope.

Consider the following "inner island" phenomena:

(82) a. *How did few people do it?
          how$_i$ [few people]$_j$ [do it]$_{S:i:j}$
      b. That is how few people do it.
          [that is how few people$_i$ [do it]:j]:i

(82a) illustrates a scope constraint and (82b) a loophole in the constraint. The constraint seems to be as follows:

(83) *Nested Scope Constraint* (NSC)
      *XP$_i$ ...[... YP:i ...]:k

That is, if the scope of XP is contained in the scope :k of another element, then XP must be contained in that scope as well. In (82a) the scope of *how* is contained in the scope of *few people*, but *how* itself is not, so the result is bad. (82b) shows that embedding the offending configuration improves it. In (82b) the scope of *few people* is the whole embedding S, so the result does not violate the NSC. I will not explore here the characterization of the type of items XP$_k$ that create scope barriers.

The NSC accounts for some facts about the placement of adverbs. In (84) the adverb *carefully* has been displaced (by some limited sort of topicalization) from the position adjacent to its scope, assuming that it has VP scope in its manner interpretation.

(84) Carefully$_i$, John [lifted the box out of the well]$_{VP:i}$.

But in (85) this displacement is impossible, because of the intervening adverb *probably*.

(85) *Carefully$_i$, [John probably$_k$ [lifted the box out of the well]$_{VP:i}$]$_{S:k}$.

Here *carefully* violates the NSC. It is not the absolute position of the adverb that is at issue here, but its relation to other adverbs.

The following question is a counterexample to the NSC:

(86) How did everyone leave?
     how$_i$ everyone$_k$ [leave]:i:k

Only certain quantifiers are counterexamples: exactly the ones that provide suitable contexts for functional dependence, giving the so-called multiple questions interpretation (see chapter 6 and Chierchia 1992). Hence, the NSC should be revised as follows:

(87) *Nested Scope Constraint*
     In XP$_i$ ...[... YP:i ...]:k XP depends on *k*.

Now, turning to *wh*-islands, we find that the embedding effect observed in (82) does not occur:

(88) a. *How$_i$ do you remember when he [did it]:i?
     b. *That is how$_i$ I remember when he [did it]:i.

The account of the difference between (82) and (88) comes down to the difference in types of linguistic scope that we have been discussing. *When* in these examples is in an adjunct position, and so is interpreted by the Adjunct Scope Rule, which fixes the scope as the sister to the adjunct. But in that configuration the relation of *how* to its trace violates the NSC, and embedding the offending configuration will not change this, since the scope assigned by the Adjunct Scope Rule to *when* is fixed.

A second scope constraint is illustrated by the following examples:

(89) a. John is everything his father was.
     b. Someone ate everything I left.
        Everything [Someone[...]]
     c. Someone (or other) is everything that John was.
        *Everything [Someone[...]]
     d. Someone or other has every property that John had.

(89a) shows that English has second-order universal quantification. (89b) shows that a universal following an existential can have scope over the existential, even though this is not the preferred interpretation: the existential covaries under the influence of the universal. But (89c) shows that when the universal is second-order, then the existential cannot covary in this way. (89d), which has the intended meaning, is not ruled out, because here the scope interaction is between two first-order terms. Put another way:

(90) *Constraint on (Skolem) Dependence* (CSD)
      A first-order term cannot depend on a higher-order term.

A general version of the constraint would require that lower-order elements cannot crucially depend on higher-order elements. In natural language we may identify first-order terms, second-order terms (predicates), adjuncts, and operators (such as *wh*), in that order. Operators can depend on operators (as in multiple questions), but nothing else can depend on them.

A further illustration of the CSD can be seen in the comparative construction:

(91) At most one person is taller than Mary.

      Does not mean
      there is a height x [at most one person has x height]
      there is a height y [Mary has y height]
      $x > y$

(91) means that Mary is a fairly tall person. But suppose 2′5″ were a height uniquely instantiated by only one person; then the formula in (91) would be satisfied even if Mary was shorter than 2′5″.

In this example the higher-order element is the *-er* operator, and the wrong meaning indicated in (91) involves a strict scope subordination of the first-order term *at most one person* to that operator. But it is this sort of strict scope subordination that is barred by the CSD.

A final example concerns questions. Consider the following example:

(92) How many books did at least one person buy?

      Does not mean
      how? [at least one person x [x buy how many books]]
      (What is a number such that at least one person is such that that person bought that many books)

      Does mean
      how? [how many books b [at least one person x [x buy b]]]
      (How large is the set of books x such that at least one person bought x)

Here the higher-order operator is *how*. The reading where *at least one person* is strictly subordinate to *how* is barred by the CSD.

The NSC and the CSD together predict a wide range of scope phenomena, and in particular, account for the central cases of antecedent government, at least as far as adjuncts are concerned. Consider for example extraction of an adjunct from a *wh*-island:

(93) When do you wonder who [left t]?

Here *when* is understood to modify *left*; that is, *left* is its scope. Since the scope of the *wh*-operator on *who* contains this scope, the NSC requires that *when* be dependent on that operator. But that dependence is contrary to the general version of the CSD, if the adjunct is of a lower order than the *wh*-operator. Hence, we derive the effect of antecedent government.

As already detailed, the SECP cannot be held accountable for all of the empirical facts that led to the classical ECP. To close this section, I will consider one further discrepancy between the two. It is sometimes considered a mark of an adjunct that it cannot remain in situ in English, and theories of the ECP have been written to take this into account (see, for example, Lasnik and Saito 1992:42). In fact, though, only *why* is so barred:

(94) a. *Who left why?
       b.   Who left how?
       c.   Who left when?

It is unhelpful to classify the adjuncts other than *why* as nonadjuncts, since in other respects, they show the same properties as *why*—in particular, they are not extractable from weak islands.

(94) shows a difference between *why* and the other adjuncts. The question is whether this difference is a feature of the in-situ position. In chapter 6 I will suggest that in multiple questions the unmoved *wh*-word is "dependent on" a moved *wh*-word; given this, we might suppose that what distinguishes *why* from the other adjuncts is that it cannot be dependent on a moved *wh*-word to form a multiple question. The examples in (95) suggest that this is so:

(95)		Multiple answer (with respect to times)
	a. Why have you danced?	no
	b. How have you danced?	yes
	c. When have you danced?	yes
	d. Where have you danced?	yes

Here, the failure of dependence shows itself to be independent of in-situ positioning. Similarly *how*, but not *why*, can be dependent on universal quantifiers:

(96) a. Why did every boy leave? (not multiple question)
     b. How did every boy leave? (multiple question)

These conclusions confirm two results. First, they confirm the relevance of the notion of dependence. Second, they protect the Scopal ECP from the charge that it is not sufficient for the full set of cases that the classical ECP accounted for. The cases that bear on the failure of adjuncts to remain in situ (94) turn out not to directly bear on the ECP in the first place; rather, they come down to a special property of *why*, namely, that it cannot be dependent.

2.5.4 Scope and Percolation

Let us now turn to a tentative explanation for the difference between quantified arguments, on the one hand, and adjuncts and heads, on the other, with respect to scope assignment.

In section 2.4 we saw that the notion of relativized head applies only to complement structures, not to adjunction structures; the evidence presented was that an external argument from the adjunct cannot become the external argument of the whole in case the head has no external argument. We can use this difference to explain the difference in scope assignment.

Suppose that every phrase has a scope index—that is, an index whose assignment will indicate the scope of that phrase. Let us indicate that index as :*i*. As shown in (97), when a phrase occurs in complement position, that index will percolate to higher nodes, by the mechanism of relativized head.

(97)

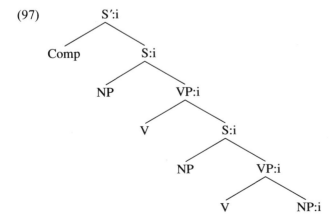

The percolation indicated here proceeds from nonhead to phrase, according to the definition of relativized head. This is permitted because the junctures are complement junctures, and the heads in these cases are not marked for the feature that is percolating. Thus, scope assignment is another instance of percolation under the definition of relativized head.

A quantifier in adjunct position cannot percolate its index to higher nodes, since the adjunct is not in head position, and the head position is not relativized for adjunct junctures, as has already been established. This is illustrated in (98).

(98)

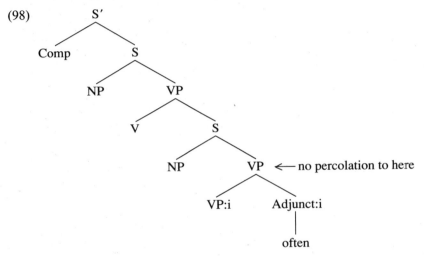

As a result, an adverb like *often* has only the VP it is attached to as its scope.

We thus derive the scope differences between adjuncts and arguments from the definition of relativized head. And having done so, we automatically derive the movement differences.

We conclude, then, that the same mechanism that determines the category of a form, and the external argument of a phrase, also determines linguistic scope: namely, the relativized head. The fact that category and scope behave in a uniform way, despite their different characters, lends support to the formal apparatus developed.

Thus, we have related the restrictions on movement to restrictions on scope, via the SECP; and we have related restrictions on scope to the percolation mechanism that is implicit in the definition of relativized head. Ultimately, then, we have related restrictions on movement to percolation.

Manzini (1992) has proposed a theory of the ECP which is homologous to the one presented here, and which inspired it. Her account differs from the one presented here in two respects. First, it lacks the notion of percolation that is derived from relativized head and must therefore have a different explanation for why adjuncts do not undergo long movement. Second, it does not relate the percolation of the licensing feature to scope. Such a relation would be impossible under this theory, for it seeks to include NP-movement under the ECP and scope is clearly irrelevant for the locality of NP-movement.

Like the proposal made here, Manzini's proposal recalls Kayne's (1984) g-projections, and also Gazdar's (1982) proposal for long-distance dependencies. The percolated feature *:i* here is similar to the "slash" features of Gazdar's original proposal for the treatment of long-distance dependencies. It is worth emphasizing, however, that in this account the very same percolation mechanism is used throughout—all types of features are percolated in the same way. Gazdar draws a distinction between "head features" and "foot features"; the foot features, which include the slashed category feature for *wh*-movement, behave differently from the head features. In the account presented here, all features exhibit uniform behavior, determined solely by the X-bar notion of head, appropriately relativized.

2.5.5 Extraction of Adjuncts versus Extraction from Adjuncts

There is a difference between extraction from an adjunct and extraction of an adjunct that is not accounted for in the theory of section 2.5.4.

(99) a. *With whom do you wonder whether Mary left t?
      b. ?Who do you wonder whether Mary left with t?

In the theory we are considering, there is no reason for this difference in grammaticality, since the same deficit occurs in both cases: no scope index of the trace reaches the top S.

These facts may ultimately force us to discard the percolation theory of scope of section 2.5.4. They will not, however, touch the conclusions reached in section 2.5.1 about the relation of scope to the ECP. I will assume for the time being that we want to preserve both theories, and offer the following proposal to account for the relative acceptability of (99b). Suppose there is a reanalysis rule that moves the adjunct from adjunct position to complement position. In that position it will be able to participate in feature passing under the definition of relativized head:

(100) $[[\text{leave}]_{VP} [\text{with t}]]_{VP} \Rightarrow$
        $[\text{leave} [\text{with t}]]_{VP}$

The reanalysis will not affect the fact that the adjunct is not an argument and so will not endow it with the ability to originate a scope index; but it will permit it to pass up scope indexes that originate in arguments within it. So the trace, which is an argument of the preposition *with*, will be able to pass up its scope index in the reanalyzed structure. The reanalysis rule must be regarded as a "marked" possibility, to account for the semi-ungrammaticality of extraction from adjuncts.

This reanalysis finds support in the binding theory. Solan (1978) has observed the following type of difference between adjuncts and complements:

(101) a.   We [arrested her$_i$]$_{VP}$ before Mary$_i$ left town.
        b.   *We [told her$_i$ that Mary$_i$ should leave town]$_{VP}$.

He attributes this contrast to the indicated difference in bracketing, which ensures that *her* c-commands *Mary* in (101b) but not in (101a). But if our reanalysis rule is correct, then when it is forced by long extraction, we should find the pattern in (101b), not the one in (101a). This is correct:

(102) *What should I warn her$_i$ before giving Mary$_i$ t?
        (cf.: We warned her$_i$ before giving Mary$_i$ a speedboat.)

The reanalysis will permit an index that originates with the adjunct to be passed up through the adjunct by the definition of relativized head, since the adjunct now bears the complement relation to the verb. Therefore, long extraction will be countenanced from adjuncts.

This quite independent prediction confirms the proposition that adjuncts that have been extracted from have a different structural relation to the VP than ones that have not.

2.6   Events

The theory of functors and theta assigners outlined so far is really part of X-bar theory, and the X-bar calculus determines the interactions. But the system is sufficiently constrained that it is incompatible with various possible and even plausible proposals about how semantics works. A good example is the theory of the Event variable.

It has been proposed that a verb's argument structure contains an Event variable, in addition to the other theta roles that it contains. This proposal is quite at odds with the one just outlined. Here we will consider the evidence on both sides and will try to fill the deficits that the Event variable was posited to address, but without accepting the Event variable proposal in full.

In Higginbotham's (1985) implementation of Davidson's (1967) ideas about this, the verb itself contains, in addition to its other arguments (Agent, etc.), a variable that ranges over events. It is by connection to this variable that adverbs such as *recently* modify VPs—the external argument of the adverb is identified with the Event variable of the verb. But this runs afoul of the definition of external argument, since the argument will have to be an external argument if it is to be accessible to adverbs like *recently*, and verbs will then need to have two external arguments (argument positions that are not saturated internal to the VP)—the Agent, say, and the Event variable. What is wrong with this? Two things. First, if two, then why not three?—a question one is not tempted to ask when there is only one in the first place. Second, the external argument of the verb is identified as the head of the argument structure, and this is why it (or its index) percolates to the top of the VP. But of course there cannot be two heads, or two indexes. We thus cannot use the mechanisms of X-bar theory to determine the theta potentiality of phrases.

In Higginbotham's (and others') view, it is the identification of the Event variable of the verb and the external argument of the adverb that permits modification of the verb by the adverb:

(103) Mary walked quickly.
        $(E_i, A) (X_i)$

The Event variable itself is never saturated by a linguistic expression, but instead is covertly existentially quantified.

In fact, adverbs cannot saturate theta roles. (104a) is often taken as an example where this does happen, but (104b) shows the conclusion to be hasty.

The following evidence suggests that if the Event variable existed, it could not be located in the verb or in the VP, but would have to be associated with Tense. However, I will suggest further that it cannot be a variable at all on a par with the other variables that we have discussed, the theta roles.

Consider the following paradigm of adverbial modification:

(104) a. Mary has recently been talking to Fred.
      b. *Mary has been recently talking to Fred.
      c. Mary has been quietly talking to Fred.

What is the adverb modifying in these cases? Clearly, the adverb *recently* is modifying the Tense of the sentence, since it must be adjacent to the Tense, and not the verb, though it is sometimes accidentally adjacent to the verb when the verb bears Tense:

(105) Mary recently talked to Bill.

Thus, if the adverb is modifying by virtue of its relation to an Event variable, then that variable is located in the Tense structure of the sentence, rather than in the main verb (of course, *main verb* is a misnomer anyway, since the verb bearing the Tense is probably best regarded as the main verb). Importantly, (104b) is not ruled out by a prohibition against adverbs, even sentential adverbs, from intervening between *be* and its complement:

(106) John was recently talking to Bill.

Here, of course, *recently* modifies Tense, which it is adjacent to.

But not all adverbs modify the same thing: *quietly* can appear in the slot in (104b) where *recently* cannot. Clearly, *quietly* is modifying something different from *recently*, namely, the VP or the verb. If modification by adverbs were accomplished in both cases by identification with an Event variable that originated in V, then this distinction between *recently* and *quietly* would not be expected. Not enough distinctions are drawn by positing a single Event variable, wherever it is located.

In the problem just reviewed, it appears that different sorts of modification make different and conflicting demands on the Event variable. But even if we restrict ourselves to one sort of modification, a single Event variable per clause will not suffice. Consider the following sentence:

(107) John ate breakfast twice three times.

According to (107), John ate breakfast six times. Why the multiplication? If a time modifier modifies the Event variable, then (107) will be represented as follows—

(108) $\exists x$ eat(x) &...& three-times (x) & two-times (x)

which is at best contradictory, at worst incoherent. If, on the other hand, the time modifiers bind the Event variable, then only one such modifier should be allowed, since a variable can only be bound once:

(109) three-times$_i$ [twice$_i$ [...eat(e$_i$)...]]

Once again, it appears that the Event variable, although it allows a description of some simple cases, fails to generalize to the full set of relevant cases.

Chapter 3
Small Clauses

In listing environments of predication in chapter 2, I ignored an important controversy, the controversy surrounding the notion "small clause." If the generalized "small clause" theory is correct, then the environments of predication may well reduce to a single one, clausal predication, [NP VP]$_S$. In this chapter I will review the controversy.

The issue is not whether there are "small clauses." Jespersen settled that issue in 1924 when he observed the *nexus of deprecation*—a clause with no tense and no agreement, just a subject and a predicate:

(1) Me dance? [How ridiculous.]
    (Jespersen 1924:130)

Instead, as noted above, the issue is whether all cases of predication reduce to clausal structures.

3.1 The Theta Criterion and the Opacity Condition

3.1.1 The Extended Projection Principle and the Theta Criterion
The small clause hypothesis says that there is only one instance of predication, which is in some clausal structure YP, as shown in (2). All others reduce to this.

(2) [NP XP]$_{YP}$

For example, the complement to *consider* cannot be as shown in (3a), but must be as shown in (3b), for some YP.

(3) a. John [considers Bill silly].
    b. John [considers [Bill silly]$_{YP}$].

Why would the small clause hypothesis be true? Chomsky (1981:29–30) attributes it to what he calls the Extended Projection Principle hypothesis.

The Projection Principle insists that lexical properties be satisfied in the same way at all levels, in particular, at S-Structure and LF. Given this, and given that *seem*, for example, is a monadic predicate in LF (as (4c) suggests), Chomsky argues that (4a) must be represented as (4b) in S-Structure.

(4) a. John seems sad.
    b. John [seems [t sad]]
    c. It seems that John is sad.
    d. John [seems sad]$_{VP}$

His argument rests on a notion of uniformity across different uses of a lexical item. If (4c) is the correct S-Structure analysis, and not (4b), then *seems* in this usage must be dyadic in S-Structure, and with a new strange notion of S-Structure argument, such that *John* and *sad* wind up in LF as a single argument, violating the Projection Principle.

I think, though, that the notion of functor developed here will permit the uniformity that Chomsky seeks and permit (4d) to be the correct structure. Recall that *seems* in this usage is a propositional operator. In the case where the proposition is closed, as in (4c), the result of adding *seems* to it is closed as well; however, when the propositional element is open—that is, when it is a one-place predicate, like *sad*—then the result of applying *seems* to it will be open as well. In other words, *seems* uniformly applies to objects and preserves their state of closure. This behavior of *seems* ultimately reduces to the way that the notion of relativized head applies to the external argument, as detailed in chapter 2.

As a result, there is no need to construct a proposition *John sad* in the LF representation of (4a). It is enough to derive the complex property, *seem sad*, and apply it to *John*. The argument based on the Projection Principle does not lead to any conclusion here.

Chomsky (1981) eliminates structures like (2a) in another way: he suggests that they violate not only the Projection Principle, but also a principle that says that if an item is in the VP, then it is assigned a theta role by the verb ("subcategorization entails theta-marking"; pp. 39–40). This principle indeed eliminates the analysis (3a), since *John* is in the VP and does not receive a theta role from V, but it is purely stipulative and has no other consequence. In fact, the stipulation is incorrect as well, since adjunct modifiers are in the VP and are not assigned theta roles by the verb:

(5) a.   ... and [eat the meat raw] he did t.
    b. *... and [eat the meat] he did t raw.

(5) is an example of VP-fronting, which clearly indicates that the adjunct modifier *raw* is in the VP, but it is not assigned a theta role by *eat*.

One could claim for these cases that *raw* is in the VP, but is not subcategorized for. This would not serve Chomsky's purposes, however, since it would allow the NP object in (3a), so long as it was not subcategorized for. In other words, for Chomsky's proposal to have the effect he wants, nothing in the VP can escape the effect of subcategorization.

The example with *raw* is especially troublesome for Chomsky's analysis of examples like (6a) (p. 107). Chomsky proposes that such cases have the structure in (6b) and are ruled out by the PRO Theorem under the assumption that small clauses are not barriers to government.

(6) a. *John wants dead.
    b. John wants [PRO dead]$_{SC}$.

However, adjunct cases are allowed, and the adjunct cases are in the VP, as (5) shows. Why are these not ruled out as well?

In my view, explored in Williams 1983, (6) is ruled out by the Theta Criterion. Consider (7).

(7)

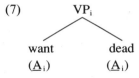

Here the index on VP binds two arguments, the external arguments of *want* and *dead*, and thus violates the Theta Criterion. The parallel case with *arrive* (*John arrived dead*) does not violate the Theta Criterion, because *arrive* and *dead* are not part of the same argument complex (see chapter 2), even though *dead* is undoubtedly part of the VP:

(8) a. John arrived dead.
    b. ... and arrive dead he did.

In section 3.2 I will present arguments against the PRO theory of control for these cases.

3.1.2 Opacity

The debate about small clauses boils down to whether predication is syntactically "trivial," in that it is always a reflex of something else, specifically, the configuration [NP VP]$_S$. I believe that so-called subject opacity effects show clearly that this reduction is incorrect.

In Williams 1980 I proposed that the opacity ordinarily attributed to subjects was actually a fact about one-place XP predicates:

(9) *Predicate Opacity Condition* (POC)
    a. An anaphor cannot occur free in XP, if XP is a predicate.
    b. A pronoun must occur free in XP, if XP is a predicate.

(10) a. *John$_i$ considers Mary$_j$ [mad at himself$_i$]$_j$.
    b. John$_i$ considers Mary$_j$ [mad at herself$_j$]$_j$.
    c. *John$_i$ considers Mary$_j$ [mad at her$_i$]$_j$.
    d. John$_i$ considers Mary$_j$ [mad at him$_j$]$_j$.

When the reflexive is contained in a VP and not bound within it or by it, as in (10a–b), it violates the POC. Likewise, as (10c–d) show, if a pronoun is bound within the smallest predicate that contains it, or is bound by it, it violates the condition.

In the special case where an anaphor is related to the subject of the predicate, it will be bound by the index on the predicate itself and thus not be free in it. For almost all cases, this matches the ordinary Subject Opacity Condition (SOC) (as in Chomsky 1973) or Condition A of the binding theory (Chomsky 1981).

Under the POC, a subject-bound reflexive can occur in a predicative XP (as in (11)) if it is bound to the subject that the XP is predicated of, because it will then be coindexed with the predicative XP itself; that in turn counts as being bound in the XP, since the external argument index on VP is a binder.

(11) John [saw himself$_i$]$_{VP_i}$.

Here, *himself* is bound in VP because it is coindexed with VP. It should be easy to see why the POC matches the SOC so closely in empirical prediction: wherever there is a subject, there is a predicate. So it might seem difficult to distinguish the two ideas.

Recently though, some evidence favoring the POC has come to light. The difference between the following pair, observed by D. Lebeaux and K. Johnson (personal communications), follows from the POC but not from the SOC:

(12) a. John$_i$ wondered [which picture of himself$_i$] Mary would like.
    b. *John wondered [how mad at himself]$_{AP_i}$ Mary$_i$ would be.

In (12a) the reflexive occurs in no predicative XPs except the one predicated of its antecedent, so it satisfies the POC. In (12b), however, the reflexive occurs in the AP predicated of *Mary* and so must be bound in that AP; coindexation of the reflexive with the AP would satisfy the POC but would give the wrong meaning, for then the reflexive would be bound by *Mary*. So the POC correctly discriminates between the two cases, the important difference being that the *wh*-fronted XP is predicative in (12b) but not in (12a).

The SOC cannot discriminate these—in both cases, the reflexive has been moved out of the domain of the subject. It is not clear what prediction the SOC makes here—it depends on whether it applies to the pre- or post-*wh*-movement structure—but whatever the prediction, it should be the same for both cases and therefore incorrect for one of them.

The SOC can mimic the effect of the POC by including a "subject" inside the AP; this subject—clearly not the surface subject—can then induce opacity effects. This would give the following analysis for (12b):

(13) *John$_k$ wondered [t$_i$ how mad at himself]$_{AP}$ Mary$_i$ would be.

Since the surface subject is not in the AP subject position, movement must have taken place—hence the trace. The opacity effect can be attributed to the trace.

We have here one of the "VP-internal subject" theories, about which more in the next chapter. To some extent, the VP-internal subject theories overlap in motivation and mechanism with small clause theories. In connection with the present topic, one problem with the VP-internal subject theories is that the VP-internal subject must be endowed with all the same properties as the VP-external subject, and so we wind up reconstructing the clause inside the VP, with no gain. Such is the case here, where the VP-internal subject is not simply another verbal argument, but has the opacity-inducing effects of a VP-external subject, including those of a *derived* VP-external subject, such as the subject of a passive. So both positions have this property.

I believe there is no version of these theories that resolves all the issues. In this version, essentially Stowell's (1983), the category of the predicate matches the category of the predicate it dominates. Paradox arises when one attempts to determine the internal structure of the small clause. The question is, Is the predicate of the small clause a maximal projection or not?

If we look at the *consider* complement, alleged to be clausal, it would seem that the predicate is a maximal projection, since it can be fronted, without its subject, by *wh*-movement:

(14) How tall do you consider John?

But in order for (13) to work, the predicate cannot be a maximal projection, for if it were, then we could derive (15).

(15) *John$_k$ wondered [how mad at himself]$_{A?P}$ Mary$_i$ would be [t]$_{A?P}$.

Here, the predicate has been fronted, leaving behind the trace. This should lead to a canceling of the opacity effect, just as in (12a), but it does not.

In sum, in one kind of structure the predicate is a maximal projection, and in another it is not.

One could perhaps evade paradox by analyzing the *consider* complement as consisting of two subject positions, one inside an AP, and another in some higher category different from AP, as in (16).

(16) consider

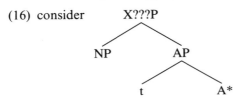

In this theory, A* is not a maximal projection, that is, not frontable without *t*. This theory maintains a distinction between XP-internal subjects (the *t* in AP in (16)) and small clause subjects (the NP under X???P). There are two problems with this theory. First, nothing forces the extra layer of structure (X???P), since AP is already propositionally closed. Second, since X???P is (and must be) categorially different from AP, it will prevent selection of the type of the predicate, but such selection does take place:

(17) *I consider John in the garden.

Again, I believe we have a paradox: selection suggests that some projection of AP is directly the argument of *consider*; on the other hand, the opacity facts suggest that some category different from AP must intervene between the verb and the maximal projection of AP.

I will return to VP-internal subjects and small clauses in chapter 4. For the present I think the considerations just given are sufficient to show that the small clause theory is not a reasonable alternative to the POC for the facts in (12).

Further evidence for the POC comes from an observation by Higginbotham (1983):

(18) a. *John$_i$ is [his cook].
      b.   John$_i$ likes his$_i$ cook.

There is no ready means for the binding theory to discriminate these two cases, which are structurally identical, at least in all relevant respects. However, under our proposals, and under the assumption that the post-copular NP in (18a) is a predicate, the POC (9b) rules out (18a) but not (18b):

(19) *John$_i$ is [his$_i$ cook]$_i$.

In this representation, *his* is bound by the external argument operator *i* of the smallest predicate that contains it.

3.1.3   The Theta Structure of Complement Small Clauses

What is the theta structure of the complement small clause constructions? Clearly, as the previous arguments indicate, either of the two elements of a small clause construction can be selected by the verb, thus implying argument status.

At the one extreme, *see* (*I saw John leave*) selects both the subject and the predicate: the subject must be seeable, and the predicate must be something the subject can be seen doing. At the other extreme, *consider* selects neither.

Now, we are prone to view *consider* as a verb of the type that takes a proposition as its internal argument. I would suggest instead that in the usage we are discussing, it is more like *think* or *say of* in the following examples:

(20) a. I said of John that he was an idiot.
      b. I said of Mary that she was similar to John.
      c. I said of John that he was similar to Mary.
      d. I think that John is similar to Mary.
      e. I think that Mary is similar to John.

Here, *say* is really a three-place predicate, with a special relation between the last two places: the second is a comment on the first. So, for example, (20b) and (20c) are very different in meaning, whereas (20d) and (20e) are not so different. Both (20d) and (20e) have readings in which my "thought" can be either about John or about Mary; but (20a) and (20b) are not ambiguous in this way.

Note that although *John* is an argument of *say*, the verb does not impose any semantic selection—the only requirement is that the argument be something that a comment can be made on. So absence of selection does not guarantee that the "argument of" relation will be absent.

A similar paradigm is found with *consider*:

(21) a. I consider Mary similar to John.
     b. I consider John similar to Mary.

In the first case my consideration concerns Mary, in the second case it concerns John; and neither of these is ambiguous. To this exent, *consider* is a three-place predicate.

Of course, *consider* also exists in a dyadic version:

(22) I consider that John is similar to Mary.

Does our hypothesis about triadic *consider* cost us a generalization—namely, the claim that all related verbs have the same adicity? Yes, it does; but that generalization goes out the window in the face of the examples in (20).

The following example shows that *think* selects the heads of both of its complements:

(23) I think of John as silly.

Here, the subject argument is an *of*P, and the predicate argument is an *as*P. This dual selection suggests dual arguments.

In their VP, *consider* in (22) and *think* in (23) are playing a role similar to the role that Infl plays in the clause: they "bind together" subject and object. The fact that *consider* has semantic content, and Infl has relatively little, does not change this formal similarity. In fact, several of the instantiations of Infl—the modals, for example—do have a semantic content, to varying degrees.

3.2 Adjunct Control

In this section we again ask, How extensive is predication? Consider an innocent case:

(24) Sad, John left the room.

What is the relation between *John* and *sad*? I will insist that it is one of *direct predication* (DP), though it is not immediately clear that it is not a relation of control. To see this, consider the following paradigm:

(25) a. The device arrived (while) still explosive.
     b. John would not take a life, while a doctor.
     c. The device arrived (while) spewing forth sparks.
     d. The device arrived (while) still in its case.

I will assume that anyone inspecting these examples would conclude that they should be given a unified account; but if (25a) is a case of predication, and (25c) is a case of control, this is impossible. I will refer to the phenomena in (25) as *adjunct control*, without prejudicing the issue of what the relation actually is.

Some theorists, notably Stowell (1983), have in fact reduced the relation in (24) to control, by positing a controllable subject (PRO) in every category:

(26) [PRO sad]$_{AP}$

This achieves the unity of (25) in one way. I will achieve it in another, by suggesting that all of (25a–d) are cases of DP. The argument will be simple, given the preceding discussion: I will demonstrate that the relation shown here differs in obligatoriness and locality from other known cases of control, and in fact has the obligatoriness and locality of DP.

The picture is complicated by the fact that there are undoubted cases of control that are not DP, which I will call cases of *logophoric control* (LC). However, once these are separated out and properly characterized, a tight theoretical picture emerges in which there are two and only two sorts of control, LC and DP, and these are clearly distinguishable.

3.2.1 Logophoric Control

3.2.1.1 The Difference between Logophoric Control and Direct Predication
The logophoric cases of adjunct binding can be identified first by the absence of any sort of locality condition, and second by the inference that the antecedent is the "logophoric center" of the sentence. For example, in (27a) the controller is not strictly local to the adjunct (it does not c-command it, for example); furthermore, the antecedent is the "logophoric" center of the sentence, since it is the person whose views of the world the sentence is reporting.

(27) a. Having just arrived in town, the main hotel seemed to Bill to be the best place to stay.
     b. *Having just arrived in town, the main hotel collapsed on Bill.
     c. Believing in ghosts, John dismissed Bill's fears.

In (27b), on the other hand, the control must be logophoric; but *Bill* is not logophorically appropriate, and so the sentence is odd. In (27c) *John* is the only available antecedent. Bill's psychological state is mentioned in the sentence, but the main sentence is not a report of his psychological state, and so he is not the logophoric center of the sentence.

Even when the antecedent c-commands the adjunct, if it is not strictly local to it, only LC is available, not DP:

(28) *This open window$_i$ proves that before breaking$_i$, it was raining.

This cannot be a case of DP, because the antecedent is not local; nor can it be a case of LC, since the antecedent is not a plausible logophoric center. Hence, it is ungrammatical.

The empirical content of the theory derives from the correlation of a strict locality requirement with the absence of a logophoric requirement, for the case of DP, and the reverse for LC.

The correlation between logophoric selection and lack of a structural condition can be demonstrated for the case of PP adjuncts with the following pair:

(29) a. *John repaired the car several times while in the possession of the Mafia.
     b. The car was repaired several times while in the possession of the Mafia.

In these cases, since *the car* is not available as a logophoric antecedent, only the DP interpretation is available. Consequently, the antecedent, *the car*, must strictly c-command the adjunct—hence the anomaly of (29a), where it does not. In (27a), on the other hand, *Bill* can serve as a logophoric antecedent, and hence need not c-command the adjunct.

In order to be the logophoric center of a sentence, an NP must at least be a thinker, a perceiver, or some such, whose thoughts or feelings are reported by the sentence. Sells (1987:445) identifies three independent conditions of logophoricity: "... the source of the report, the person with respect to whose consciousness (or 'self') the report is made, and the person from whose point of view the report is made [PIVOT]." Sells refers to the NP meeting one of these conditions as the *logophoric center* of the sentence.

It is not even necessary for the logophoric antecedent to be physically present in the sentence; it can be "implicit":

(30) Having just arrived in town, the new hotel seemed like a good place for a stop.

Here the implicit experiencer role of *seem* is the antecedent. If the implicit argument is not the logophoric center, then it is not an admissible adjunct controller:

(31) *The box was wrapped beautifully thinking it was for Mary.

Here, the implicit controller is human. However, it can hardly be considered an appropriate antecedent, since it is not the logophoric center of the matrix, being a wrapper, and not a thinker, a perceiver, or some such. Hence, DP is the only possibility, and so *the box* is the only structurally available antecedent. But it is not clear that even an implicit argument is needed, so long as the "point of view" of the sentence is clear:

(32) Having travelled all day, the hotel was a vision indeed.

3.2.1.2 The Availability of Logophoric Control Reinhart and Reuland (1991) have argued that binding of a certain class of reflexives (specifically, reflexives in (subjectless) picture noun phrases) and other "incomplete functional complexes" is logophoric. The account of LC here is inspired by their work. In fact, though, it seems to me that the case for including a logophoric component in the description is even stronger for control than for reflexive binding—there are simply many more circumstances in which non-c-commanding antecedents are allowed for superequi, than for the binding of picture noun reflexives. For example, an implicit argument is not sufficient for the binding of a definite picture noun reflexive, even when the implicit argument is understood as definite; however, "argumental" or adjunct control by an implicit argument is quite acceptable:

(33) a. *Pictures of himself were upsetting.
      b. Standing in the corner was upsetting.
      c. Standing in the corner, everything seemed fine.

In (33b–c), the controller is the implicit experiencer argument of *upsetting* and *seemed*, respectively. I will use the term *argumental control* to refer to control of the subject of an infinitive in an argument position. It thus includes control of subject infinitives and infinitives in complement position, but it does not include adjunct control.

Logophoric adjunct control is available not just for infinitives, but for any NP-modifying adjunct. Thus, we find the following examples with bare APs and PPs:

(34) a. Unaware of Bill's activities, it nevertheless seems to Sam that
          something was amiss. (LC)
          While in a coma, it seemed to me that the world was on fire. (LC)

b. John approached Bill unaware of Bill's activities. (DP)
   I talked to Bill while in a coma. (DP)

In each case, the non-c-commanding antecedent can be construed as the logophoric center of the sentence and hence as a possible logophoric controller.

The availability of a logophoric interpretation is governed by a number of complex factors, most of which I do not understand.

First, there is an effect of pre- or postposition, the former being greatly more hospitable to LC:

(35) a. ?Mary was a wonderful change, having spent my day with Bill.
     b. Having spent my day with Bill, Mary was a wonderful change.

Second, for many speakers, it appears that the logophoric interpretation is unavailable, or is marginal, if a DP interpretation is available, especially when the adjunct follows, rather than precedes, the main clause. Thus, the pair in (36) will contrast less sharply than the pair in (35).

(36) a. It was clear that the sheriff was asleep, on first arriving in town.
     b. On first arriving in town, it was clear that the sheriff was asleep.

Finally, there is an effect of intonation, the logophoric adjunct being set off with commas, whereas the DP case can at least as one possibility be intonationally a part of the matrix. The intonational difference may follow from the structural difference that is indicated in section 3.2.3.1.

3.2.2 Nonlogophoric Adjunct Control as Direct Theta Role Assignment

In this section we will see that the mechanism of nonlogophoric adjunct control is a case of direct theta role assignment that arises automatically from the possibility of "vertical binding" discussed earlier in connection with the notion of relativized head. The conclusions reached here will hold for the adjunct constructions we have already discussed, and also for attributive adjective constructions.

3.2.2.1 Adjuncts Suppose that the relation of adjunct control was exactly the theta assignment relation, as shown in (37).

(37)

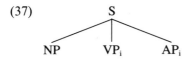

Here, the external argument of the head A has percolated to the top of the AP_i; and once it is there, the entire AP can be predicated of the subject.

Actually, a more realistic picture might have the AP adjoined to the VP as in (38), since by several constituency tests the adjunct seems to be part of the VP (see section 3.2.3 and chapter 1):

(38)

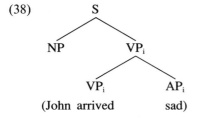

(John arrived   sad)

One question that arises is why this structure doesn't violate the Theta Criterion, since two predicates assign a theta role to the subject NP. This question was addressed in chapter 2, where it was proposed that the Theta Criterion is relativized to argument complexes. Since the adjunct is not an argument of the main verb, it and the subject constitute a separate argument complex. See Williams 1983 for full discussion.

Looking at (38) and (39), one can see a kinship between how the Theta Criterion holds in adjuncts and how it holds in the case of conjoined VPs, which themselves at first appear to violate it.

(39) John [sang$_i$ and danced$_i$]$_{VP_i}$.

Here, the two external arguments of the verbs are bound in an ATB fashion by the predicate operator on the embedding VP. Likewise in (38), I claim.

A second question is how the representation in (38) is arrived at in the first place. The answer is that the Theta Criterion forces it. Suppose that an AP with external argument is generated as an adjunct of the VP. The external argument of the AP must be satisfied, but the AP has no NP sister to satisfy it. The only recourse is for the external argument of the adjunct to be "vertically bound" by the containing phrase, and this is what is represented in (38). No special rule is needed for this; free indexing will suffice. The vertical binding relation will be enforced by the Theta Criterion, since no other means of satisfying the AP's external argument is available.

A special locality problem arises in cases like (25c–d). It would appear that *while* would interfere with a strictly local theta role assignment relation between the subject and the participle. (25d), for example, has either of the structures shown in (40) and (41).

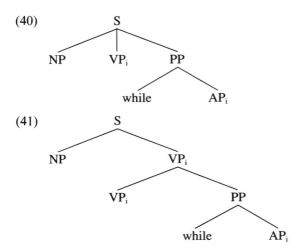

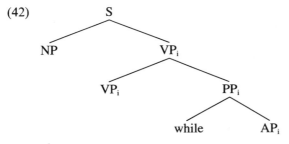

In both of these cases the PP node would seem to act as a barrier against direct theta role assignment to the subject by the XP in the adjunct (or, in the case of (41), against the vertical binding of the XP's external argument by the matrix VP).

Suppose, however, that *while*, like *seem*, lacked an external argument of its own. Then the representation of (41), for example, would be (42).

(42)

Here, the external argument of the AP is represented on the PP, from which it can be bound by the index i on the matrix VP under strict (daughter) locality.

In connection with (40), we may also ask what relation the vertical binding has to the interpretation of the adjunct. Actually, very little. Certainly, the interpretation (or "full interpretation licensing") of the adjunct does not reduce to the identification of the external argument of the adjunct with the external argument of the VP. In all of the following (repeated from (25)), the identification of external arguments has taken place, but the force of modification is different in each case:

(43) a. The device arrived (while) still explosive.
  b. John would not take a life, while a doctor.
  c. The device arrived (while) spewing forth sparks.
  d. The device arrived (while) still in its case.

The identification of external arguments is incidental. This can be seen from the fact that the same relations exhibited in (43) occur in the following sentences, where no such identification takes place:

(44) a. The device arrived while it was still explosive.
  b. John would not take a life, before he became a doctor.
  c. The device arrived after it spewed forth sparks.

The relation of the adjunct to the VP is therefore not the "argument of" relation in the theta-theoretic sense, but some other relation, something like the "function composition" relation identified in chapter 2; at least, the relation is "transparent" to the percolation of theta roles.

What happens to the adjunct if the matrix VP does not have an external theta role, as when it is headed by *seems*? Then the adjunct must also lack an external theta role. Contra Chomsky (1981), I believe this is possible:

(45) It can seem that someone is guilty without seeming that they actually committed the crime.

In theories in which the subject of the *without* adjunct is subject to control, (45) would have to count as a case of control by an expletive. Needless to say, PRO in the subject position of an infinitive in argument position is never liable to such control, since it is restricted to logocentric antecedents. Here, then, is another reason to remove the subject of these adjuncts from the realm of control and to reassign it to the realm of direct theta role assignment.

3.2.2.2 Attributive Adjectives The ordinary assumption is that an adjective modifies a noun in an "intersective" way. In (46), for example,

(46) The bright star suddenly dimmed.

the referent of the subject is calculated by intersecting the set of bright things with the set of stars, in this discipline. The intersection of the two predicates clearly turns on the external argument of each; the interpretation of the N′ in (46) is the equivalent of (47),

(47) $\lambda x(\text{bright } (x) \ \& \ \text{star } (x))$

where the x's are the external arguments of the two predicates.

The faults of the intersective theory are well known. In some cases the intersection is skewed:

(48) The tall elephant suddenly knelt down.

Here, the intersection of *tall*(x) and *elephant*(x) presupposes a universal scale of tallness to establish the first set. But (48) suggests that the elephant in question was tall among elephants, not among things in general.

Still, in these cases it appears that the external argument of *tall* is involved in the interpretation. In some other well-known cases this is not clear at all:

(49) The alleged murderer was deported.

The adjective *alleged* functions in a peculiar way. First, as in the case of *tall*, there is no set of universally alleged things. Further, it makes no sense to say of the set of murderers, for example, that some are alleged. The fact is, someone can be alleged for one thing and not alleged for another, and in *alleged murderer* the murderer is not just alleged, but alleged to have murdered. In other words, it is not just the set of the N that is combined with *alleged*, but rather the label on the set.

Interestingly, when *alleged* is in postnominal position, it has an entirely different character:

(50) a. *The murderer alleged since yesterday ...
     b. The murderer alleged to have stolen the car ...

In postnominal position, *alleged* does not have the special relation to *murderer* that it has in prenominal position. In (50b) the referent is not alleged to have murdered, but alleged to have done something else. In (50b) *alleged* bears that special relation to its complement. This suggests that the relation of *alleged* to *murderer* in (49) is the head-complement relation, and that *alleged* is an A_0 in this usage.

Some cases similar to *alleged* are the following:

(51) a. a secret drinker
     b. a compulsive gambler
     c. the apparent leader
     d. the presumed leader
     e. a would-be senator

In an example like (51a), a reading like (52)

(52) a drinker who is secret

is entirely inappropriate. Rather, (51a) seems to have the meaning in (53).

not in omni

BwB
✓

ONE DAY BOOK

To be returned
following
morning

(53) a person who drinks secretly

This suggests that although the adjectives in these cases have external arguments, the semantics of the modification is not exhausted by coindexing the adjective's external argument with the noun's.

In another sort of case, there seems little reason to posit an external argument at all:

(54) a. A mere boy saved the king.
     b. The only/sole survivor denied cannibalism.

I would suggest that the semantic relation of adjective to noun is not one of intersection of sets, even in the simple cases. Perhaps the most that can be said is that the adjective restricts the reference of the noun, but without saying how. The *how* will be determined contextually.

Why, then, is the external argument implicated in the modification relation at all? As in the case of adjuncts discussed in section 3.2.2.1, the Theta Criterion forces it. If adjectives have external arguments, then those external arguments must be satisfied. Given the representation in (55), the adjective has little choice but to identify its external argument with the external argument of the dominating N'.

(55) a.

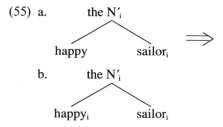

The vertical binding of the adjective's external argument is simply the only means available for satisfying it. Now, the representation in (55b) does not fully determine the meaning of the expression; some rule of interpretation must tell us what it means. One simple rule is the intersective rule, but others are imaginable, and there must be others in general. But any rule will be constrained by the indexings that have occurred. For example, (55b) probably cannot refer to sailors whose wives are happy, since the external arguments of *sailor* and *happy* have been coindexed.

Here, the coindexing is a by-product of the Theta Criterion and the availability of vertical binding; in other words, no special rule is needed to bring about the coindexing. Again, this is just what we found in the case of adjuncts in section 3.2.2.1.

To summarize: The external argument of an adjective plays a role in the interpretation of a [A N] construction, but the semantic relation of the A to N does not reduce to the identification of the external arguments of the two. It is very likely that some adjectives, like *alleged* and *mere*, do not have external arguments. When the adjective does have an external argument, it must be bound to the containing predicate, by the Theta Criterion, and this will constrain, but not determine, the interpretation. In other words, there are no special mechanisms of theta theory for interpreting attributive adjectives.

3.2.3   Further Differences between Direct Predication and Logophoric Control

In this section we will consider further differences between direct predication (DP) and logophoric control (LC) for adjuncts. We will first note some differences in syntactic structure between the two and will then extend the distinction to argumental (nonadjunct) control.

3.2.3.1 Syntactic Differences   Aside from having different "control" properties from the DP adjunct, the LC adjunct bears a different relation to its matrix clause. The difference is roughly that the LC adjunct bears a "looser" relation to the matrix clause than the DP adjunct. This can be shown in a couple of ways.

First, the LC adjunct does not admit extraction, whereas the DP adjunct does. In general, extraction from adjuncts is marginal, though possible:

(56)   ?Who did John go to New York [after talking to t]?

Consider the following LC/DP pair:

(57) a.   John's fears always go out of control, when listening to LaRouche.
     b.   John loses control of his fears when listening to LaRouche.

(57a) is necessarily logophoric, since the antecedent is not the subject, but (57b) at least admits a DP reading (the preferred reading), since the adjunct is in postposition.

Now, (57b), but not (57a), admits extraction from the adjunct:

(58) a.   *LaRouche, who John's fears always go out of control when listening to t, ...
     b.   LaRouche, who John loses control of his fears when listening to t, ...

I am not sure what the difference is; perhaps it is a structural difference, in that the DP adjunct is adjoined to the matrix VP, whereas the LC adjunct is outside VP. Inside VP, the adjunct would count as marginally "L-marked," permitting extraction, whereas when it is outside, extraction is impossible. (See chapter 2 for an account of the ECP in terms of the notion of relativized head.)

That this is something like the correct approach is indicated by the following VP-fronting cases, which show that the LC adjunct is not contained in the VP, whereas the DP adjunct is:

(59) a. *We told him his fears would go out of control when listening to LaRouche, and go out of control when listening to LaRouche they did.

   b. We told him he would lose control of his fears when listening to LaRouche, and lose control of his fears when listening to LaRouche he did.

Again, there is a detectable contrast. We tentatively conclude that the LC adjunct is external to the VP; though the more limited point here is simply to show that the two adjuncts are distinct.

3.2.3.2 Argumental Control Logophoric control may extend beyond adjunct control to control in general. Among infinitives appearing in argument position (argumental infinitives) without a subject, we can distinguish two cases. The first are the most extensively studied cases of control, the lexically regulated (or "complement") cases, involving verbs like *want* and *try*. These cases seem to require c-command. It is worth noting that although a tight structural relation holds for these cases, it is still not as tight as predication; when the subject is the controller, it is not a structural sister of the infinitive, which is contained in the VP. So the adjunct control cases that are governed by DP are tighter than even the complement control cases. The complement control cases generally involve a thinker or perceiver and thus are similar to the logophoric cases— so similar that it is difficult to know whether logophoricity is relevant to complement control. There are a few known cases where the controller is not a plausible logophoric antecedent:

(60) The book served to hold open the door.

In addition to the complement control cases, there are the so-called *super-equi* cases:

(61) John thought that it would be inappropriate to shave himself.

And there are the "backward" cases of control (of the subject of an infinitival subject):

(62) To find himself alone there would increase John's fears.

In general, the antecedent for super-equi and backward cases must be plausible as a logophoric antecedent (a thinker, perceiver, etc.); and in general, there is no c-command requirement if this logophoric requirement is met:

(63) a. To find himself alone in Times Square became one of John's most abiding fears.
     b. *To find himself alone in Times Square became one of John's aunt's most abiding fears.
     c. *To find himself alone in Times Square would frighten John's aunt.
     d. John thought that shaving himself would upset Mary.
     e. *John's aunt thought that shaving himself would upset Mary.
     f. *John's fears brought it about that shaving himself would upset Mary.

Structurally, (63a) and (63b) are similar; but in (63b) *John* is not a plausible logophoric center, since it is his aunt's point of view, not his, that is being reported. The phrase structure of (63c) is identical to that of (63a), but here again *John* is not a plausible logophoric center and so cannot be the controller. In (63d) and (63e) the same point is made with super-equi, though there appears to be no special reason to separate backward argumental control from super-equi, since both seem to fall together as LC cases. (63f) is included because it uses the same containing NP as (63a), and yet control is blocked. This shows that it is not the structural or local lexical context of the putative antecedent that determines whether the control relation will hold or not; rather, it is whether the putative antecedent can be understood as the logophoric center of the sentence.

Cases of super-equi with inanimate antecedents do not exist; this is because nonhumans are inappropriate logophoric antecedents. With logophoric control of adjuncts, however, there are some surprising cases. (64a) was pointed out to me by an anonymous reviewer, and (64b) by A. Marantz (personal communication).

(64) a. Having run smoothly for years, it was finally time for my car to be serviced.
     b. The train has a track to run on.

To maintain the view defended so far, it will be necessary to hold that these sentences express the "point of view" of the car or train. The point of view may inhere in the position x in *time for x to* ... or *x has*; note that the active of (64a) is not grammatical:

(65) *Having run smoothly for years, it was finally time for Joe to service my car.

What causes this difference is unknown to me. It will clearly involve identifying the position x in *it is time for x to do y* or *x has* as the logophoric center, and permitting an inanimate object's point of view to serve as the point of view of the sentence in certain cases. Certainly a car cannot be the source of a thought or a report; however, these cases may fit into Sells's third category ("PIVOT"), which includes simple physical point of view. When this is possible in general I cannot say.

   In sum, we will assume that PRO is involved in the cases of argumental control, and of logophoric control of adjunct clauses. The adjunct control cases stand apart as cases that do not involve PRO, but rather direct theta role assignment.

3.2.4   The Structure of Infinitives and Participles
In this section I will review the theory of the structure of controllable infinitives proposed in Williams 1987. I will then be in a position to predict, for a variety of adjunct control structures, whether they will be cases of DP or LC.

3.2.4.1   The "Nominalization" of Infinitives in Control Structures   So far we have looked at four kinds of infinitives:

1. Adjunct infinitives controlled by direct predication
2. Logophorically controlled adjunct infinitives
3. Argumental infinitives with lexically specified control relations (VP-internal complement infinitives)
4. Argumental infinitives without lexically specified control relations (infinitives in subject position)

I have suggested that although PRO may be implicated in the last three cases, it cannot be in the first. DP adjuncts are like raising structures, not like control structures.

   Among the four types of cases, there seem to be three modes of control. DP infinitives are assigned their understood subjects under the theta role assignment relation; argumental infinitives in complement position are assigned theirs by the lexical control relation (whatever that turns out to be); and argumental infinitives in subject position and logophorically controlled infinitives are assigned theirs by LC.

The empirical basis of the theory rests on tying together a number of properties in a particular way. Theta role assignment is characterized by strict locality and obligatoriness—these are the basic elements of the theory. The properties of DP (which we have identified with theta role assignment) are (1) obligatoriness, (2) distributivity and strict locality, and (3) lack of a logophoric requirement.

Because infinitives with null subjects are of two sorts—theta-role-assigning and controllable—there must be two distinct structures for them.

In Williams 1987 I proposed that the difference between the controllable infinitive and the raising infinitive is that in the former case the one-place predicate VP has been turned from a theta role assigner into an object that can serve as an argument, or theta role assignee, whereas in the latter case the one-place predicate remains a one-place predicate.

Support for a difference in structure between the raising and control infinitives derives from the fact that in some languages the infinitive can serve one purpose but not the other. In Russian, for example, infinitives are allowed only in control structures, not in raising structures. Here, I am arguing that the DP adjuncts have the same internal structure as raising infinitives, and the LC adjuncts have the same structure as the control structures.

We may instantiate the difference between control and raising structures in the following terms, again following Williams 1987. Suppose that PRO is an NP that satisfies a theta role. Then raising and control structures must differ as shown in (66a) and (66b).

(66) a. 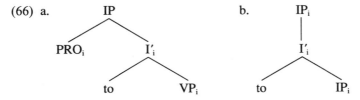 b.

In the control structure the theta role i, the external argument of the VP, has been vertically bound to I' and assigned to PRO. In the DP structure it has been vertically bound to I', then vertically bound to IP; it is still unassigned, and still must be assigned. If the raising infinitive is itself embedded in a VP, its external argument is vertically bound yet again by the matrix VP, and ultimately assigned to the matrix subject.

A crucial feature of this analysis of DP is that the path of vertical binding must be free of heads with external arguments, for a head with an external argument would block the vertical binding of the external argument of the complement of that head, as outlined in chapter 2 in the definition of relativized head; the actual head always takes priority. In particular, suppose that Comp always has an external argument. Then raising will never take place out of an infinitive with a Comp, since (as shown in (67)) the theta role of the Comp must become the external argument of the CP, by the definition of head; hence, the external theta role of the IP cannot be passed up to the CP.

(67)

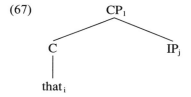

Since it is not passed up farther, the theta role *j* is no longer available for theta role assignment, and since it cannot be passed up and out of IP, it must be assigned within IP, to PRO. On the other hand, the external argument *i is* available, and in fact must be, in order for the CP to serve as an argument of a predicate. This is the controllable infinitive. (See Williams 1987 for fuller discussion.)

To borrow a term from Chierchia (1984), the complementizer thus "nominalizes" the IP, in the sense that it "encapsulates" its predicate and turns it into an item that can serve as an argument.

In fact, "nominalization" is quite an apt view of what has happened. Consider ordinary nominalization. The predicate *intelligent* is strictly a predicate and must assign its theta role. However, the form *intelligence* does not assign the theta role that *intelligent* assigns. In fact, it has "internalized" that theta role (call it the A-role) and supplied another one (call it the R-role) that permits it to head a phrase that occupies an argument position, as shown in (68).

(68)

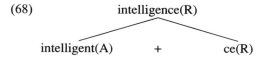

The A-role of *intelligent* is no longer available for assignment; only the R-role is. This is precisely parallel to what happens to the IP role when it is embedded in a CP: the IP's free theta role is no longer available for theta role assignment.

Both the A-role and the free IP role are available for lexically specified control, though or for free interpretation:

(69) a. John was to be intelligent.
     b. John has intelligence.

In addition, each can be logophorically controlled. Thus, the parallel is nearly perfect.

In sum, then, I am suggesting that in three of the four cases discussed at the beginning of this section—cases 2–4—the infinitive is "nominalized," in Chierchia's sense; in fact, the "nominalizer" is the complementizer. In case 1, however, the infinitive is not nominalized, but in fact remains an active theta role assigner, because this structure has no CP encapsulating the IP.

3.2.4.2 A Brief Survey of Infinitive Constructions in English   Armed with these categories, and the means of distinguishing them, we may now survey the various infinitival constructions in English to see if they fit one or the other of the patterns. If we ignore the case of lexically specified control, we are left with two patterns: DP, for adjuncts, and LC, for LC adjuncts and for infinitives in subject position.

As (70) illustrates, the infinitival indirect question clearly has a Comp, filled with *wh*; consequently, its subject is PRO. It fails to show obligatoriness or locality, and it cannot be controlled by a nonhuman.

(70) *The note$_i$ specified where PRO$_i$ to be filed.

So the properties all point in one direction: the infinitival indirect question is controllable.

As (71) illustrates, the purpose clause (with two gaps) shows indirect evidence of a Comp. Its second gap must be controlled by an operator in Comp; therefore, the subject must be a controllable PRO, since the Comp would interfere with any theta role assignment. Thus, the purpose clause is not theta-role-assigning, but controllable; hence, the antecedent is nonobligatory, necessarily logocentric, and therefore human.

(71) *The cabin$_i$ contains a brush PRO$_i$ to be scrubbed with t.

However, when the purpose clause has a single gap in subject position, everything is different. That gap is obligatorily filled, but not necessarily logocentric, or even human:

(72) I bought the shelf$_i$ [to hold books]$_i$.

In this case the infinitive is not a CP, and it is theta-role-assigning. Similar remarks hold of infinitival relatives, which also may have either one or two gaps: the two-gap variety involves PRO and control of the subject position; the one-gap variety (when the gap is in subject position) involves direct theta role assignment.

Perhaps the most controversial element in this description of these constructions is the suggestion that the purpose clauses with only a subject gap are not CPs, but simply IPs; this is entailed because IP can be theta-role-assigning, but CP cannot be.

On the other hand, the *in order to* rationale clause with null subject has a single gap in the subject position. It is therefore possible that this is a theta-role-assigning infinitive; and in fact it appears to be, in that it shows none of the properties of PRO. For example, it admits nonhuman subjects:

(73) This book was written in order to be read.

It is also subject to strict locality; for example, the matrix direct object cannot be construed as the infinitive subject. There is some question about whether control in this case is obligatory. Roeper (1984) has claimed that this construction admits implicit controllers, which of course is impossible for theta role assignment, but his conclusion has been questioned (see Williams 1985b). At any rate, the sort of example Roeper gives for this is marginal and appears to be restricted to humans, so perhaps this construction also permits LC:

(74) ?The boat was sunk PRO to collect the insurance.

There is also the case in which the entire matrix is the controller of the subject:

(75) [The boat was sunk] to make the river overflow.

Here, it is the sinking of the boat that makes the river overflow. But there do not seem to be cases of implicit control by a nonhuman:

(76) *The strop was rubbed [with the knife] in order to become sharp.

Thus, we may conclude that the purpose clause is essentially a case of an "open" theta role assigner, but perhaps may have a marginal "closed" structure with PRO, as in the case of the adjuncts.

Adjunct participles with null subjects are generally theta-role-assigning and therefore not CPs. In fact, as noted in Williams 1971, participles in general are never CPs; this is why they do not undergo *wh*-movement. The fact that they are not CPs explains a fact discussed by Johnson (1988). (77a) is ambiguous in a way that (77b) is not.

(77) a. John left before he said he would.
     b. John left before saying he would.

The two readings of (77a) can be expressed as a difference in binding by an abstract operator in the Comp of the *before* clause, as Johnson, following Geis (1970), suggests:

(78) a. ... before Op_i [he said [he would]$_S$ t_i]$_S$.
     b. ... before Op_i [he said [he would t_i]$_S$]$_S$.

However, the adjunct in (77b) cannot have a Comp, because it is a participle; hence, there can be no ambiguity of binding by an operator. The example is therefore unambiguous, corresponding most closely to the reading given in (78a), the "short" binding.

   The accuracy with which the theory predicts the clustering of properties across these diverse constructions strongly supports the idea that there are two distinct relations. If one of these is the control relation, then the other must be DP, and the effort to reduce all predication to clausal [NP VP]$_S$ structures must be abandoned.

3.3   Complex Predicates and Small Clauses

In previous work (Di Sciullo and Williams 1986) I suggested that small clause constructions were to be analyzed as complex predicate constructions, the governing verb and the small clause predicate together forming a complex verb taking the small clause subject. This analysis has a long ancestry, going back at least to Chomsky 1955.

   I now feel that this conclusion is not correct. The class of objects called "small clause" is not a homogeneous class. It is composed of truly clausal structures, of the kind discussed in the previous two sections, along with a limited set of constructions that involve complex predicates.

   I will argue that there are two sorts of complex predicates, lexical and phrasal, which behave differently, but predictably according to their nature. I will first consider a contrast in English between certain lexical complex predicates and parallel syntactic constructions (small clauses), suggesting that despite superficial similarities, fundamentally different processes derive them (section 3.3.1). I will then suggest that the French causative construction might be viewed in a similar light (section 3.3.2).

3.3.1 True Complex Predicates

As observed in Di Sciullo and Williams 1986, certain "small clause" constructions can appear in the form "V Predicate NP" even without the conditioning environment of heavy NP shift, whereas others cannot:

(79) a. John wiped clean the table.
  b. John wiped the table clean.
  c. *John considers clean the table.
  d. John considers the table clean.
  e. John considers clean any table with a reflectant surface.

(79a) is a plausible candidate for a lexical rule of complex predicate formation:

(80) V → V A

There is no evidence, however, that such a rule should be extended to the cases with *consider*, and facts in (79c–e) in fact suggest no such extension.

Further evidence that strongly discourages a uniform account comes from small clause structures in which "extraposition" has taken place within the small clause:

(81) a. John made it clear that he wouldn't help.
  b. John made clear that he wouldn't help.
  c. John considers it clear that he won't help.
  d. *John considers clear that he won't help.

It would appear from these examples that *consider* takes a clausal complement structure (whose exact nature I take up shortly), but that *make* does not, on the assumption that clauses associated to a sentential subject position are tagged with *it*, whereas other clauses are not.

As observed by Emonds (1976), and more recently by Neeleman (1992), whenever the second member of the complex predicate is complex itself, the V-Pred-NP order is ungrammatical:

(82) a. *I picked right up the paper.
  b. *I wiped very clean the table.

Both Emonds and Neeleman take this as evidence that a rule of extraposition has applied, a rule that applies obligatorily here, but optionally otherwise:

(83) I wiped the table very clean.

I would entertain a different sort of explanation. If we suppose seriously that (80) is a lexical rule, then we might suppose further that it is incapable of generating (82b) in the first place, since the supposed D-Structure unit in (82b), *wiped very clean*, is not a possible lexical unit, as it contains a syntactic phrase.

This solves the problem of (82), but leaves no source for (83). I think (83) involves no complex predicate, but is a true small clause structure, whose nature was explored in section 3.1. In fact, then, (82b) and (83) are not related in syntax.

The English particle constructions entail a similar analysis. As observed in Williams 1974, these constructions fall into two classes. In one class are verb-particle combinations that concern the "intrinsic" properties of the thing denoted by the object; in the other class are ones that denote the "extrinsic" relation of the object to other things. Many verb-particle combinations are ambiguous; for example:

(84) John put the planes together.
　　　a. assemble [intrinsic]
　　　b. side by side [extrinsic]

(85) John kicked the vase over.
　　　a. on its side [intrinsic]
　　　b. over to me [extrinsic]

For the (a) meaning, the order V-Prt-NP is not grammatical in the absence of heavy NP shift effects (Williams 1974):

(86) a. *I put together the planes.　(in the side-by-side meaning)
　　　b. I kicked over the vase.

This seems to be exactly the same phenomenon as before: two constructions, one lexical, and the other not:

(87) a. V → V P　(for the intrinsic cases)
　　　b. VP → V NP P(P)　(for both the intrinsic and extrinsic cases)

The lexical rule cannot admit phrases, so when the particle is syntactically complex, only the syntactic rule is possible (Emonds 1976):

(88) *I put right together the planes.

It may be that the English pseudopassive is an extension of the rule in (87a); at any rate, it is clear that the English pseudopassive is a rule of the type we have been calling lexical. In general, phrasal material is excluded from the construction:

(89) a. John was [talked to Mary about] t.
　　　b. *John was [taken great advantage of] t.

The verb and the material up to the direct object trace (bracketed in these examples) must be construable as a lexical item, perhaps derived by rule (87a), and must therefore contain no syntactic phrases. (89b) shows just how tight that restriction is. There is perhaps a good reason why the material must be so construed: in the pseudopassive, just as in the passive, the engine of the construction is the retraction of the verb's Case-assigning ability. If, as seems likely, structural Case assignment is a property of lexical items, and not of syntactically derived items, then in the case of the pseudopassive, it is necessary for the bracketed material to be a lexical item, since it is only from a lexical item that Case can be retracted.

The semantics of pseudopassives seems to be different from the semantics of the V-A cases, but it is not clear whether this is an obstacle to identifying them. The semantic relation of the predicate A to the V seems to be that the A specifies a property that is an intrinsic part of the meaning of the V. But in the case of the pseudopassive, the semantics seems to be function composition. In categorial terms, the P is a PP/NP, and the V is a VP/PP, so the composition is "transitive": VP/NP.

The lexical character of the V-A rule can be seen in the following nominalizations, since only lexical items can nominalize:

(90) a.   the wiping clean of the table
     b.   *the considering silly of Bill
     c.   *the considering of Bill a fool

In sum, we observe a rule in English that derives a complex predicate by appending a V with a P or an A. The rule is purely lexical in that neither of the constituent elements can be syntactically complex. Furthermore, the derived unit has the characteristic properties of lexical items: it can assign Case; it is liable to retraction of Case assignment; it excludes syntactically complex subunits; it can be nominalized; to which we might add, it is referentially opaque (see (89)).

The rule itself is left-headed, in that the verbal inflections are added to the left member, not to the derived unit as a whole: *makes clear*, not *make clears*. This is not so when the verb is nominalized:

(91) a.   do some push ups
     b.   *do some pushes up

There is no mystery about this, though: since the nominalization is derived by a rule that does not obey X-bar theory (N → V), the X-bar transmission of features from head to whole therefore cannot penetrate to the verbal interior of the expression.

3.3.2 French Causatives

In section 3.3.1 I noted that English has the rule (92), a left-headed lexical rule of complex predicate formation.

(92) $V \rightarrow V \begin{Bmatrix} A \\ P \end{Bmatrix}$

I also discouraged the idea that English has nonlexical complex predicates, that is, instantiations of the rule in (93),

(93) $V \rightarrow [V \; XP]_{V^x}$

where the V^x constituent is some argument-taking nonmaximal unit, in other words, a syntactically derived complex predicate.

In this section I would like to explore the notion that such items do exist, in some languages. The candidate I will put forward is the French causative construction, suggesting that at least one variety of this construction involves a syntactically derived complex predicate.

There are three varieties of the French causative. First, there is the *faire-par* construction, which I will put aside as not involving complex predicate formation at all.

Second, there is the *faire*-accusative construction. This construction, which can be formed only with verbs that do not take a direct object, compounds (with head on the left) *faire* with a predicate, internalizing as direct object the external argument of that predicate:

(94) a. faire + partir → faire-partir [+DO]
              +subj
       b. J'ai fait partir Pierre.
           I made leave Pierre

In other words, it is identical to the *wipe clean* construction in English. It is in fact more typical of French to have such compounds than English, since in French, to the extent that compound terms occur, they are left-headed. The limitation to predicates without direct objects is easy to understand in light of the fact that the derived form puts the embedded subject in direct object position, and only a single direct object is ever allowed.

The semantics of the construction is either function specification (as in the English *put-together* case), or perhaps function composition, as in the pseudopassive; function composition gives

(95) $V = VP/S$; partir $= S/NP$; $V \circ VP = VP/NP$

Third, French has the *faire*-dative causative construction, used when the predicate to be causativized already has a direct object. It is this construction that I will argue is a syntactically derived complex predicate, of a sort not found in English:

(96) a.   V + VP → [V + VP]$_{V^x[+\text{dative}]}$
      b.   Jean a [fait   [manger la   pomme]$_{VP}$]$_{V^x}$ à   Pierre.
           Jean has made eat   the apple   to Pierre
           'Jean made Pierre eat the apple.'

Importantly, the derived V^x is not lexical, but it is not maximal either. It is not lexical, because it contains phrasal material. And it is not maximal, because it is the head of a VP that contains its internal dative argument.

Since it is not lexical, it cannot assign accusative Case, this being exclusively the right of lexical items, as we saw in the case of the English pseudopassive.

However, its being nonlexical does not prevent it from assigning theta roles. Now, in general syntactically complex units—not just atomic heads—can assign theta roles—witness the VP, which assigns a theta role to the subject. What is special here is that the assigned theta role is an internal one (external to the embedded VP, but internal with respect to the V^x complex)—that is, contained within its maximal projection.

The semantics of this construction is identical to that of the *faire*-accusative; it is either function specification or function composition:

(97)   V = VP/S; VP = S/NP; V ∘ VP = VP/NP

Ordinarily, the *faire*-accusative and the *faire*-dative constructions are treated as the same construction. This is because they are in perfect complementary distribution—if the embedded verb has a direct object, then the *faire*-dative is used, and if not, then the *faire*-accusative is used. Various schemes have been devised to achieve this result.

Even if there are two distinct constructions, as I am claiming, it is clear enough why when the embedded verb takes a direct object, the *faire*-dative construction is the only possible causative: the *faire*-accusative is excluded to the extent that two accusative objects are not possible.

What remains unexplained if there are two constructions is why the *faire*-dative construction cannot be used when there is no direct object. I think that the Blocking Principle could be invoked here. Typically, a lexical possibility blocks a syntactic possibility (e.g., *happier* blocks **more happy*), except where the lexical form is impossible (in the case of the

comparative, when the base has more than two syllables). So, in the case
of the causative, it is natural for the lexical causative (the *faire*-accusative)
to block the syntactic causative (the *faire*-dative) when both otherwise
would be applicable.

In fact, in some languages—for example, Japanese—the blocking does
not occur. Japanese has the same two causative strategies, the causative-
accusative and the causative-dative. The causative-accusative is impossible when the embedded verb has a direct object, just as in French. However, the causative-dative is possible even when the embedded verb lacks
a direct object (as well as when the embedded verb has a direct object).
Hence, the blocking effect has no force in Japanese. Native speakers tell
me that there is a subtle difference in meaning between the two forms with
an intransitive, thus perhaps explaining the absence of a blocking effect.

In Spanish as well the causative-dative is not blocked for intransitives:

(98) Le   hicimos [llamar a sus padres] a Pedro.
     to-him we-made call   to his parents to Pedro
     'We made Pedro call his parents.'
     (Chomsky 1981:171, from Jaeggli 1980)

A further piece of evidence that these two constructions are not grammatically related is that the causee (the *à*-NP) must be a possible agent in
the *faire*-dative, but not in the *faire*-accusative:

(99) a. *J'ai fait toucher la table   à la chaise.
          I made touch   the table to the chair
          'I made the chair touch the table.'
     b. J'ai fait tomber la chaise.
          I made fall   the chair
          'I made the chair fall.'

Yet another is that English has only one of the two constructions (the *wipe
clean* construction), whereas French has both.

The analysis in (96) entails further that the V + VP forms a constituent
apart from the dative NP:

(100) [[V VP]$_{V^x}$ à NP]

It thus predicts that the dative causee NP will follow all complements of
the embedded V. In this, the theory differs sharply from theories in which
the dative is simply an ordinary dative argument of a compound verb
(V + V). The prediction entails that the dative NP should follow PPs that

are strict complements of the embedded verb, since these would be contained within the V^x. The following facts suggest that this is so:

(101) a. Jean l'a fait retirer de la table   à Pierre.
          Jean it made remove from the table to Pierre
          'Jean made Pierre remove it from the table.'
      b. ??Jean l'a fait retirer à Pierre de la table.

Here the dative PP must follow the *de* PP, as the theory under discussion would predict. This despite the fact that in cases where a single verb takes both a dative and a *de* phrase, they can occur in either order:

(102) a. Jean a parlé de cela à Pierre.
          Jean talked of that to Pierre
      b. Jean a parlé à Pierre de cela.

Thus, the ordering illustrated in (101) does not reflect principles governing the ordering of coarguments. See also the Spanish example (98).

It remains to be explained why (101b) is not judged fully ungrammatical. It is probably because there is a rule of right dislocation that can derive (101b) from (101a), no matter what the structure, and because this rule is motivated in these constructions by a tendency for the complex predicate to be as light as possible.

Still more evidence for the proposed dissociation of the dative and accusative causatives comes from the fact that (at least for some speakers) the *faire*-accusative strategy allows a passive, whereas the *faire*-dative does not:

(103) a. Pierre a été fait travailler.
          Pierre was made to work
      b. *La maison a été faite construire à Casimiro.
          the house was made built   by Casimiro
          (Zubizarreta 1985:284)

Passive is possible in (103a) because *Pierre* is a direct object of a lexical verb: *faire-travailler*, which has the properties of underived verbs, including the ability to assign accusative Case and thus to participate in the passive construction. But in (103b) the direct object of *construire* is not the direct object of *faire-construire*, which is not a (complex) active verb in the proposed analysis and so, naturally, cannot be a passive verb either:

(104) [V [V NP]]
      faire construire

This observation is not by itself enough to eliminate the possibility of passive in this construction, since the lower verb by itself could become a passive verb:

(105) J'ai fait [être construit]$_{VP}$ à cette maison.
I made to-be built   to this house
'I made this house be built.'

This could plausibly be ruled out on grounds of the "agentivity" selection on the dative NP illustrated in (99).

As observed by Burzio (1986), unlike its French counterpart, the causative dative in Italian permits a passive:

(106) Quei brani   furono fatti leggere (a/da Giovanni).
these passages were make read   by Giovanni

But for Italian, it is very plausible that the causative-dative is purely lexical, as suggested by the following example from Di Sciullo and Williams 1986:

(107) il fare scrivere delle poesie
the make-write of poetry

That is, the complex verb can be nominalized, just as an ordinary infinitive can. French has no such nominalizations.

Further evidence for the account given here of the difference between French and English is that French has syntactic complex verb formation for epistemic small clauses, a possibility that English lacks:

(108) a.   Jean trouve   très important que Pierre est ici.
Jean considers very important that Pierre is here
b.   *John considers very important that Peter is here.
c.   John considers it very important that Peter is here.

In (108a) French exhibits another instantiation of the structure [V XP]$_V$, as shown in (109).

(109)

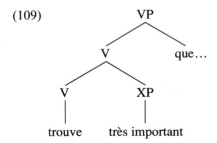

Trouve plus *très important* form a V constituent capable of assigning an internal theta role to the *que* clause. There is no need for an expletive, because there is no subject position in this construction, thanks to the operation of function composition in building the complex predicate. Since English in general lacks the syntactic complex predicate construction, this construct is unavailable, and so the expletive is required in English.

It is intriguing to try to relate this difference between English and French to another one, which is discussed in chapter 5 and illustrated by the following sentences:

(110) a.   Jean a vu récemment Pierre.
      b.   *John has seen recently Peter.

Di Sciullo and Williams (1986) argue that this difference arises from the possibility in French, but not English, of the following syntactic construction:

(111) [V AdvP]$_V$

But this is very close to the difference already needed in the present context: in a sense, (111) is another instance of a "syntactically derived complex predicate." Adjunction to a lexical head seems to be disallowed in English altogether. There remains a discrepancy between the two cases in French, however. In the case of the *faire*-dative, the resulting V^x cannot assign accusative Case, but if our speculation about (110) is correct, the complex V in (111) must have this ability. This is surely related to the fact that in V + VP the VP is connected to the complement structure of V, and in V + AdvP the AdvP is not, but I have no particular suggestion at the moment.

If these proposals are correct, then we may conclude that French has four instances of the syntactic form [X YP]$_X$: the dative causative; the epistemic construction with *trouver*; the [V AdvP]$_V$ construction just discussed; and the [N AdjP]$_N$ construction also discussed in chapter 5. Since English lacks all of these, it is plausible that the presence of these forms in French and their absence in English reflect a single *syntactic* typological dimension that separates the two languages.

Chapter 4
NP-Movement and the Subject

The topics covered in this chapter are more diverse than its title would suggest. I will divide the cases of NP-movement that have been proposed in the literature into three classes and treat them separately, arriving at quite different conclusions for each; but the upshot will be that there is no job for the rule of NP-movement to do. By saying that there are no cases of NP-movement, I am of course not denying the phenomena that NP-movement has played a role in explaining; rather, I will say that the phenomena do not exhibit properties in common with *wh*-movement, which I take to be the crux of the movement theory. On the other hand, I will not be giving a purely "lexical" account of NP-movement either. The relations, at least in two cases, will be syntactic in the full sense.

The three classes of NP-movement are

1. Raising, NP-movement to subject position from object
2. Movement of a VP-internal subject to VP-external subject position
3. Local (roughly, clause-bounded) scrambling

The first is the traditional case of NP-movement; the last two have been recently proposed as additional cases.

I will argue that traditional raising reduces to theta role assignment. The mechanisms are already in place. The notion of relativized head and the vertical binding that it gives rise to were outlined in chapter 2; all that remains is to determine the structure of infinitival clauses.

I will then argue that the VP-internal subject hypothesis (of Koopman and Sportiche (1988) and others) is not correct, except perhaps for some languages for which it was not intended, such as Hungarian.

In these first two cases, I believe that movement was proposed to account for a real relation between two items in syntax: the object and the subject in the first case, and the verb and the subject in the second. Here I will simply argue that movement is not part of the correct account. However, in the case of local scrambling, I will argue that there is no relation to account for.

4.1 Assumptions

4.1.1 Binding Theory
In this chapter, especially in section 4.4 on object scrambling, it will be necessary to make certain assumptions about the binding theory and movement. We will assume here the model of grammar outlined in Van Riemsdijk and Williams 1981, especially as revised in Williams 1986b. We will have to delay full discussion of the consequences and rationale of the model until chapter 6, but for the purposes of this chapter it is enough to say that in this model, theta role assignment, binding, and weak crossover effects hold at D-Structure, and quantification scope holds at S-Structure. As a consequence, *wh*-movement exhibits "reconstruction" effects; that is, binding, Case assignment, and so on, can be computed from the pre-*wh*-movement structure. However, the relations represented in NP-Structure —namely, the passive and raising relations—show no reconstruction effects; binding and weak crossover relations are computed solely from the NP-Structure representation of those relations. The usefulness of this model, then, is that it allows us to determine the nature of a number of relations whose status is not clear.

4.1.2 A Note on Scope
In this chapter I will also make quite specific assumptions about the representation of the logical notion of scope. We will use these assumptions in three distinct ways: first, in determining the scope properties of raised NPs, in section 4.2.1.4; second, in the discussion of expletives in section 4.2.2; and third, in the discussion of some arguments pertinent to the VP-internal subject hypothesis in section 4.3.1. These assumptions will be crucial in chapter 5 as well.

The most important assumption is that there are three sorts of linguistic scope: head scope, adjunct scope, and quantified argument scope.

Head scope is the scope that a head has over the phrase it projects, or at least over its complement structure:

(1) $[\ldots X \ldots]_{XP}$

The scope of X is XP.

This is perhaps nothing more than to say that a head takes its complements as arguments. So, for example, *believe* has scope over its complement clause, giving rise to narrow scope readings for quantified NPs contained in it: *John believes that everyone left*. *Believe* does not have scope extending beyond the range of its projection; for example, it does not have scope over its subject.

Adjunct scope is the scope of an adjoined phrase—namely, the phrase adjoined to:

(2) [XP YP]$_{YP}$

The scope of XP is YP.

For example, the scope of *probably* in (3) is the VP.

(3) John will probably [see no one].

Here, *probably* does not have scope over *John*, because *John* is not included in the phrase to which *probably* is adjoined.

Finally, quantified argument scope is the scope of a quantified argument:

(4) [... XP ...]$_{YP}$

The scope of XP is YP, if XP is an argument.

The scope is some phrase that includes the quantified NP; how large a phrase is determined by factors not at issue here. This last sort of scope is what has been treated by the rule of Quantifier Scope Assignment (QR, or "RA" in Chomsky 1973).

There has been a tendency to assimilate all cases of scope to the last case. In fact, it is only arguments that are subject to the rule of Quantified Argument Scope Assignment. I think no economy is achieved by this assimilation, and many questions are left unanswered. As far as I can tell, there is no reason to assign either a verb like *believe* or a modal a scope different from its own projection. No one has in fact proposed that "QR" apply to main verbs. However, analyses of this sort have been proposed for modal constructions; in some accounts, modal scope has been assimilated to quantified argument scope by submitting them to the same scope determination discipline.

Quantified NPs in argument position can be assigned arbitrarily wide scope. For example, with some strain, it is possible to understand the following sentence as a statement involving multiple students and professors, indicating that the embedded subject has scope over the matrix subject:

(5) At one time or another, some student or other has accused each of those professors of incompetence.

Although a special intonation is perhaps needed to get this reading, the reading is at least possible. But no amount of special intonation will render (6) the equivalent of (7).

(6) John thinks Bill must have left.

(7) John must think Bill has left.

This is not simply a matter of a lexical variability in the scope potential; such variability certainly exists and distinguishes, for example, the wide scope of *each* from the relatively narrow scope of *every*. The failure of *must* to take matrix scope is categorical. The fact is that modals do not undergo QR; that is to say, they are not subject to a rule that assigns them some containing phrase as their scope.

Now, modals do have scope, and their scope interacts with the scope of quantified NPs. How is that scope determined?

Modals are assigned scope by the Head Scope Rule, which says that a head of a phrase has scope over the whole phrase. Since a modal is the head of S, the modal has scope, for example, over the subject:

(8) No one must be there.

This has a reading in which *no one* is subordinate to *must*.

We now have established two of the scope rules: a quantified NP argument is assigned some arbitrary containing phrase for its scope (argument scope), and the head of a phrase has its phrase as scope (head scope). There is one further type of scope, namely, adjunct scope: an adjunct's scope is whatever it is adjoined to. This is illustrated in (9).

(9) a. Quickly everyone will arrive.
    b. Everyone will have quickly arrived.

In (9a) *quickly* is adjoined to S; hence, it has S as its scope and is interpreted as superior to *everyone*. In (9b), on the other hand, *quickly* is adjoined to the VP and is strictly subordinate to *everyone*.

The Head Scope Rule and the Adjunct Scope Rule interact in an interesting way when an adjunct is adjoined to a head. The adjunct has the head in its scope, and the head has its phrase as its scope; by transitivity, then, the adjunct can have the phrase as its scope. This is illustrated in (10).

(10) Everyone [will quickly] arrive.

Here, since *quickly* is adjoined to *will* and the projection of *will* contains *everyone*, *quickly* can have wider scope than *everyone*.

I think that the ECP provides some evidence that this view of scope is correct, as outlined in chapter 2.

4.2 Movement to the Subject Position

I will first treat the relations between the subject and the VP that have been traditionally described in terms of NP-movement to subject position: passive and raising. I will argue that these relations are nothing more than instantiations of ordinary subject theta role assignment. I will then provide an alternative analysis of expletives that nullifies the strongest classical argument for NP-movement to subject position.

4.2.1 NP-Trace and Movement
The analysis of NP-movement constructions here is not based on movement, but neither is it "lexical." In my account, there *is* a relation between the direct object position and the subject position in a passive; it is just that this syntactic relation is fully explicated in terms of theta theory.

4.2.1.1 Raising and Passive Constructions We have seen that in the "small clause" raising cases such as (11), the mechanisms of theta role assignment by themselves—in particular, the definition of relativized head—are sufficient to determine fully the properties of the construction.

(11) John [seems [sad]$_i$]$_i$.

[Seems sad] is a predicate by virtue of binding the external argument of *sad*. Neither movement nor NP-trace plays a role in determining the relations involved.

The same is true of the infinitival raising construction. The only difference is the element *to*. Suppose that *to* is a lexical item with no external argument. [To VP] will therefore have the same theta potentiality as VP; it can then be embedded under *seem*, to give the following structure:

(12) John [seems [to VP$_i$]$_i$]$_i$

Here *John* gets its theta role from the head V, just as in (11) it gets it from the head A; the only difference is that (12) has one further layer of structure. Hence, for infinitival raising constructions, neither NP-movement nor NP-trace is involved in the relevant syntactic relations.

Note that the same locality holds here as in the small clause raising construction: every link in the relation between the embedded verb's external argument and the matrix subject is either an instance of predication, under sisterhood, or an instance of "vertical binding," which is subject to the constraint of immediate domination that follows from its being an instance of X-bar theory inheritance, under the definition of relativized head.

Finally, let us turn to passive. Is there any evidence for NP-movement in the description of this family of constructions? We will conclude, essentially as in Williams 1982b, that there is no evidence for movement, although there is evidence for NP-trace. Most importantly, the relation of the subject of a passive to a verb is determined entirely by theta theory, not by movement theory.

We will consider several different types of passive, and we will assume a rather "standard" analysis of what makes a passive, despite the fact that no movement is involved. The element common to all the passives is dethematization of the subject (Williams 1981a); in this respect, passive forms resemble raising verbs. We will assume further that passive verbs do not assign accusative Case.

Let us begin, then, with the passives that most resemble the raising verbs, the "raising" passives:

(13) John was believed to have left.

Suppose for a moment that *believed* is subcategorized for *to*P. Then (13) is identical to a case of raising—we have simply exchanged *believed* for *seems*. There is one problem with this assumption: the uniformity of subcategorization. The active of *believe* subcategorizes for a clause; in fact, in English a *to*P is ungrammatical in the active:

(14) *John believes to have left.

We will return to this problem in section 4.2.1.2; essentially, (14) will turn out to violate the Theta Criterion.

Now let us turn to the ordinary verbal passive. To begin, let us make some very particular assumptions about theta roles and Case. Let us assume that the arguments of verbs are annotated for "conditions of realization"; so, for example, the dative of *give* is marked as being realizable as a *to*P. Let us assume further that the verb assigns accusative Case. Specifically, it does not assign accusative Case to an argument; rather, it assigns "structural" accusative Case, under some form of government. Not to an argument, because of the exceptional Case-marking constructions, in which the verb assigns Case to an NP that is not an argument of the verb. These assumptions should not be controversial.

The direct object will not be marked with a realization condition, since its realization is accusative Case, and so it can be realized if and only if accusative Case can be assigned.

We are assuming as well—again, not controversially—that the passive cannot assign accusative Case, and that the "old" external argument has been assigned the realization condition *by*P (and hence is not an external argument).

Given these assumptions, a passive VP will have the form shown in (15).

(15) VP

Now, the Theme argument must be assigned internally, but there is no Case-marked position to which it can be assigned. Therefore, let us assume a Caseless empty category for this purpose. This will give the structure shown in (16).

(16)   VP
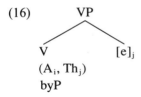

Assuming further that Caseless NPs cannot satisfy theta roles, theta role *j*, now on the empty category, is not satisfied. However, since it is the external argument of the empty category, it can now be vertically bound by the VP as in (17a), just like the external argument of the predicative phrases discussed earlier (*seems sick*, etc., as in (17b)).

(17) a.   VP$_j$ b.   VP$_i$
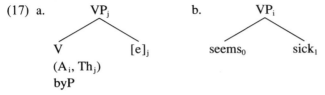

But this is now a one-place predicate on the Theme argument; it can be applied to a subject, to yield a passive sentence.

Note the connection between this analysis and the analysis for existentials introduced in section 4.2.2.2.2: in both cases a theta role assigned to a VP-internal NP does not satisfy that theta role, and the index of the theta role is vertically bound by the VP. The difference between NP-trace and ordinary NPs is that an ordinary NP can, but need not, satisfy a theta role, but NP-trace cannot do so. We will return to the case of the existential in section 4.2.2.

Note further that this analysis involves "trace," but not movement. The trace is nothing more than the empty Caseless NP, which we assume to be base-generable, and which has the further property that it cannot satisfy a theta role. That it does not arise through movement simply means that we cannot appeal to the theory of movement to explain any of the properties of the constructions in which it occurs; but in fact we have just provided an alternative account of those properties in terms of X-bar theory and theta theory.

There is no movement in the description of the passive construction here. But what has replaced it? Exactly the same thing that has replaced it in the case of raising: the vertical binding of an argument. In this case it is the argument index on the VP that is vertically bound. What prevents the vertical binding of the index on an ordinary NP? Two things, generally acting together. First, the binding theory, which says that a referential NP cannot be bound, prevents the vertical binding of a referential NP. The special thing about Caseless [e] is that it cannot be referential, which is why it cannot satisfy a theta role. (See chapter 6 for a fuller discussion of the binding theory in the current context.) Second, the Theta Criterion in general prevents the vertical binding of an internal NP: the index on the VP is reserved to bind the external argument of the verb. Hence, an internal argument will be vertically bound only under the special circumstances that (1) the verb itself has no external argument, and (2) the internal argument is not a referential item.

Note that the relation between the verb and the subject in a passive now has three components:

1. The relation of the verb to the internal argument position
2. The binding of the internal argument position to the VP
3. The predication relation between that VP and the subject

Note further that these are all instances of the theta role assignment relation, so that the theory of that relation should exhaust the description of the "movement" relation in passive.

Although this description of passive does not involve movement, it is not a "lexical" description of passive, at least, no more so than any other description. What has happened in the lexicon is the dethematization of the subject and the retraction of accusative Case; but this is what happens in the lexicon under all accounts. What has not happened in the lexicon is the externalization of the Theme argument. This externalization happens in the syntax—not by movement, but still, irreducibly in the syntax— namely, in the vertical binding of the Theme argument.

Is there any reason for not fully lexicalizing passive—so that the passive form, rather than resembling the raising verb, resembles an ordinary adjective like *big*? I think several of the considerations that favor the movement analysis favor my analysis as well, over one that is fully lexical. It is in fact the syntactic environment that determines whether the Theme argument can be realized in object position or not, not the lexical verb by itself. This cannot be seen in English, but in Spanish it is quite clear. Spanish has a mechanism whereby Case can be assigned to the direct object not by the verb, but by the nominative Case assignment mechanisms. When this happens, the direct object can remain VP-internal, in which case it is not vertically bound:

(18) Fue presentada María. (see Jaeggli 1986:594)
      was introduced Maria(nom)

(German and Icelandic behave similarly.) Of course, the raising case is possible as well:

(19) María fue presentada.

(19) corresponds to the English case; (18) is particular to Spanish and follows from the availability of the extra Case assignment mechanism in Spanish but not in English. We may reduce the difference between English and Spanish to this Case assignment mechanism and maintain that the passive forms in the two languages are identical. But if we fully lexicalize passive, then not only will English and Spanish passive forms be different, but Spanish will systematically have two passive forms, one like the English passive, and another that has internal Case and no external argument.

We have eliminated NP-movement, but we have not eliminated NP-trace. Can NP-trace be eliminated as well? I think not. We could imagine a theory that allowed direct vertical binding of internal verbal arguments, yielding (20), which is just like (17a) except that the mediation of the internal trace is eliminated.

(20)

VP_j

V

(A_i, Th_j)

byP

However, I think there is a good deal of evidence that weighs against this. Furthermore, it would require a complication of the difference between internal and external argument, something beyond the notion of relativized head, which is all that we have used thus far.

The evidence concerns the syntactic transitivity of passive VPs. For example, passive VPs are rejected by the Head-Final Filter on prenominal modifiers:

(21) a.   a [proud (*of his children)] man
     b.   *the [promised t] people
     c.   the promised book

The picture is complicated by true lexical passives, which are just adjectives, and hence have their own designated external arguments, like any ordinary adjective. But since lexical passives seem to be restricted to Themes, (21b) is probably reliably a verbal passive, and it is properly excluded so long as the trace is forced to be present.

Another kind of evidence for the transitivity of passive VPs derives from the evidence adduced by Burzio (1986) for the analysis of unaccusative verbs in Italian. Burzio shows that the partitive clitic *ne* in Italian can be related only to internal arguments. He then shows that it can be related to the subject argument of certain "unaccusative" verbs:

(22) a.   Ne   arriveranno molti.
          of them will arrive   many
     b.   *Ne   telefoneranno molti.
          of them will telephone many
     c.   *Ne   examineranno il caso   molti.
          of them will examine   the case many
          (Burzio 1986:chap. 1, (5))

This would follow if we assume, as Burzio does, that *ne* is restricted to internal arguments, and that *arrivare* has only a single internal argument, whereas *telefonare* has a single external argument. *Arrivare* has the theta structure of a passive form, shown in (23).

(23)   VP$_j$

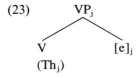

(Th$_j$)

But now, *ne* can be related to the internal argument position [e], which will exist only for *arrivare*, not for *telefonare*.

The main reason why internal arguments cannot be vertically bound, however, is theoretical. Vertical binding is simply X-bar percolation, which by definition is only open to heads—and the external argument is the head of its argument structure. But when an internal argument, such as the Theme argument in (20), is assigned to the direct object, it is identified with the external argument of the direct object and thereby becomes eligible for vertical binding under the definition of relativized head.

4.2.1.2 Exceptional Case-Marking Constructions   In analyzing exceptional Case-marking (ECM) constructions in the present context, there are four things we want to achieve. The first is of course to analyze all forms without recourse to anything beyond the theta theory already given —in particular, without NP-movement. The other three all have the same goal: to preserve sound generalizations established by previous work on these constructions. First, we want uniformity of subcategorization for related lexical items—specifically, for the active and passive forms of the verbs. Second, we want to preserve the correlation, noted by Bresnan (1972), of lack of a passive and possibility of control. Third, we want the Case of the subject of the ECM construction to be licensed by the matrix ECM verb, and not from within the ECM embedded clause.

The first question is, What is the type of the embedded complement of the ECM construction—or is it in fact a single constituent? The left member of the clause is an NP that does not get Case from the clause itself; the right member is a *to*P. Assuming the notion of clause structure espoused in chapter 1, we should analyze the clause type as follows:

(24) [0, to]P

That is, it is a complex projection whose left member is 0 and whose right member is *to*; hence, it consists of the sequence 0P *to*P. The 0P indicates that no Case or features are assigned to the left element. Given this, if the left element is to satisfy the Case Filter, its Case must be assigned by something outside the clause.

Now, suppose that a verb like *believe* both assigns structural accusative Case and subcategorizes for (24). This gives an ECM structure like (25).

(25) John believes [him to have left].

Him to have left is a [0, toP], and the Case on the left element is assigned by *believe*.

If we passivize *believe*, then accusative Case assignment is eliminated, and the left element of the ECM clause cannot be realized. This gives the representation in (26).

(26) John was believed   [0, toP]

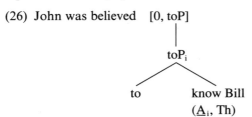

$$\text{toP}_i$$

to   know Bill
          $(\underline{A}_i, \text{Th})$

Since the external theta role of the *to*P cannot be satisfied at the [0, toP] level, it is vertically bound by it, then bound by the VP headed by *believed*, and then assigned to *John*. Thus, this analysis achieves uniformity of subcategorization, and the notion that the Case on the embedded subject comes from without.

Importantly, [0, toP] is not in a theta relation to *believe*, but rather is in the functor-complement relation; otherwise, it would not be theta transparent. In this regard, *believe* ____ [0, toP] is not uniform with *believe* ____ *that*P, since the latter is a theta complement.

As discussed in chapter 3, control verbs differ from raising verbs just on this dimension: the complement of a control verb is a theta complement (e.g., *want* takes its complement as a theta argument, as in (27)). We may suppose that it is *to* that makes this possible, by virtue of having an **R** external argument (recall: to be a theta argument, an element must have an external argument).

(27) want   [to   leave]$_{\text{toP}_i}$
     $(\underline{A}, \text{Th}_i)$ $(\underline{R}_i)$ (A_j)

In constructions with a *for* phrase, *for* plays this role.

The answer to the question "Why do *want* verbs not permit passive like *believe*?" is now simply this: the infinitive itself is a theta argument and therefore cannot be a means of passing up an argument. For example, in (27) the *j* argument of *leave* cannot be passed up through the *to*P, since the *to*P itself already has an external argument (the *i* argument of *to*), which takes priority.

Thus, given uniformity of lexical items, control verbs will not permit passive. For control to obtain in the first place, the complement must be a theta complement (and not a functor complement); and if it is, then it will be opaque to theta roles.

Note that the word *to* is ambiguous under this account, since it occurs in both raising and control structures. In raising structures it has no external argument, but in control structures it does. One way to make *to* uniform across these two constructions would be to posit a null complementizer, with external argument, for the control infinitive; but this simply relocates the ambiguity. I think, though, that the ambiguity is tolerable, given that there are some languages that are clearly unambiguous. Russian, for example, has raising constructions with XPs for X = A, N, but does not have raising from infinitives:

(28) a. Ivan kažetsja (*byt') umnym.
         Ivan seems   (to be) smart (instr)
     b. Ivan kažetsja xotet' pojti domoj.
         Ivan seems   to want to go home
     c. Ivan kažetsja (*byt') durakom.
         Ivan seems   (to be) a fool (instr)
         (L. Babby, personal communication)

This would follow if the infinitive in Russian always has an external argument and hence can serve only as a theta argument.

4.2.1.3 Movement in General   In this account of the passive and raising constructions, movement plays no role. Rather, the relations are established by the calculus of theta role assignment and its relation to X-bar theory. I do not believe that this analysis paves the way for the elimination of all movement. In particular, I believe that *wh*-movement is untouched by the arguments presented here.

In a way, it is misleading to pose the problem in terms of movement. What is more important is what grammatical relations are akin to. I have argued that the relation of surface subject to embedded verb in raising constructions, and surface subject to object position in passive, is an instance of a theta relation—that is, a relation established by theta theory pure and simple. *Wh*-movement is not such a relation. Thus, I am arguing that the NP-movement relation is akin to the "subject of" relation, and not akin to the operator-binding relation of *wh*-movement.

Some theorists (Gazdar (1982), for example) have argued that all movement rules reduce to an annotation of phrase structure rules. This may or
may not be correct, but it is quite a different proposal from the one made
here. Here, I have proposed first, that there is a calculus of theta role
assignment tied to X-bar structures, and second, that the passive and
raising relations are instances of that calculus, which is moreover the same
calculus that assigns the theta role to any subject.

That *wh*-movement cannot be subsumed under the system outlined here
is easily demonstrated. For example, the NP-movement relation cannot
"cross" a head with an external argument; clearly, though, *wh*-movement
can and (in all but the most degenerate cases) does.

4.2.1.4 Raising and Scope   A striking feature of the raising construction
is that the raised NP can be scopally subordinate to the raising predicate:

(29) No one tends to be there.
   "It tends to be the case that no one is there"
   tends (not exist x (x is there))

The natural interpretation of (29) is the one in which *no one* is subordinate
in scope to *tends*, though of course the opposite reading is available as
well. The puzzle is to determine how the reading illustrated in (29), the
"narrow" reading for the subject, comes about.

Two possibilities present themselves in the literature. First, there is the
notion of reconstruction, applied here to NP-movement. Under this theory, *no one* is returned to its (supposed) D-Structure position, and then
QR applies to derive the structure in (30).

(30)   [e] tends [[no one]$_i$ [[e$_i$] to be there]]

The other proposal, suggested by May (1977), is quite similar: QR, the
scope assignment rule, is capable of deriving (30) from (29) directly, by
lowering the quantified NP to a position adjoined to the lower clause,
without benefit of the intermediate step provided by reconstruction.

The problem with the reconstruction solution is that it does not work
generally. Reconstruction into *wh*-trace positions accounts correctly for
binding facts in many cases, but not scope facts; it seems that the structure
derived by reconstructing into *wh*-trace positions is not appropriate for
scope determination, as shown in Williams 1986b. Second, reconstruction
into NP-trace positions does not even account for binding facts. For
example:

(31)   *Each other seems to John and Mary t to have won.

If antecedency of reciprocals could be licensed under reconstruction into NP-trace positions, then (31) should be much better than it is, given that the position of *t* is c-commanded by the position of *John and Mary*, as shown by the applicability of Condition C in (32).

(32) *It seems to him$_i$ that John$_i$ has won.

Given that reconstruction does not work for NP-traces, and that even for *wh*-traces it does not work for scope assignment, it seems like a bad bet for the solution to the question posed by the narrow reading of (29).

A different solution emerges from viewing (29) as the result of an interaction between the Head Scope Rule and the Adjunct Scope Rule. The Head Scope Rule says that a head has scope over its projection; by this rule, the scope of *tend* is the VP in (29). The Adjunct Scope Rule says that in the structure (33),

(33) [XP YP]

the scope of XP is YP. In a way, this is the default interpretation: the interpretation that arises when the Quantified Argument Scope Rule does not apply. If the Quantified Argument Scope Rule does not apply in (29), then the Adjunct Scope Rule will determine that the scope of *no one* in (29) will be *tends to be there*.

As a result of these two scope determinations, both the NP subject and the verb *tend* are assigned the VP as their scope. Since linguistic rules assign them the same scope, their relative scope is not linguistically determinate, meaning that the sentence is ambiguous, with wide and narrow scope for the subject. In this way, the puzzle of the narrow reading is solved.

It remains to be explained why the "lowering" effect does not occur except with raising verbs. Specifically, why is there no interpretation of the following sentence in which *no one* is subordinate to *wants*?

(34) No one wants to be there.
      *(wants (no one . . .))
      (A, B)

The difference, of course, is that *wants* has an external argument that is assigned to *no one*. Why does this make a difference? Suppose an interpretation were assigned in which *no one* was subordinate to *wants*. Then *no one* would not include the external argument of *wants* in its scope, since it does not include *wants* itself in its scope; but then this argument would be unbound. Hence, this reading is unavailable.

Next we turn to the fact that an argument itself—that is, a theta role on a verb—must be in the scope of a quantifier that it is assigned.

The result just derived depends on a conception of linguistic quantification that is problematic under the usual assumptions. In saying that the scope of *no one* is the VP, we are saying that the scope does not include the quantified NP itself. This is a problem if the position of the quantified NP is taken to be the variable of the quantified structure.

Under the most standard assumptions, a quantified structure consists of the following elements:

(35) a. A quantifier
      b. A restriction on the quantifier
      c. A variable
      d. A scope

Given these four things, it is reasonable to think that the full interpretation of a sentence with a quantified NP can be derived. In all standard theories, the variable must be included in the scope. The theory of QR (Chomsky 1973 and subsequent work) is a theory of this kind, as is the theory outlined in Williams 1986b.

What, though, is a variable? We have assumed, following general assumptions, that a variable is a syntactic position—in fact, the position occupied by the expression of the quantifier and its restriction. However, it would be more consistent with the conclusions drawn in chapter 6 if we were to take the variable to be a theta role, rather than a syntactic position. In chapter 6 we will see that as far as the binding theory is concerned, it is the theta role itself that has the property of reference, and the NP to which the theta role is assigned is simply a qualification of the reference. Here the same consideration would lead us to say that the variable is the theta role itself, not the NP to which the theta role is assigned. So, for example, (36) has the quantificational structure shown in (37).

(36) [Every boy]$_i$ likes carrots]]$_s$.
          ($\underline{A}_i$, B)

(37) Quantifier: every
      Restriction: boy
      Variable: A_i
      Scope: S

This differs from the ordinary theory of quantification only in identifying the variable as the subject theta role, rather than the subject position.

If this view is assumed, then giving the subject VP scope in (29) is not a problem, since the VP contains the variable of which the subject is the quantifier.

May (1977) treats the problem of the narrow reading for (29) in a different way. He proposes that the subject NP is "lowered" by his rule of QR, which adjoins it to the embedded S, as discussed in connection with (30). Because this sort of lowering operation is not a part of quantifier interpretation as conceived here, it becomes especially interesting to know which analysis is correct.

I think that the following sort of fact favors the analysis presented here: a quantified NP cannot be interpreted as subordinate to more than one predicate that it c-commands. I will first show that this is the case, and then demonstrate that it follows from the present conception, but not the "lowering" or reconstruction theories.

In the following double raising construction, the subject cannot be understood as subordinate to both of the verbs that follow:

(38) No one could have tended to be there.
    NOT: could(tend(no one

As indicated, (38) cannot mean 'It could have been the case that there tended to be no one there'.

A lowering analysis must equip itself with an otherwise superfluous "subjacency" condition in order to explain this fact, a prohibition against lowering across more than one predicate. But the theory defended here derives it immediately: if the Quantified Argument Scope Rule does not apply to *no one*, then the subject is interpreted as having *could have tended to be there* as its scope. This means that *no one* will have indeterminate scope with respect to *could*, the head of that phrase, but the structure will fully determine that it is superior in scope to *tended*.

Corroboration of the empirical conclusion comes from another sort of example:

(39) a. A democrat couldn't have done that.
        not(could(a democrat
    b. A democrat could have not done that.
        *not(could(a democrat
        a democrat(could(not

(39a), but not (39b), has the reading 'not(a democrat'; (39b) has only the opposite reading. This is because in (39a), but not (39b), the negation is in the head of the phrase that the subject has as its (smallest possible) scope.

Reconstruction theories fare especially badly with these examples, for reconstruction obeys no subjacency effect at all. But lowering theories are really just as unsatisfying, since the prohibition against lowering across two predicates would be perfectly arbitrary.

4.2.2 Expletives and Idioms

Expletives and idioms are thought to provide a special argument for NP-movement. In this section we will see that they do not.

For idioms, the argument runs, "Idioms are D-Structure units because they are lexical units. The fact that they are not units in S-Structure is evidence of transformation." Similarly, expletives are regarded as evidence for NP-movement because they are raisable.

4.2.2.1 Idioms   The thesis we have been exploring is that NP-movement reduces to theta role assignment mechanisms. This view can be discounted if constructions can be found that exhibit the phenomena of NP-movement constructions, but in which the mechanisms of theta role assignment are not operative. Idioms might be such a case. For example, if a VP idiom is passivizable, what theta role could be involved, if idioms have no internal semantic structure, let alone no internal theta role analysis?

I believe the argument for NP-movement has already been answered by Fiengo (1974), who observes that when raising or passive is applied to an idiom, then the idiom can independently be shown to be analyzable in certain ways. Specifically, it can be shown that the moved NP occupies a quantifiable (and hence argument) position within the idiom.

For example, consider the idiom *to cross that bridge when we come to it*, which can be passivized. In addition, the object can be quantified:

(40) a. That bridge will be crossed when we come it.
      b. We will cross those bridges when we come to them.

But in the case of *kick the bucket*, the idiom cannot be passivized, nor can the object be quantified (even though it would be perfectly sensible to do so):

(41) a. *The bucket was kicked by Bill.
      b. *They kicked many buckets.

Fiengo's correlation tells us something about the theta structure of idioms. One tends to think of idioms as unanalyzed fixed expressions to which an unanalyzed meaning is assigned. Part of the meaning of an item is of course its theta structure: how many theta roles there are, what the theta relations are, and so on. However, idioms are not all fully unanalyzable. For example, although (40a) is an idiom, it may nevertheless have a theta structure, in that the object bears a theta role with respect to the verb. To the extent that this is so, the meaning of the idiom has structure and is not "unanalyzed," although it of course remains idiosyncratic. Although we cannot assign meanings to the parts of the idiom from which the full meaning of the idiom can be derived, the assignment of a theta structure to the idiom means that we can locate different parts of the meaning of the idiom in different parts of the idiom. For example, in (40a) we can say that *cross* corresponds to *solve* and that *bridge* corresponds to *problem*. Once this correspondence is established, it is easy to see how the idiom can be generalized to, for example, several problems. The idiom then is not deviant in its theta structure: *bridge* really is an argument of *cross*. Instead, these words are deviant in their reference: *bridge* does not refer to bridges, but to something else, and *cross* does not refer to crossing, but to something else.

But if the idiom has theta structure, then it is passivizable under the theory entertained here, since the relation of the subject to the direct object position is established by the mechanisms of theta role assignment. On the other hand, if the idiom has no theta structure, as in the case of *kick the bucket*, then no passive is possible.

It should come as no surprise that some idioms have a theta structure; a theta structure, like a syntactic structure, is a partial determinant of meaning, and nothing requires that idioms be completely unanalyzable by the rules of semantics, just as they are not completely unanalyzable by the other rules of grammar.

4.2.2.2 Expletives   If we suppose that expletives are simply incapable of fulfilling the theta requirements of predicates, but are capable of fulfilling Case requirements, then we derive most of the properties of expletives, at least for *it*. (We will return to *there* in a later section.)

4.2.2.2.1 **It**   First consider *it*, supposing for the moment that it is the only expletive in English. Assume that it lacks the R̲ external theta role of most nouns. Now, what about its distribution follows from this and this alone?

It follows that *it* can occupy only nontheta positions to which Case is assigned. Let us make the usual assumptions about Case, and let us assume as well Burzio's generalization (Burzio 1986), or anything from which it follows: a verb that assigns accusative Case must assign an external theta role. Then I think our account of *it* is 99% right.

It will occur as the subject of weather verbs. These will not be transitive (Burzio's generalization). It will occur as the subject of verbs that take S as a complement, but not those that take NP (again, Burzio's generalization). And it will occur as the subject of a number of verbs that take oblique complements,

(42) It is tight/small/suffocating/scary under the porch.

but again, by Burzio's generalization, not transitives:

(43) *It is tight the space under the porch.

It will occur as the subject of passives. In English this construction is quite limited, since the passive morpheme can attach only to verbs that take a direct complement; and if the complement is an NP, then it must appear in subject position to get Case, thus excluding *it*. This leaves verbs that take the only other sort of direct complement—a clause—and *it* does occur with them:

(44) It was believed that Sam had left.

As has been discussed elsewhere, other languages are different, permitting a wider set of passives with expletive subjects:

(45) a. *German*
          Es wurde getanzt.
          it was   danced
      b. *French*
          Il a été tiré sur le bateau.
          it was fired upon the boat

For this discussion, the important thing is that these differences between languages do not entail different analyses of expletives; rather, the differences reduce to different conditions on the attachment of the passive morpheme.

We have explicated the distribution of the expletive purely in terms of its not having a theta role. We have not, for example, imagined that in a sentence like (44) the expletive is related in any way to the clausal complement itself. We are assuming that the clausal complement is directly an argument of the verb, and that the assignment of the theta role is not mediated by *it*.

Our theta theory is a theory for interpreting junctures, coupled with the X-bar inheritance device. To add a chain of the sort that has been pro-

posed for the assignment of theta role to clauses in these sorts of structures would undermine the whole enterprise. Simply on the grounds of
conserving the power of the theory, then, we would reject anything other
than direct theta role assignment by the verb to the clause in (44).

At the same time, we are assuming that the mechanism that underlies
the passive and the raising constructions is not NP-movement, or indeed
any sort of movement, but rather theta role assignment. It might be raised
as a problem for this view that the expletive *it* seems to be raisable and
passivizable. How could this be so if the mechanism of raising and passive
is theta role assignment, and if *it* simply has no theta role?

This is not a real problem. Consider an actual case where *it* raises:

(46) a.   It seems [t to have been believed S]
     b.   *(It) seems it to have been believed S

A problem only arises if one is tempted to regard the matrix *it* as related
in any way to the embedded clause. In fact, there is no need to; if we
assume what we have assumed all along, that *it* simply occupies Cased but
thetaless positions, then only (46a) is possible. In (46b), for example, *it*
occupies the embedded subject position, which is Caseless. So in fact no
relation at all—and in particular, no theta relation—is needed between
the two subject positions. They are both thetaless; one is Cased and is
filled by *it*, and the other is Caseless and remains empty.

A further argument against relating the extraposed S to the expletive thematically, or in any other way, can be gleaned from the fact that
pseudopassive is incompatible with extraposition:

(47) a.   That John had arrived was talked about.
     b.   *It was talked about that John had arrived.
     c.   That John had arrived we talked about t all night.

As (47a,c) show, neither the unextraposed nor the topicalized clause is
incompatible with pseudopassive. I believe it is because in these cases the
S is assigned its theta role indirectly, via the trace position. Note that
these constructions do not require a match between the S, which receives
the theta role, and the trace (an NP-trace) from which the theta role
emanates.

Now, if the S in extraposed structures were licensed purely by receiving
a theta role via transmission from the expletive, there would be no reason
that (47b) is ungrammatical. (We know that the S need not match the
category of the source position, so that cannot be the reason.) Suppose,
though, that there is no such thing as theta role transmission through an

expletive, an incoherent idea in the present framework in any case. Then
the clause in (47b) must receive its theta role directly in the VP. That theta
role is assigned to the object of the preposition; since an S cannot occupy
that position, it cannot receive that theta role; hence, (47b) is bad.

4.2.2.2.2 The Existential Expletive

4.2.2.2.2.1 There   The remaining obstacle to the thematic theory of NP-
movement is *there* insertion constructions. The problem is this. If *there*
is an expletive, as it is supposed to be, then it needs no theta role. In
that case, however, it bears no theta relation to the sentence in which it
appears—so its distribution should follow from the fact that it does not
satisfy a theta role, and from this fact alone. This almost works, but it fails
to account for the distribution, and it leaves a number of other important
questions about this construction unanswered.

To begin with, some distinction must be drawn between the two expletives *there* and *it*. They cannot simply both be thetaless NPs, since then
they would be interchangeable, which they are not (in standard English).
Having argued that *it* is fully accounted for by the assumption that it does
not need (and cannot get) a theta role, we need to look more closely at
there as a way toward solving the dilemma.

Since *there* (unlike *it*) is quantificational, one way to draw the distinction is to view *there* as a scope marker of the indefinite; *there* would then
have a semantic role that *it* did not have. This was the proposal that I
made in Williams 1984. I now feel that this is not correct, for reasons I will
give shortly.

As a step toward a new theory, I propose to start with the observation
that *there* insertion sentences do not violate the Theta Criterion, though it
is not clear why they do not:

(48) a. There is a god.
     b. There was [a man eating leaves]$_{NP}$.

In (48a) *a god* is not the argument of any predicate, so this sentence
should violate the Theta Criterion. Even in (48b), I would contend that
the NP *a man eating leaves* is not the argument of any predicate, though
other theorists would claim that the constituency need not be as indicated
there; instead, they might posit an NP *a man* as a subject of the predicate
eating leaves, perhaps in a small clause structure. Whatever we say about
(48b), though, (48a) remains problematic; and even if the alternative
analysis is allowed, the constituency actually indicated in (48b) is surely
allowed as well, and so both (48a) and (48b) violate the Theta Criterion.

Moro (1991) has suggested that *there* is a predicate. If so, then the postposed NP is the subject of that predicate, and the Theta Criterion is not violated. I think this is untenable. First, *there* can never occupy a true predicate position. Second, *there* undergoes raising, just like a regular NP. Although there are indeed sentence types (*there* sentences not among them) that are best analyzed as inverted subject-*be*-predicate sentences, the precopular NP in these sentences does not undergo raising or show any other subject-like properties. I have argued that the specificational pseudocleft is such an inverted structure, but (49a) shows that the precopular clause does not undergo raising. (49b) shows that *there*, by contrast, does undergo raising.

(49) a. *What John is seems to be important to himself.
     b. There seems to be a man in the room.

The difference between the two suggests that *there* is not a predicate. Further facts concerning extraction to be detailed later lead to the same conclusion.

Let us therefore suppose instead that *there* is a subject and that the indefinite NP is a predicate—this is, after all, what the surface suggests. Then at least we have an explanation for why *There is a god* does not violate the Theta Criterion—it involves a normal subject-predicate relation.

A second type of support for this idea comes from VP-deletion. VP-deletion is really XP-deletion, where XP is a predicate. This can be seen from the behavior of the inverted specificational pseudoclefts mentioned earlier:

(50) a. *What John is is callous, and what Mary is is too.
     b. What John is is amazing, and what Bill is is too.

Here, *callous* is really the subject of the clause and hence cannot be deleted. ((50b) is provided for contrast, showing that when the pseudocleft is not specificational, and hence not an inverted structure, then VP-deletion is possible.) But the indefinite NP of *there* insertion sentences can be deleted:

(51) We thought there would be a lot and there were $[t]_{NP}$.

This suggests that the *there* construction is not an inverted copular sentence and in fact that the indefinite NP is a predicate.

A third kind of evidence comes from scope interpretation. In the theory of Williams 1984, in which *there* is a scope marker, the understood scope of the indefinite is kept small by the presence of *there*. But in fact, the scope of the indefinite is actually smaller in general than the c-command domain of *there*. Consider the following sentence:

(52) In order for the illusion to work, there must seem to be nothing in the box.

Here, the only interpretation is 'must(seem(nothing'. In other words, the indefinite must have scope subordinate to both predicates, despite the fact that *there* c-commands both predicates.

But if the indefinite NP were a predicate, then its narrow scope would be explained, since predicates are not subject to QR (which is applicable only to NPs in argument position). So the indefinite NP has scope limited to its surface position, which seems to be exactly right; in (52) it is c-commanded by both predicates in S-Structure, which predicts that it will be semantically subordinate to both in interpretation.

If the indefinite NP is a predicate, as I am suggesting, one consequence of course is that it cannot be the subject of a small clause. This makes impossible the analyses in which the structure of *there* insertion sentences is (53).

(53) There is [NP Pred]$_{SC}$

I have argued elsewhere (Williams 1984), as has Jenkins (1975), that these analyses are wrong. If the arguments there are correct, then the standing of the present proposal is thereby enhanced, since it is incompatible with these analyses.

In order for *there* insertion sentences not to violate the Theta Criterion, it is not enough to say that the indefinite NP is a predicate; for if it is, it must have a subject. The only candidate is *there*. Suppose that *there* is the subject. The immediate benefit is that the close relation between *there* and the indefinite NP is exactly the relation that must hold between any predicate and its subject—essentially, the relation of theta role assignment outlined in chapter 2. And factually, this seems to be the case: the relation between *there* and its NP is neither more nor less local than the relation between any predicate and its subject. So the obvious locality of the principal relation of a *there* insertion sentence is immediately accounted for.

On the other hand, the idea that *there* is the subject of the indefinite NP raises a perplexing question: Why must the predicate be an NP? Why could it not, for example, be an AP?

(54) *There was red.

(Meaning 'There was some redness', or 'There was something red', or some such.) I do not have an answer to this question. It is clearly connected with the question of what it means for the nonreferential *there* to be the subject of the predicative NP, and with the existential interpretation of the clause, but I do not understand this.

Another perplexing question is, Why is the copula necessary? For example, why do we not find (55a), even though we do find (55b)?

(55) a. *I consider there a man in there.
     b. I consider there to be a man in there.

I have no answer to this question either, though of course I can think of numerous ways to stipulate either one of these facts.

A final argument that the indefinite NP is a predicate comes from its behavior under extraction, where it patterns exactly like other predicates, and not, for example, subjects.

First, the postcopular NP is extractable, as are predicates in general:

(56) a. Who was there at the party?
     b. How big was John?
     c. Who do you think that there was at the party?
     d. How big do you think John was?

However, it is not extractable from *wh*-islands; in this, it resembles other predicates, as well as adjuncts, and does not resemble regular NP arguments, even subjects (once *that*-trace effects are put aside):

(57) a. *Who do you wonder why there was at the party?
     b. *How foolish do you wonder why Bill considers anyone t?
     c. *Why do you wonder [who left t]?
     d. ?Who do you wonder why Bill likes?
     e. ?Who do you wonder why Bill considers foolish?

I conclude from these considerations that the indefinite NP is a predicate, and that *there* is its subject. But if this is so, then the same mechanisms of theta role inheritance and assignment that work for ordinary subject-predicate pairs will work for these as well, and no mechanism beyond these, such as NP-movement, is called for.

The same conclusion can be drawn from the "presentational" *there* construction, as in *There arrived a man*. Belletti (1988) has argued that the definiteness restriction exhibited in the presentational construction is due to partitive Case assigned to the NP under government. This untenable conclusion is based on a misinterpretation of the following fact:

(58) *There talked to John a man.
        (Belletti 1988:(6b))

Belletti concludes that the postverbal NP must occupy object position.
However, the following examples show that it does not—that in fact the
NP is adjoined to VP:

(59) a.   There [came into the room] a man.
        b. *There came a man into the room.

Two significant conclusions follow. First, the restriction to verbs like
arrive that this construction manifests is not related to unaccusativity,
which in any case has little to do with English grammar, apart from the
absence of certain pseudopassives. The restriction seems to derive from
the special "presentational" semantics of this construction.

Second, in the face of (59), the definiteness constraint cannot reduce to
verbally governed Case marking, as Belletti proposes.

(59) shows that presentational *there* sentences have the structure shown
in (60).

(60)

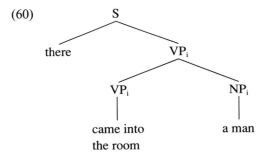

We may now relate this construction to the existential *there* construction in a simple way. (60) has two junctures, the upper [there VP] and the
lower [VP NP]. The lower juncture is an adjunct theta juncture, in the
sense of chapter 2, and the adjoined NP is a predicate NP, so the external
theta role of *a man* is bound by the embedding VP. The top juncture is the
subject-predicate relation. Thus, from the point of view of theta structure,
(59a–b) are the same as (61).

(61) John arrived a fool (but left a wise man).

The *there* in this sentence is the same as in the existential *there* sentences—
it is the thematic subject of the top VP, and consequently of both the
embedded VP and the adjoined predicative NP.

4.2.2.2.2.2 Other Expletives   French has expletive *il*, which is ambiguous. In sentences like (62) it is a theta-neutral empty expletive, like English *it*.

(62) Il est clair que Pierre est ici.
     it is   clear that Pierre is   here

But it is also an existential, as in sentences like (63).

(63) Il   est arrivé   trois hommes.
     there is   arrived three men

We know that an existential is involved, because there is a definiteness effect (the NP in the position of *trois hommes* must be indefinite), just as with *there* insertion sentences in English. This sentence will receive the structure shown in (64).

(64)

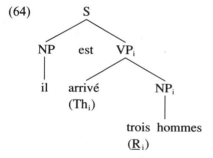

As noted in chapter 2, the NP *trois hommes* does not satisfy, but simply passes up, the Theme theta role of *arrivé*; this theta role is ultimately satisfied when the matrix VP is predicated of the NP subject expletive.

In effect, *trois hommes* is acting like a predicative NP in this construction, in that it becomes the source of the VP_i's external argument. As in the passive construction, the VP cannot bind an internal theta role (here, the Theme role of *arrivé*), but when that role is assigned, it becomes the external role of the item it is assigned to, and is then available for binding.

Importantly, the NP does not satisfy the theta role that is assigned to it. We might ask, When is this possible, in general? The Theta Criterion answers this question: only when the matrix verb has no external argument—that is, only in the case of unaccusatives, passives, and raising verbs. If the matrix verb does have an external argument, then the dominating VP must bind it, and cannot bind the argument of the complement constituent; but then that argument cannot be satisfied, if it has not already been.

How does the NP in (64) get Case? I see two options. First, it can get Case by agreement, as predicative NPs do in general—they agree in Case with the NP they are ultimately predicated of. Alternatively, it can get a special Case for predicatives, as is found in many languages. It cannot get structural accusative Case from the verb, under Burzio's generalization, since the verb does not assign an external theta role.

Some scope facts surrounding examples like (63) have been pointed out to me by V. Déprez (personal communication):

(65) Il doit   arriver   trois hommes.
     it ought to arrive three men

This sentence has solely the interpretation 'doit(trois' and not the interpretation 'trois(doit'. This is just what we would expect if the NP in (64) is not an argument, for, as noted in connection with the parallel English cases, QR is applicable only with referential NPs, that is, theta role satisfiers. Since QR does not apply, the NP has only the scope it has in situ.

A long-standing counterexample to Burzio's generalization can perhaps be solved in a similar manner:

(66) Il faut   un bateau pour faire ça.
     it needs a boat   to   do   that

This appears to be a case of a verb, *falloir*, that takes no external argument but assigns accusative Case. However, suppose that the postverbal NP is a predicative NP, and suppose that *il* is its (ultimate, not direct) subject. Then this is not a counterexample to Burzio's generalization.

We are in danger, though, of reducing Burzio's generalization to a triviality; it would be simple enough to declare that any counterexamples could be reanalyzed in this manner. In order to preserve the generalization, we will need to restrict the applicability of this analysis.

I think the means of doing this lie in lexical semantics. Suppose that *falloir* had all the properties that it does have, but meant 'x is destroyed' or 'x falls apart' or 'x rolls down a hill', rather than 'x is needed'. In that case I think that the analysis of the verbal NP as predicative would be far more suspect, for in *x falls apart* and the like, the NP seems to denote an object to which something happens—a sort of denotation we may exclude from the possible denotations of a predicative NP, even if it remains unclear what denotation a predicative NP is capable of in general.

What case does the NP get in (66)? A predicative NP gets Case in two different ways: either by being assigned a nonaccusative Case by the governing verb, or by agreement with its subject. In either case, Burzio's generalization is preserved in its widely assumed form.

Italian has two related null subject constructions, distinguished by Belletti (1988). One occurs with unaccusative verbs, as in (67a–b), and the other occurs generally (67c).

(67) a. ∅ È   stato [messo un libro sul   tavolo]$_{VP}$.
        it has been put   a   book on the table
     b. *∅ È stato [messo il   libro sul   tavolo]$_{VP}$.
        it has been put   the book on the table
        (Belletti 1988:(18a–b))
     c. ∅ Ha [mangiato un dolce]$_{VP}$ il   ragazzo.
        it has eaten   a cake   the boy
        (Belletti 1988:(12f))

Since Belletti shows that the unaccusative cases are subject to the definiteness effect, we might suspect a null existential expletive for such a case and analyze it like the French case in (64) (except that the expletive is null in Italian). (67c) must have an entirely different analysis. In particular, Belletti shows that when the subject is not in the VP, there is no definiteness effect; hence, in (67c) *il ragazzo* is simply an ordinary subject. It may be that in addition to [Nom, Tense], Italian also has a construction [Tense, Nom], simply the reverse. If this is so, then of course (67a) and (67c) have very little to do with each other.

A further difference between the French and Italian constructions is that Italian has verbal agreement with the postposed NP, whereas French does not. I suppose this to be an unrelated difference between the two languages; the null expletive is ambiguously singular or plural, whereas *il* is strictly singular. The behavior of *there* in English, sometimes agreeing and sometimes not, prevents us from concluding that the correlation of overt expletive and lack of agreement is a general one.

4.3   The VP-Internal Subject Hypothesis

Given the theory developed so far, there are two types of argument: internal and external. If we are able to identify subjects independently of this distinction (say, as Agents), then we may identify two types of subjects: internal and external. Internal subjects will be subject to the theta directionality parameter. External subjects will not be.

Some theorists have claimed that all subjects are VP-internal in D-Structure. They argue this for languages for which it could not possibly be the case, for the postulated internal subjects do not obey the theta directionality parameter. A good example is English.

In the following sections, we will sort out the possibilities, paying particular attention to arguments that there are internal subjects not subject to the theta directionality parameter; these arguments will turn out to be uniformly faulty.

4.3.1   The Koopman-Sportiche Theory

Koopman and Sportiche (1988) (K&S) and Sportiche (1988) propose that the subject position is an argument internal to the VP in D-Structure, being moved to its VP-external position in the derivation of S-Structure. They argue that in D-Structure the subject is in a preverbal position even where the theta directionality parameter requires internal arguments to be on the right; hence, their proposal violates the parameter.

This theory of the subject (the *movement theory*, or *MT*) is much closer than it at first appears to my own theory, which I will call the *external argument theory* (*EAT*). I will outline K&S's theory, and then comment on its relation to mine.

K&S's theory can be summarized as follows:

(68) a. All arguments, including the subject, are generated inside the VP
        in D-Structure (see K&S's (2)):

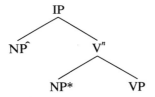

        NP* is the D-Structure position of the subject; NP̂ is its
        S-Structure position; V^n is the maximal projection of V; and
        VP is what is called the "phrasal projection" of V.
     b. All theta role assignment is "internal" in the sense that a verb
        assigns theta roles strictly to items internal to its maximal
        projection.
     c. NP* is moved to NP̂ under the canons of NP-movement.

The similarity between the MT and the EAT lies in their both having some kind of representation of the subject argument within the VP in S-Structure. In the case of the EAT, the representation is the *i* on the VP that defines the abstraction; in the case of the MT, it is the trace of the subject inside V^n. In this, both theories differ from the standard theories, past or present. The similarity between the two theories can be seen in the two surface trees of (69).

(69) a. *Movement theory*   b. *External argument theory*

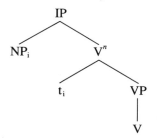   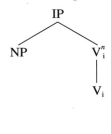

The trace in the MT diagram serves much the same purpose as the subscript i on V^n in the EAT diagram. A translation from the EAT representation to the MT representation would proceed as follows: where the EAT representation has an indexed VP, remove the index from the VP and adjoin a trace with that index to the VP, labeling the newly created node V^n.

Are these two then notational variants? More closely than I think K&S realized, though perhaps not totally.

Consider the involvement of NP-movement in the derivation of S-Structure. Here, the theories appear radically different, but in fact they are merely "symmetrically opposite." The MT determines the surface position to which the subject theta role is assigned in terms of NP-movement and NP-trace (the role is assigned internally, and then the NP to which it is assigned is moved out). The EAT does the opposite; it first posits a theory about how the external theta role is assigned, and it then explains the properties of (so-called) NP-movement in terms of that, as outlined above and elsewhere (Williams 1982b, 1985a). So here the theories are more alike than they would at first appear to be, one having a notion of "NP-movement" as primitive, and the other a notion of "external argument," but each accounting for the nonprimitive in terms of the primitive.

The theories are not really notational variants, though the above remarks should show that theory comparison requires care. I think some of K&S's arguments for their position do not take into account the symmetries that hold between the two.

4.3.1.1 The Idiom Argument   K&S present an argument for their structure based on the notion "possible idiom." The assumption of the argument, surely true, is that an idiom is a phrase of some type, and not an arbitrary string of words.

K&S demonstrate the existence of clause-sized idioms in which the tense of the clause is not fixed; for example:

(70) The shit will/would/should/did hit the fan.

Idioms of this kind, they suggest, imply that the phraseology of the clause in general is as shown in (71),

(71) Infl   ^ (rest of clause)

since in this case "rest of clause" can be a constituent idiom, still leaving Infl free to vary. "Rest of clause" in their theory is a VP with internal subject.

There are two problems with this argument that invalidate K&S's conclusion about clause structure.

First, there are idioms in which Infl elements are fixed, and the subject is free; for example:

(72) John can't/*will/*did see the forest for the trees.

Idioms of this kind suggest the more traditional clause structure (73).

(73) NP   ^ (rest of clause)

Of course, there is an alternative description of (72). Without committing ourselves to (71) or (73) as the basic structure of the clause, we might simply conclude that (72) is an S idiom, with the subject unfilled. Clearly, idioms must contain unfilled positions; for example, in (74) NP* is simply an open position in an S idiom.

(74) The cat has got NP*'s tongue.

But if Ss can have open positions, then what happens to K&S's argument? It would seem that in addition to S idioms with subject fixed and Aux elements free, we should also find the reverse: S idioms with subject free and Aux elements fixed.

If there is any argument at all, it will have to be a statistical argument, along the following lines. Idioms with no free positions will be the most common, or least marked; hence, the relative plenitude of S idioms with subject fixed and Aux free versus the scarcity of S idioms with Aux fixed and subject free argues for K&S's proposal, since under their analysis the plentiful idioms will receive an unmarked analysis.

But—and this is the second problem with K&S's argument—the statistical analysis founders on the fact that the two things being compared,

Aux and subject, are functionally so different. An idiom with a free Tense position will be twice as useful as the same idiom with fixed Tense, since it can be used to describe both the present and the past. Hence, there will be great pressure for the idiom with fixed Tense to have its Tense freed up. The effects of this same pressure can be seen in the lexical category of verbs: nearly every verb has both a present and a past form, a generalization that is clearly independent of clause structure. An idiom with a free subject, on the other hand, is a one-place predicate, and is simply not comparable to an S idiom with its subject fixed; hence, there will be no pressure to free up the subject.

For example, consider (74). There is a clear way to abstract Tense from *The cat has your tongue* to get a meaning for *The cat had your tongue* and hence generalize to an idiom with unfixed Tense. But there is no comparable way to get a meaning for *The dog has your tongue*, and so on.

These considerations are probably sufficient to account for any statistical differences in the frequencies of the two types of idioms under discussion, and hence render K&S's account unnecessary. In any case, the markedness stipulation on which the statistical argument hangs is questionable in the first place.

4.3.1.2 The Argument from Extraction in Italian   K&S review Rizzi's (1982) original generalization about extraction in Italian and suggest that it is a misgeneralization. Using the possibility (or not) of the clitic *ne* as an indicator of the pre-extraction position, Rizzi concludes that all long extraction in Italian takes place from postposition. Essentially, the preverbal subject position does not permit *ne*, and extraction is incompatible with absence of *ne* when *ne* is possible. (For discussion, see Rizzi 1982, K&S 1988.)

The fact that Rizzi failed to notice, and that K&S take as crucial, is that Rizzi's paradigm for preverbal subject position is correct for unaccusative verbs, but not for ergative verbs:

(75) a. Quante   hai   detto che *(ne) sono cadute?
       how-many have (you) said   that   *ne* are   fallen
       'How many have you said have fallen?'
   b. How many do you wonder whether ([e]) saw it?[1]

As the absence of *ne* shows, (75a) (K&S's (57)) is an example of the long extraction of a preverbal subject; but contrary to Rizzi's generalization, it

---

1. (75b) is as it appears in Koopman and Sportiche 1988. It is a word-for-word translation of the relevant Italian example.

is grammatical. The difference between (75a) and (75b) (K&S's (58)), the expected case, is that the verb is ergative in (75a).

In light of this fact, the generalization that K&S suggest, which I will accept, is that long extraction is possible only from nonderived positions. The nonderived positions include of course the (surface) subject and object position of an active transitive and the object position of an unaccusative, but not the subject position of an unaccusative, under the hypothesis that these subjects are D-Structure objects.

K&S realize this idea in the following way. In their view, only VP-internal positions are theta-marked, including the VP-internal subject position. The VP-external subject position is never directly theta-marked, but is always derived by movement of some VP-internal argument. Given this, it is possible to understand the condition on long extraction as a prohibition against extraction from nontheta positions–namely, from the VP-external subject position. Then the reason (75b) is grammatical is that the subject is actually in the VP-internal position, not the VP-external one (neither allows *ne*). This is impossible for (75a): the deep position of the unaccusative subject is postverbal, so if it is found preverbally, it is in a derived position.

Can K&S's generalization be realized in a theory without their notion of subject? Yes, so long as the theory has some notion of either derived subject or theta position. The standard theory, and the theory of this book, of course have both of these. Under the unaccusative hypothesis, the theta positions are the subject of active transitives, and objects; the nontheta positions are the subjects of unaccusative verbs and passives. So stated, the generalization is identical to K&S's position.

The difference, of course—and this is the only difference—lies in the definition of theta position, namely, that in the standard theory the external surface subject position of a transitive verb is a theta position. If we accept K&S's generalization about long extraction, then, the only difference between the two extraction accounts comes down to the difference between the two theories in the first place: whether or not the external surface subject position is a theta position.

The two theories do make subtly different predictions: K&S's theory predicts that when the subject of a transitive is long-extracted, its trace will be VP-internal, whereas the standard theory predicts it will occur in the usual VP-external position. In principle, such a difference could be decisive.

A further difference, which again could be decisive, lies in the definition of A-position in the two theories. The notion of A-position is required in

both theories for the statement of the binding theory. In particular, because of the following type of example, the surface VP-external subject
position must be identified as an A-position for the proper action of Conditions A, B, and C:

(76) He seems to John [t to have won].

If *he* were not in an argument position, then *John* would not be marked as
disjoint from *he*, clearly a wrong result.

In the standard theory, A-positions are all positions accessible to theta
role assignment, and in fact A-position is defined in terms of this. But if
the surface external subject position is never the target of direct theta role
assignment, as in K&S's theory, then the usual definition will not do. In
order to match the effects of the usual definition, the following definition
is required:

(77) A-positions are NP specifiers and complements of theta-marking
      categories.
      (K&S 1988:(19))

This definition is unsatisfying because it is disjunctive; but apart from that
it does not distinguish the two theories, since it could serve in the standard
theory as an extensionally equivalent substitute definition of A-position.

Finally, in the two theories under consideration, what is the difference
between Italian and English? Under K&S's account, the difference lies in
the obligatoriness of raising the subject from its VP-internal theta position
to the Spec of IP position. In Italian this movement is optional, so that
wh-movement can apply to subjects in theta positions. In English it is
obligatory. K&S supply a particular means of expressing this obligatoriness in terms of Case marking: in English Infl can assign Case only to Spec
of IP, whereas in Italian it can also assign it to the VP-internal subject
position. Thus, NPs that need Case must move in English, but may remain in the VP in Italian.

This difference between English and Italian is a difference without any
further consequences; hence, it amounts to a stipulation of the difference
between English and Italian. Any other stipulation will do as well, so we
will not explore the possibilities.

4.3.1.3 The Argument from Quantifier Float   K&S, and in a more extended way Sportiche (1988), argue that quantifier float supports the VP-
internal subject position.

Sportiche proposes that floated quantifiers enter D-Structure in the position of French *tous* 'all' in (78).

(78)

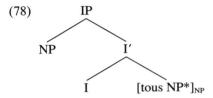

If NP* is moved to Spec of IP, the appearance of a floated quantifier arises; if the larger NP is moved, the quantifier stays with the subject. As a possible alternative to his own view, Sportiche considers the hypothesis that the quantifier is simply an adverb, not attached to the subject. He rejects this hypothesis for the following reason: the quantifier can appear in positions in which it is not adjacent to the subject it modifies, as in (79), thus violating a general principle of modification (nothing more than the basic law of theta theory; see Williams 1982b, Di Sciullo and Williams 1986, and section 2.4).

(79) They have both left.

But this argument is based on the notion that the floated quantifier directly modifies the subject. It is my view that the floated quantifier modifies the VP; in particular, it modifies an aspect of the theta structure of the VP, namely, the distributivity of the external argument. That is, *both* says of the VP it is attached to that the VP will be true of the subject it applies to only if that subject denotes two individuals, and the VP is true of each of those individuals separately.

Suppose the adverb is adjoined to the VP as shown in (80).

(80)

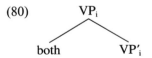

Here, *both* modifies the relation of the external argument of VP' to the external argument of VP_i, where the external argument is the index i, and where the relation established is *i of VP' is the distribution of the (plural) argument i of VP*.

Under this view, outlined in Williams 1982b, 1989, the adverb *both* is immediately adjacent to the thing it modifies (namely, VP'_i), as the locality of theta relations requires, and so the fundamental law of theta theory is observed in these cases. *Both* does not modify the subject directly; instead, it modifies the external argument of the VP and therefore *seems* to modify the subject. Here again, we see that the two theories under discussion are nearly notational variants; the *i* index marking the external argument of the VP gives something like a VP-internal representation of the subject.

Sportiche bases part of his case for the implausibility of the adverbial account of floated quantifiers on the notion that these quantifiers do not behave like other adverbs. But in fact there are adverbs that behave rather strongly like floated quantifiers, and for which something like the interpretive account just given, in which adverbs modify the distributivity of variables, would be needed anyway, even if floated quantifiers did not exist. The adverbs *jointly*, *separately*, and a number of others work in exactly this way:

(81) a. They jointly/separately carried out the orders.
     b. They carried out the orders jointly/separately.

The semantic contribution of these adverbs is exactly that of the floated quantifiers.

It is very unlikely that these adverbs, being true adverbs, originate as part of NPs. And in any case, although they can occupy the same position as the floated quantifiers (81a), they need not (81b). At least in the cases in (81b) these adverbs do *not* occupy positions adjacent to putative traces of NP-movement. Hence, there must be some mechanism for interpreting such entities as modifying the VP. Any such mechanism will automatically apply to the floated quantifiers, rendering any analysis other than the VP-modifying adverbial one superfluous.

The only difference between these adverbs and the floated quantifiers is that floated quantifiers cannot occupy postverbal position. However, this does not disqualify them from being adverbs. It is well known that different sorts of adverbs have different distributions; for example, only the floated quantifiers and the -*ly* adverbs can freely occupy the preverbal position. Many other adverbs are excluded (**John hard ran*). In the case of adverbs, distribution is very sensitive to subtypes, and morphology has as much to do with defining the subtypes as semantics.

Sportiche's overall generalization is that wherever there is a floated quantifier, there is an NP-trace of the NP the quantifier is related to, and conversely, wherever there is an NP-trace, a floated quantifier should be possible. But the latter is patently untrue of English passives:

(82) *They were seen all t.

In the face of this, Sportiche suggests that clause-bounded passive (but not ECM passive) does not involve a postverbal trace, a position for which there is no independent evidence, and against which considerable evidence can be adduced (see Williams 1978a, for example). In fact, in Sportiche's own terms, since a postverbal trace is involved in ECM passives, it is not clear how he could avoid the postverbal trace analysis of clause-bounded passive, even if some alternative means of generating passives, like the one he suggests (p. 444), were available.

I think the absence of postverbal floated quantifiers simply reflects the special distribution of these "adverbs" to preverbal position, just as adverbs like *hard* are restricted to postverbal position.

A further consideration that favors the account discussed here, and disfavors Sportiche's, is that (as noted in Williams 1982b) floated quantifiers do not have the scope properties of ordinary quantifiers, but in fact have the scope properties of adverbs. Thus, contrasts like the following arise:

(83) a.   Someone or other has said that each of the candidates is
          unqualified.
     b.   ?Someone or other has said that the candidates are each
          unqualified.

(83b), if grammatical, does not share the meaning of (83a) in which the embedded subject has wide scope. Why not? Under the view that quantifiers are adverbs, this is because adverbs do not take scope wider than their c-command domain; in this, they differ from quantified NPs in argument position, as I argued earlier in this chapter and in Williams 1984.

However, under Sportiche's account, the floated quantifier is really just a quantified NP (with missing head NP), and so there is no reason for the discrepancy:

(84) ... the candidates are [t each]$_{NP}$ unqualified.

It is a mystery why the quantified NP [t each] cannot be assigned wide scope. Note that it cannot be because the *t* it contains would then not be properly bound; such unbound traces exist in profusion in K&S's theory, where every fronted VP, or predicative XP, contains an improperly bound trace (t_i):

(85) ... and [t$_i$ give Mary a book]$_j$ we think he$_i$ will t$_j$.

Some kind of reconstruction or its equivalent will be needed to handle these traces, and will handle the trace in (84) as well. The problem with (84) is that the quantifier is liable to scope assignment in the first place. If floated quantifiers are simply adverbs, then the fact that they never take wide scope follows, since adverbs are not subject to scope assignment by QR, always taking their S-Structure sister as their scope.

4.3.1.4 The Burton-Grimshaw Argument   Burton and Grimshaw (1992) have given another sort of argument for the VP-internal subject hypothesis. Their argument is based on the conjoinability of active and passive VPs:

(86) a. The criminal will be arrested and confess to the crime.
   (Burton and Grimshaw 1992:(3b))
   b. The criminal will [be [arrested t]] and
      [confess to the crime].
   c. The criminal will [be [arrested t]] and
      [t [confess to the crime]].

If we assume a structure like (86b), then this example appears to violate the across-the-board (ATB) principle on movement, since there is a trace of movement in the first conjunct and not in the second. But if we assume the VP-internal subject hypothesis, as represented in (86c), then there is a trace in both conjuncts, and the movement can be said to have obeyed the ATB constraint.

As Burton and Grimshaw are careful to point out, however, if one assumes the theory of passive in this chapter, a theory in which the binding of the trace is accomplished "internal" to the VP in passive, then the ATB constraint is not violated, even in (86b). In the theory proposed here, the only rule relating the interior of the conjunct to something outside it is the assigning of the external theta role of the VP as a whole, and this rule applies across the board to begin with, since the representation of the theta structure of the coordinating VP is as follows:

(87) $[VP_i \text{ and } VP_i]_{VP_i}$

Here, the containing VP dominates coordinated VPs, each of which bears the index i. In general, a theta-role-assigning coordinate VP must dominate two theta-role-assigning VPs. Presumably, this is a consequence of the nature of the coordinate juncture:

(88) *John [[likes bears]$_{VP_i}$ and [seems that it will rain]$_{VP_0}$]$_{VP_i}$.

In the theory proposed here, the passive VP is simply another theta-role-assigning VP and so can be coordinated with any other theta-role-assigning VP.

4.3.2   The Diesing-Kratzer Hypothesis

The theta directionality parameter says that all arguments in a given language should be on the same side of the predicate; therefore, if the subject is internal, it will be on the same side as the object. In a language like English, this is patently impossible, and in the previous section we argued that in fact the subject is not internal. However, in an SOV language, the subject could be internal or external; it is impossible to tell which. It could be always external, always internal, freely internal or external, or internal or external with a difference of meaning. Diesing and Kratzer defend the last of these alternatives for German.

In German the strandability of a quantifier expression signals an internal argument. Kratzer (1989), following Diesing (1990), assumes that the ECP is responsible for this discrimination. Then the following example (Kratzer's (21b)) suggests that the subject is external:

(89) *Lehrer   wissen das viele.
      teachers know that many
      'Teachers, many know that.'
      DS: [viele Lehrer das wissen]$_{VP}$

The quantifier *viele* cannot be stranded from the topicalized *Lehrer* because it is external. If this is true, then the following example (Kratzer's (20b)) shows that the subject is not *always* external in German:

(90) Lehrer   haben uns viele   geholfen.
      teachers have us   many helped
      'Teachers, many helped us.'
      DS: [viele Lehrer uns geholfen haben]$_{VP}$

Here the stranding is possible. If we assume the D-Structure representations indicated, with the subject external in (89) and internal in (90), then the difference can be reduced to this factor. Kratzer and Diesing amply demonstrate that the discrimination between these two is along semantic lines: the verbs with internal subjects are *stage-level* predicates, which describe events, and the verbs with external subjects are *individual-level* predicates, which describe timeless properties of individuals.

Kratzer supplies an account of why the predicates behave as they do: stage-level predicates have an Event variable, whereas individual-level predicates do not. If the Event variable must be external, then the subject argument of a stage-level predicate must be internal, but the subject argument of an individual-level predicate (lacking an Event variable) at least may be external. This is an attractive explanation but one we cannot accept. First, individual-level predicates are not forced to have external subjects, but this is what is required to derive the facts about them; a further hypothesis is needed to produce the desired result. Second, if this were the reason for the contrast in German, then how could we avoid the conclusion that English individual-level predicates also have internal subjects, which they clearly do not? Finally, as noted in section 2.6, I believe that the syntactic reality of the Event variable, at least as a verbal argument, is dubious.

I will suppose, then, that the difference is a difference in verb type. Some German verbs have argument structure (91a) and some have (91b), and the difference is determined by the Diesing-Kratzer semantics.

(91) a. [A, ...] (stage)
  b. [$\underline{A}$ ...] (individual)

When the subject is VP-internal, how does it get Case? German has a well-attested process that assigns nominative Case to internal NPs; for discussion, see Den Besten 1982. It is presumably a related mechanism in Spanish that can assign nominative to an NP in object position of a passive verb; see section 4.2.1.1.

4.4 Object Scrambling

Recently A-movement has been used to account not only for movement to the subject position, but also for various cases of scrambling. Functional projections of the sort we have sought to avoid host the movement, by means of their specifier positions. I believe that the relation between these movements and movement to the subject position is spurious, and I will present a model of grammar in which these scramblings play a distinctly different role.

The model of grammar we are entertaining has two levels: NP-Structure and *Wh*-Structure. The first is the output of the base rules and is subject to the strictures of theta theory, Case theory, and binding theory; the second is the output of *wh*-movement and quantifier interpretation. This is the model proposed in Van Riemsdijk and Williams 1981, and especially in Williams 1986b.

This model limits the sort of relations that can be found. *Wh*-Structure relations will exhibit reconstruction effects with respect to binding, but NP-Structure relations will not.

In this model, two sorts of scrambling will be found: NP-Structure scrambling and *Wh*-Structure scrambling. NP-Structure scrambling will be represented in NP-Structure and *must preserve theta role assignment and Case assignment possibilities*. *Wh*-Structure scrambling is simply an instance of *wh*-movement, generalized. In English, heavy NP shift is an example of NP-Structure scrambling, and right node raising is an instance of *Wh*-Structure scrambling.

What does it mean to "preserve theta role assignment possibilities"? Internal theta role assignment is subject to absolute (sister) locality, and to the theta directionality parameter setting, which determines the theta role assignment configuration. So, for example, both (92a) and (92b) are possible in English.

(92) a.   give the book of poems to John
     b.   give to John the book of poems
     c.   *to John give the book of poems
     d.   *give the book to John of poems

In (92a) and (92b) locality and the theta role assignment configuration are observed; in (92c) the setting of the theta directionality parameter is violated, and in (92d) locality is violated. Heavy NP shift is therefore simply the variation allowed under locality and the theta role assignment configuration for English.

Now, although (92a) and (92b) are allowed, they are not on a par. There is a "normal" order, (92a); (92b) is judged as "marked" and is subject to special constraints. However, if the position taken here is correct, the "normal" order is not the only order in which valid theta role assignment can take place; any rearrangement of normal order subject to locality constraints and the theta role assignment configuration permits valid theta role assignment. We will return to the concept of normal order in a later section.

4.4.1   Heavy NP Shift in English
Heavy NP shift (HNPS) in English is a clear case of NP-Structure scrambling. It shows no reconstruction effects and is bounded just in the way an NP-Structure scrambling would have to be.

For example, consider (93a–b).

(93) a.   ?I recommended to Bill himself.
     b.   *I recommended himself to Bill.

Here we see that HNPS ameliorates binding. In (94) we see that HNPS ameliorates Weak Crossover (WCO) violations as well; that is, the input to HNPS might be ungrammatical, even though the output is grammatical.

(94) a.   I gave to every boy a copy of his grades t.
     b.   *I gave a copy of his grades to every boy.

In other words, binding and WCO are computed on the *output* of HNPS, not the input; hence, HNPS is represented in NP-Structure, not *Wh*-Structure.

   The same point can be made in the opposite way. If the input to HNPS is good, then the output will generally be bad:

(95) a.   I introduced John and Mary to each other's parents.
     b.   *I introduced to each other's parents John and Mary.

This demonstrates that HNPS does not show reconstruction effects, again consistent with the assumption.

   In general, HNPS must preserve the theta role assignment configuration of the language. The reason for this is simple: since theta role assignment applies after HNPS, the output of HNPS must meet the conditions of theta role assignment. This is shown by its failure to strand prepositions, for example:

(96) *I talked to, about Mary, John.

Here, *to* cannot assign a theta role to its complement, since the complement has been removed; furthermore, there are now three items in the domain of *talked*.

   Right node raising (RNR) shows a different complex of properties. First, it can strand prepositions:

(97) John talked to, and I yelled at, Peter.

Second, it can operate over an unbounded domain:

(98) John wants to talk to, and I would like to yell at, Peter.

It clearly does not preserve the theta role assignment configuration. It shows properties of *wh*-movement, including reconstruction:

(99) John and Mary yelled at, and then pretended to punish, each other.

So HNPS and RNR contrast exactly on the dimension at issue.

   Now, it has been argued that HNPS is an $\bar{\text{A}}$-movement (in our terms, an S-Structure rule) with properties like those of *wh*-movement. The argument is based on parasitic gaps and rests, I believe, on mistaken notions of what parasitic gaps are, and of the difference between HNPS and

RNR. The sort of example that is typically cited is (100),

(100) John read t before filing pg this book.

where supposedly the *t* is left by HNPS and the *pg* is licensed by it. However, it is easily shown that the *t* is actually left by RNR, since preposition stranding is possible in these cases, and was not possible in the cases of HNPS that we examined:

(101) John yelled at, before punishing, all of those campers.

Thus, there is no evidence that HNPS is an $\overline{\text{A}}$-movement, or S-Structure, rule.

4.4.2   Classifying Scrambling Rules
The situation then is quite simple: there are two kinds of scrambling, NP-Structure scrambling and S-Structure scrambling. The former is not a movement at all, but an alternative base order. The latter is a movement with *wh*-movement properties.

We may now turn to some of the vast literature on NP-movement. We will examine only a tiny number of the cases that have been discussed, concentrating on the ones that at first glance seem difficult to fit into this model.

We may begin with a case from Persian, described by Browning and Karimi (1990). ((102a–b) are Browning and Karimi's (6a) and (20), respectively; OM = object marker.)

(102) a. Ali ketab-ash-o   fekr nemikard ke   man be Hassan goftam
          Ali book-him-OM not-think-3s   that I   to Hassan say-1s
          ke   tu   bardashti.
          that you take-2s
          'Ali doesn't think that I told Hassan that you took his book.'
       b. Mehry Alii-ra   midone ke   madar-ashi sar-e een kar
          Mary   Ali-OM know-3s that mother-his on   this job
          gozashete.
          put-3s
          'Mary knows that his mother got Ali this job.'

(102b) exhibits long-distance scrambling, of the embedded object to matrix position, clearly a movement that does not preserve the theta role assignment configuration. Hence, this cannot be NP-Structure scrambling. However, Weak Crossover violations seem to be computed on the *output* of this rule, not the *input*:

(103) Mehry Ali-ra   be madar-ash goft   ke   Hassan zadeh.
      Mary Ali$_i$-OM to mother-his$_i$ tell-3s that Hassan beat-3s
      'Mary told his mother that Hassan beat Ali.'

This would indicate that the scrambling does take place in NP-Structure—
hence, a contradiction.

However, I think there is a reasonable reanalysis of these structures that
does not lead to contradiction. Notice first that the supposedly scrambled
NP in (102b) occupies the matrix direct object position. I think it is not a
wild assumption that this NP is actually a matrix object, and an argument
of the matrix verb. English has a number of constructions that exhibit this
pattern:

(104) a. What I think of John is that he is an idiot.
      b. Mary said of John that he was an idiot.

Say here is a three-place relation, with a special connection between the
last two arguments: the third must be about the second. In Persian the
connection is somewhat stronger than the "aboutness" relation; here the
third argument must have an open variable and thereby be predicable of
the second argument. But apart from this difference the Persian and English constructions are the same. So this sort of case is simply not relevant
to scrambling.

A more troubling case is presented by Webelhuth (1989). He shows that
in German scrambling not only shows reconstruction effects, but also
licenses parasitic gaps—a contradictory set of properties in the present
model. In fact, with the following example, he shows that the properties
hold simultaneously:

(105) Peter hat die Gäste [ohne   e anzuschauen] einander   t
      Peter has the guests [without looking at]   to one another
      vorgestellt.
      introduced

Webelhuth assumes that the D-Structure form of this sentence cannot
support binding, because the antecedent of the reciprocal would follow it:

(106) *Peter hat [ohne anzuschauen] einander die Gäste vorgestellt.

I would adopt with modification the analysis that Wyngaert (1989) has
already given to such examples, namely, that they involve two scramblings. First, there is an instance of NP-Structure scrambling, which gives
(107).

(107) Peter hat [ohne die Gäste anzuschauen] die Gäste einander
      vorgestellt

This scrambling is simply an alternative base order. Second, there is an
instance of S-Structure scrambling, which operates in an ATB fashion to
give the parasitic gap:

(108) Peter hat die Gäste [ohne e anzuschauen] t einander vorgestellt

(108) is just like (106) except that the trace is to the left of the reciprocal,
permitting binding.

   This adaptation answers Déprez's (1990a:(48b)) counterexample to
Wyngaert's original proposal:

(109) ... weil   Maria die Gäste [ohne   einander   e vorzustellen]
            because Maria the guests without one another   introducing
         allein t läßt.
         alone   leaves

The problem posed by (109) is that the antecedent for the reciprocal is
the parasitic gap itself, but the configuration in (109) will not allow binding. However, we may suppose that NP-Structure scrambling holds in the
embedded clause, giving (110),

(110) weil Maria [ohne die Gäste einander vorzustellen] allein die Gäste
      läßt

which permits the licensing of the anaphor, and to which S-Structure
ATB extraction can apply, giving (109).

   Hence, the recalcitrant cases in German fall in line with the sort of
derivation we have found in English.

   The importance of the theta role assignment configuration for NP-
Structure scrambling is shown by a contrast developed by Moltmann
(1990):

(111) a.   ... weil   Maria Bilder   voneinander$_i$ diesen Leuten$_i$
              because Maria pictures of each other these   people
           sicher   welche e zeigen   wollte.
           certainly some   to show wanted
           '... because Maria certainly wanted to show these people
           some pictures of each other.'
      b. *... weil Maria Bilder voneinander$_i$ diesen Leuten$_i$ sicher e
           zeigen wollte.

In German two sorts of movement are possible. One "strands" a quantifier, the other does not. The rule that strands the quantifier changes the theta role assignment configuration, because where there was one NP, there are now two: the moved NP and the stranded quantifier. Hence, this is S-Structure scrambling, and it will show reconstruction effects (111a). (111b), where the theta role assignment configuration is maintained, is an instance of NP-Structure scrambling, which consequently does not show reconstruction effects.

Scrambling of the object over the subject in German is a particularly interesting case. The predictions of the present theory are clear, even if the facts are not. The predictions are these. If the subject is VP-internal, then NP-Structure scrambling of the object over the subject is possible, since the theta role assignment configuration is maintained; on the other hand, the scrambling in this case could be S-Structure scrambling as well. But if the subject is VP-external, then only S-Structure scrambling of the object over the subject should be possible. If we combine this prediction with the Diesing-Kratzer hypothesis discussed earlier, we derive the prediction that stage-level predicates should permit S-Structure scrambling of the object over the subject, but that individual-level predicates should not. Unfortunately, I have not been able to obtain any reliable data bearing on these questions.

The question of scrambling in Scandinavian languages will be delayed until chapter 5, because of its dependence on verb movement and the description of negation.

4.4.3   Normal Order

I am claiming that scrambled VPs are base-generated as such. This is possible because the strictures on theta role assignment do not prescribe the order of the arguments themselves, only the order of the arguments with respect to the head verb. Nevertheless, there is a preferred order. In English we observe the following preferences:

(112) object precedes prepositional phrase
       prepositional phrase precedes S
       *to*P precedes *while*P
       pronoun precedes particle

I believe that listing these preferences is misleading, for they derive from different sources. One source is surface heaviness, as Ross (1967) noted. Heaviness is complex, with both the number of words in a phrase and its category contributing to its weight:

(113) a.   I said to Mary to leave.
      b.   ?I said to leave to Mary.

(113b) is worse than (113a) because Ss "weigh more" than PPs, even with the same number of words. A second source of preference is Case marking: a Case-marked NP prefers adjacency to the verb. A third is cliticizability: weak pronouns must be in cliticizable positions. Often these preferences conflict with one another.

But beyond these factors, there is a preference for certain orderings purely in terms of theta role identity. For example, when a *to*P and a *for*P cooccur, the preferred order is *to*P-*for*P:

(114) a.   I gave it to Bill for Mary.
      b.   *I gave it for Mary to Bill.

D. Perlmutter (personal communication) shows that there is a preference for locatives to precede temporal PPs, although both orders are possible; his clever example is the following:

(115) John worked in the 40's in the 50's.

This means that John worked on 42nd Street in 1955, not on 55th Street in 1942.

The preference for ordering elements according to theta roles comes closest to being what we might call "normal order" or "base order." Let us call this *t-normal order*. T-normal order is a relatively weak effect; it takes a carefully contrived example like (115) to bring it out.

I think that t-normal order is simply one of the factors that determines order, and a weak factor at that. There is little reason to posit a representation more abstract than NP-Structure just to represent this order. And it is certainly not the case that t-normal order is always the "unmarked" option, and that other orders are always marked deviations from it. Sometimes t-normal order is impossible:

(116) *John looked up it.

It is thematically normal for the particle to be next to the verb, since it determines the meaning of the verb, but the need for the pronoun to be in a cliticizable position overrides this normal order. The same point can be made with pairs of verbs where the theta roles are reversed:

(117) a.   John robbed Bill of $3.
      b.   John stole $3 from Bill.

Presumably the same, or barely distinguishable, theta roles are involved in (117a) and (117b); but the verbal arguments are reversed in the two cases. If there is any t-normal order effect here, it is completely swamped by the need of the direct object to be adjacent to the verb.

In general, a number of factors determine normal order of VP arguments: t-normal order, order derived from Case requirements, order derived from cliticization requirements, order derived from heaviness requirements. To this we could add specificity: in German pronouns not in t-normal order must be specific. And so on.

If we identified t-normal order with a level of representation, call it D-Structure, and derived NP-Structure by reordering elements, we would be left with a peculiar question: Why does the reordering effected in deriving NP-Structure never result in a configuration that is not a valid theta role assignment configuration (i.e., one in which direction of assignment, and locality, are respected)? For example, why is there no rule that resembles heavy NP shift in that it shows no reconstruction effects (hence is an NP-Structure rule) but differs from heavy NP shift in that it moves the object from the right of the verb to a position preceding the verb?

(118) Bill [John saw t]?
       ↑_____|

The answer I think is simple: there is no level other than NP-Structure at which theta role assignments are computed. Such a rule applying to derive NP-Structure would violate the uniformity of the directionality of theta role assignment, so a child exposed to such a rule would assign it to the set of rules deriving S-Structure—but then it would necessarily show reconstruction effects.

Chapter 5
Verb Movement

We can divide the verb movements discussed in the literature into two types: "long" and "short." Long verb movement moves the verb from the VP beyond IP, and short verb movement moves it to some position within IP. I will contend that short verb movement, like NP-movement, does not exist, and that the relations it means to express are in fact best expressed by the combinatorics of X-bar projection and theta theory, along the lines of chapters 1 and 2. Long verb movement, on the other hand, does exist.

Short verb movement is typically posited to solve a conflict between theta role assignment and something else: adverb order, binding theory, and so on. I think that in all cases the conflict is illusory, and arises through a misunderstanding of theta role assignment. When theta theory is understood as exposed here, short verb movement can play no role. The crucial notions that make possible the elimination of short verb movement are the notion of relativized head and the theta directionality parameter, both introduced in chapter 2. In addition, we will rely on the three sorts of scope we have identified in natural language: head scope, adjunct scope, and quantified argument scope, as distinguished in Williams 1982b, 1984, 1986b, and in chapter 4.

Short verb movements include the verb movements proposed by Emonds (1978), Pollock (1989), Larson (1988), and a host of others. I will provide a short sample of these, with critique and reanalysis.

Long verb movements include subject-aux inversion (SAI) in English and verb second (V2) in German. These movements have a different character from the putative short verb movements.

Apart from being unnecessary, short verb movements also generally violate the Theta Criterion. Typically, the verb moves to some position, such as Agr, Infl, or Tense, to acquire inflectional features. I have argued in chapter 1 that inflectional features are not nodes in a D-Structure tree, to which the verb must move, but are part of X-bar projection. If this is so, then fully inflected Vs are inserted in D-Structure (or, in our terms, NP-Structure), and the lexicalist hypothesis is maintained (though, as noted in the Introduction, there are probably "feature-checking" accounts of short verb movement theories that are faithful to their authors' intent, so the lexicalist hypothesis will not take us far). Strikingly, though, none of the long movements violate the lexicalist hypothesis; neither SAI in English nor V2 in German is "motivated" by the verb's need for inflectional features. If this is so, it is a resounding confirmation of the usefulness of that hypothesis, which in this case simply sorts out the real from the chimerical cases of movement.

Another feature of short verb movement is that it preserves the theta role assignment configuration, in the sense of earlier chapters, and hence is similar to NP-movement. That is, short verb movement does not reorder the verb and its arguments, hence preserving the directionality of theta role assignment, and it does not move the verb to positions where local theta role assignment is impossible, if theta role assignment is understood correctly. Hence, short verb movement should be represented in NP-Structure, where theta roles are assigned.

5.1   Emonds and Pollock on the Difference between English and French

The theory of verb movement in the work of Emonds (1978) and Pollock (1989) is essentially a theory of the distribution of negation and adverbs. These are assumed to occupy fixed, perhaps universal, slots in D-Structure, and differences in their distribution with respect to the verb in different languages or constructions are accounted for as differences in the ability or necessity of the verb to move. The verb is impelled to move by the need for Case features, which also occupy fixed D-Structure positions. In the X-bar theory that Pollock and others assume, VP is embedded in AgrP, which is embedded in IP, which is embedded in CP. Correspondingly, a verb can move to the head position of any of these phrases, but movement cannot skip over a head. The movements found in French and English are listed in table 5.1.

Adverbs are adjoined to VP; hence, movement to AgrP will be movement over an adverb. On the other hand, negation is adjoined to AgrP (or, is a head that takes AgrP as a complement); hence, movement to IP will be movement over negation.

The predictive power of Pollock's theory derives from the implications of the locality of movement: for example, if the verb can move over an

Table 5.1
Verb movement in English and French

| | FRENCH INFINITIVES | | FRENCH TENSED | ENGLISH | |
	aux	main		aux	main
To Agr	×	×	×	×	
To Infl	(×)		×	×	
To Comp			×	×	

adverb, then it can move over negation. Thus, if the order V-Neg-NP exists, then V-Adv-NP must exist as well.

(1) $[_{IP}$ NP I $[_{NegP}$ neg $[_{AgrP}$ Agr $[_{VP}$ adverb V NP]]]]

For Pollock, the difference between English and French comes down to a difference in movement: in French, but not in English, the main verb can move to Agr (and hence to IP); in French infinitives the main verb can move to AgrP but not to IP, whereas auxiliary verbs can move to IP. ((2a–c) are Pollock's (4b), (11b), and (16b), respectively.)

(2) a.　Jean embrasse souvent Marie.
　　　Jean kisses　often　Marie
　　　'Jean often kisses Marie.'
　　b.　Il n'a　pas compris.
　　　he *ne* has not understood
　　　'He has not understood.'
　　c.　*Ne sembler pas heureux ...
　　　ne to seem not happy

The parameter responsible for this difference between French and English is the strength of Agr parameter: Agr is strong in French, but not in English.

In addition, Pollock's description of French versus English adverbs and negation requires at least two other parameters.

In order to explain (3),

(3) *John not left.

Pollock must postulate that English (but not French) has a null auxiliary verb that moves from a VP-adjoined position to IP (and whose movement is blocked by *not*, giving ungrammaticality). (Chomsky (1991) instead postulates "LF" V-to-I movement, with the same effect.)

A third difference between French and English is illustrated in (4).

(4) a. John recently   was talking to Peter.
   b. *Jean récemment parlait   à Pierre.

Presumably, the auxiliary verb *was* in English occupies the same position that *parlait* occupies in French—namely, Infl. For some reason, adverbs cannot precede this position in French, but they can in English.

5.1.1 A Baseline Theory of Adverbs in French and English

As a beginning, we will use subcategorization to describe the facts that Pollock would explain by movement: subcategorization by classes, as in the case of adverbs, and by individual lexical items, as in the case of negation. Later, if more insight than this is possible, so much the better. The following facts are pertinent.

First, adverbs in English in general can occur in the pre-Tense position, and in any position in the auxiliary. Adverbs cannot occur between the verb and the direct object:

(5) a. John probably left early.
   b. John will probably leave early.
   c. *John will see probably Bill.

The distribution of *not* is similar to that of adverbs, except that it cannot occur in the pre-Tense position:

(6) a. *John not left early.
   b. *John left not early.
   c. John will not leave early.
   d. John will have not seen Bill.

Therefore, the English facts can be summarized in the following subcategorization specifications:

(7) adv: _____ VP
         (V[+aux] _____)

(8) *not*: _____ XP [−tense]
         V[+aux, +tense] _____

French differs from English in two ways. First, adverbs in French cannot occur in the pre-Tense position. Second, they can occur between the direct object and the verb:

(9) a. Jean a vu récemment Pierre.
         Jean saw recently   Pierre
   b. *Jean récemment a vu Pierre.

    c.   Jean a récemment vu Pierre.

    d.   Jean a vu Pierre récemment.

The French word *pas* is distributed in the following way:

(10) a.   Jean n'a   pas vu   Pierre.
            Jean *ne* has not seen Pierre

    b.   *Jean ne pas a vu Pierre.

    c.   *Jean ne a vu pas Pierre.

    d.   Ne pas avoir   appris ...
            ne not to have learned

    e.   *Ne* avoir pas appris ...

Therefore, the French facts can be summarized as follows:

(11) adv: ____ V[−tense]   (including negation)
             V ____

(12) *pas*:   ____ V[−tense]
             (V[+tense] ____)
             (V[+inf, +aux] ____)

If we suppose that *pas* is an adverb, then we may be able to simplify the above statements. The fact that *pas* cannot occur in the pre-Tense position would follow from the fact that no adverb can. We might adopt the following convention, a sort of "elsewhere" condition:

(13) If X is a lexical subclass of Y, then X can have a narrower distribution than Y, but not a larger. (X's subcategorization must be a subcase of Y's.)

5.1.2 Negation in English and French
I will now attempt a more refined analysis of negation. An important concept in what follows is the notion of *head* as exposed in section 2.4, and in Di Sciullo and Williams 1986 and Williams 1978b, 1981a—specifically, the notion of *relativized head*.

Recall that the absolute or semantic head determines the features of the whole, by having the features itself; but when it lacks a feature, that feature is supplied by the nonhead. This gives a sort of unification, or function composition.

The theory of negation to be outlined in terms of this notion of headedness will solve the following two puzzles. First, why is it that, although there are "negative" adverbs, like *seldom*, which provide "affective" environments, the morphologically productive affixes *in-* and *un-* do not create affective adverbs?

(13) a. *Infrequently does John come here.
     b. Seldom does John come here.

Second, why does the relative scope of the modal and the auxiliary change under SAI in the following examples?

(15) a. John mustn't be there. (nec [not [. . .])
     b. Mustn't John be there? (not [nec [. . .])

5.1.2.1 English Negation   English negatives consist of the adverbs *never*, *seldom*, etc., the negative auxiliaries *can't*, *wouldn't*, *won't*, etc., and the word *not*.

The negative auxiliaries differ in significant ways from the word *not*—ways that suggest that they are not derived by cliticization of *not* in syntax. In other words, the *n't* of the negative auxiliaries is added by lexical rule, whereas the word *not* is a free form in syntax, appearances and assumptions notwithstanding.

A first hint that this is so is the fact that the negative auxiliaries do not have a uniform sort of interpretation. From the order MODAL ^ *n't* the natural assumption is that the interpretation would be MODAL[NOT[. . . . For *mustn't* and the other necessity modals this is correct, but for the possibility modals it is wrong; *can't* is interpreted as NOT[CAN[. . . . This may be nothing more than lexical variation, but that alone suggests that the negative auxiliaries are words, in every sense. Hence, the negative auxiliary is simply another auxiliary, and occupies the same position as any other auxiliary, namely, head of an AuxP. If Aux is the head of S (or, rather, as I have speculated in Williams, forthcoming b, [Tense, Nom] is the complex head of S), then the structure of sentences with negative auxiliaries is as shown in (16).

(16)

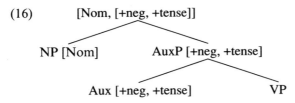

Hence, the negation on these auxiliaries will have sentential scope; in general, a head has scope over its phrase (Head Scope Rule; Williams 1984).

5.1.2.1.1 Not: *Syntax*   By contrast, the negative word *not* is a free syntactic word. It heads a projection, *not*P, and can take any XP as its complement. It lacks categorial content itself, so the category of the projection is determined by the nonhead; thus, for example, [not AP] will categorially be an AP and have the distribution of an AP:

(17) a.   John seems sad.
      b.   John seems not sad.
      c.   *John seems an idiot.
      d.   *John seems not an idiot.

In this view of *not* I depart from Zanuttini (1990), who holds that *not*, unlike *n't*, is not a complement-taking head but an adverb.

Not does have one feature of its own, namely, [−tense]. This means that its projection will be untensed and therefore can never stand as the main predicate of a tensed clause:

(18) a.   *John [not left].
      b.   I want John (not) to (not) have (not) left.
      c.   John must (not) have (not) been (not) thinking.

In (18a), although *left* is tensed, since *not* is the head, its tenseless feature dominates, and so the tense of the VP cannot become the tense of the whole clause.

In tenseless constructions, *not* does not interfere. Whatever features *to* has that make it appropriate as the head of an infinitive, *not* does not have their contraries, so *not* occurs transparently in infinitives.

Three considerations lead to the conclusion that *not* is a head.

First, complement-taking heads in English take their complement strictly to the right. The fact that *not* observes this rule indicates that it is a head:

(19) *I like him not.

Adverbs, for example, are not heads in this sense, since they can in general appear in the position of *not* in (19). There is nothing intrinsic about negation that says that it will be a complement-taking head. In fact, the negative adverb *seldom* clearly is not; and in some languages, such as German, it is likely that the negative (*nicht*) is not a complement-taking head, but is simply an adverb.

Second, in prenominal (or in general in prehead) position, modifiers must be head-final. It seems that [not XP] constructions are excluded from this position, which would follow if *not* were the head:

(20) a. *the mad at his wife man
     b. the very tall man
     c. *The [not happy] man is Pete.
     d. The man not happy is Pete.
     e. the seldom happy man

The fact that [not happy] can occur postnominally further supports the
point, since postnominal modifiers generally require a complement to the
head. A systematic set of counterexamples to the claim that *not* is a head
are such expressions as *a not impossible situation*; however, these are con-
trivances of artful language, and so perhaps should be put aside.

A final reason to consider *not* to be a head is that it supports VP-
deletion, or more generally, XP-deletion:

(21) a. ... and Bill can probably not.
     b. I consider Bill intelligent and I consider Sally not.
     c. *I consider Bill intelligent, and I consider Sally.

VP-deletion can be seen as a sort of missing-complement phenomenon. In
general, the missing complement is the complement of a modal, but in
these cases it is the complement of *not*. Even an adjunct small clause can
have VP-deletion, but only if it contains *not*:

(22) We had hoped that everyone would be cooperative, but with John
     not, we were forced to do most of the work ourselves.

"Main verb" *be* does not support a missing complement, which shows
that this property is lexically idiosyncratic:

(23) *John was being obnoxious, and Bill was being, too.

Again, as (24) illustrates, adverbs do not support VP-deletion and hence
are probably not to be analyzed as complement-taking heads. This might
be why adverbs do not take complements at all, of any sort.

(24) *I consider John ridiculously verbose, and I consider Peter hardly.

It seems, then, that the syntax of *not* can be boiled down to the following: it takes an optional XP complement, and it lacks categorial features,
except [−tense]:

(25) *not*: [−tense]; _____ XP

5.1.2.1.2 Not: *Interpretation* The principal facts of *not* interpretation
follow from the syntactic facts just given, plus the following stipulation:

(26) Only predicates and propositions can be negated.

This can be seen from the following paradigm, where prefixing *not* to anything that is not a predicate results in ungrammaticality:

(27) a. John is probably not a doctor.
     b. John seems not friendly.
     c. I consider John not friendly.
     d. *John saw not a doctor.
     e. *Not a doctor saw Bill.
     f. *You can do that not in my car.

In fact, though, *not* cannot be prefixed directly to a proposition either:

(28) *John believes not that Bill is here.

However, there are circumstances where *not* has propositional scope. Although *not* cannot be prefixed to the nonpredicative PP in (27f), when that same PP is fronted, the result is grammatical:

(29) Not in my car can you do that.

In this example, *not* has sentential scope; this is shown by the fact that SAI has taken place, which only happens in the presence of sentential negation. *Not* has sentential scope as a result of the Head Scope Rule. First, *not* is the head of *not in my car*; second, *not in my car* has been moved to the head position of the matrix clause; hence, by transitivity of the "head of" relation, *not* is the head of the matrix clause and thus includes it in its scope. Here, negation is the head of two phrases, the PP and the matrix S; but only the matrix S qualifies as a scope for negation.

The notion of scope must be carefully distinguished from some other notions. For example, it is tempting to say that in (29) it is the PP *in my car* that is "negated"; similarly for (30).

(30) You cannot do that IN MY CAR.

In fact, negation simply has sentential scope in both these examples. The sense that it is the PP that is "negated" derives from the fact that in both cases the PP is the focus of the sentence, and the sentence carries a presupposition that *you can do that somewhere*. The Head Scope Rule has nothing to tell us about the focus-presupposition structure of a sentence, only about scope.

It is significant that the immediate constituency of the negation does not fully determine its ultimate scope. The negation in (29) is what might ordinarily be termed *constituent negation* in Klima's (1964) terms; however, the configuration determines that it has sentential scope.

In (31a) both the fronted phrase and the matrix S qualify as a scope for negation; the example would therefore be ambiguous, except that SAI is compatible only with sentential negation.

(31) a. Not sad, John arrived.
   b. Not sad did John arrive.

In (31a) *not* has the predicate *sad* as its scope, and it serves simply to invert this predicate. In (31b), on the other hand, *not* takes the full S as its scope, and the meaning is the denial of *John arrived sad*. The two sentences are similar in meaning, but distinguishable.

In chapter 4 we discussed the three sorts of linguistic scope: head scope, adjunct scope, and quantified argument scope.

Adjunct scope is the scope of adjoined material; it is always the phrase adjoined to. Adverbs, for example, always have adjunct scope.

Quantified argument scope is the scope of quantified NPs. It is always some phrase containing the quantified NP. The role of this sort of scope assignment has been exaggerated in the literature. Actually, only quantified NPs in argument positions undergo Quantified Argument Scope Assignment—all other scope is determined by the other two cases.

Negation participates in all three of these scope systems. We have already seen several examples of head scope. Negation also shows adjunct scope:

(32) John comes here seldom.

Here, *seldom* is adjoined to the VP and has VP scope. And of course NPs like *no one* are assigned scope by Quantified Argument Scope Assignment, about which much has already been written.

5.1.2.1.3 Lexical versus Syntactic Negation   We can now solve the two puzzles noted earlier. The key to each is that in English the direction of complementation is different in words and phrases: in words the head is on the right, in phrases the head is on the left (see Williams 1978b, 1981c).

The negative prefixes *in-* and *un-* occupy nonhead positions. This means that their scope is determined not by the Head Scope Rule, but by the Adjunct Scope Rule—namely, their scope is determined to be exactly what they are adjoined to. This means that the scope of each prefix is restricted to the word that it is an immediate constituent of. For example, in *unnecessary* the scope of *un-* is strictly *necessary*—that is, *un-* simply inverts the predicate *necessary*. This is why words formed by prefixation of *in-* and *un-* are not affective items—they are not truly negative adverbs, in that the scope of the negation is confined to the word in which it occurs and cannot be taken to be sentential negation. So, for example, (33c) is the true paraphrase of (33a), not (33b).

(33) a. John came infrequently.
    b. It is not the case that John came frequently.
    c. John came a certain number of times, and those times were not numerous.

(33b) represents the reading in which *in-* is construed as having sentential scope. That it cannot have such scope is shown by the fact that unlike *seldom*, for example, it fails to condition polarity items or trigger SAI:

(34) a. *Infrequently did anyone come.
    b. Seldom did anyone come.

By contrast, in negative auxiliaries the negative morpheme is in the head position of the word; hence, the negation of these auxiliaries is not restricted to the word itself, but extends to anything that the word is head of, usually an entire clause. Hence, these are truly negative, and condition negative polarity items:

(35) Can't anyone do anything?

It is worth comparing these negative auxiliaries with the contractions *should've*, *could've*, and so on. As shown by Selkirk (1972), these contractions do not undergo SAI:

(36) *Could've John been there?

Why do the contractions involving *n't* undergo SAI, but not the ones involving *have*? (If Selkirk is right in her particular conclusions, the contractions involving *have* are not really contracted forms at all. But then the question remains, Why are these forms different in their analysis from the negative auxiliaries? How does the child know to treat these two types of reduction differently?)

I believe the answer lies in the fact that forms like *should've* do not qualify as possible words from the point of view of the head-complement relation. If these were words, the contracted *have* would occupy the head position. But semantically, *have* is the complement of the modal—so these cannot be words.

This analysis is bolstered by the facts relating to the second puzzle. Recall that the negative versions of the necessity modals differ from the negative versions of other modals in having negation subordinate to necessity. This interpretation is anomalous, given that the negation occupies

the head position in these cases. These words are deviant, from the point
of view of the laws of word formation.

That this is so is indicated by their behavior in syntax. When
these words are moved, their interpretation changes, so as to become
nonanomalous:

(37) a. John mustn't be there. (nec [not [...])
     b. Mustn't John be there? (not [nec [...])

Suppose, for concreteness, that there were two *mustn't*'s. The moveable
mustn't (37b) fits the laws of word formation. The *mustn't* that appears in
(37a) is perhaps similar to *must've*, which we have seen is not a true word,
in that it does not undergo inversion.

5.1.2.2 French Negation   French negation differs from English negation
in ways that are predictable from the way French word and phrase syntax
differs from English word and phrase syntax.

The French negative word *pas* has two separate functions. In one function it is a complement-taking head, just like English *not*; in the other
function it is an adverb, like English *seldom* or German *nichts*.

5.1.2.2.1 French Adverbs   French adverbs differ from English adverbs in
two ways. First, French adverbs cannot appear in pre-Tense position:

(38) *Jean souvent a vu   Marie.
      Jean often   has seen Marie

Second, French adverbs can occur between the main verb and the direct
object:

(39) Jean embrasse souvent Marie.
     Jean kisses   often   Marie
     (Pollock 1989:(4b))

It is an interesting empirical question whether these two differences
are independent of one another. Pollock (1989) claims that they are, but
V. Déprez (personal communication) has suggested they are not. I will
ignore the question for the time being.

I will insist, however, that the ability of adverbs to appear between the
verb and the direct object is of a piece with other features of French,
namely, the ability (even necessity) of adjectives to intervene between a
noun and its complement, and of compounds to be head-initial:

(40) a.   la destruction rapide de la ville
     b.   *the destruction rapid of the city

    c. poisson chat
        fish   cat
        'catfish'
    d. oiseau mouche
        bird   fly (N)
        'hummingbird'

As I have written elsewhere (Williams, forthcoming b), I believe that all three of these features of French derive from the fact that French in general permits structures of the form (41), whereas English does not.

(41)

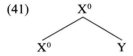

The head-initiality of French compounds shows up even in the number system, where low-number suppletion does not infect the higher compound numbers, as it does in English. This is because English, but not French, is right-headed:

(42) eighty-one   eighty-first
     quatre vingt un   quatre vingt unième
                     *quatre vingt premier

In section 3.3 we saw that French causative and epistemic constructs have the form given in (41). We will assume that structures such as (41) exist in French syntax in a general way. Further, since the derived category is of the same bar level as the head, we will assume that the derived category has the same theta potential as the head; specifically, the derived category has the whole argument structure of the head, not just the external argument. This will permit normal theta role assignment between V and NP in the structure (43).

(43)

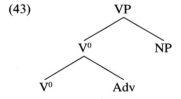

5.1.2.2.2 Pas *as Adverb* The French word *pas* is ambiguous: it is both an adverb and a complement-taking head. As an adverb, *pas* inherits the property that it cannot occur in pre-Tense position:

(44) *Jean pas est arrivé.
     Jean not is arrived

But it also inherits the possibility of adjoining an X^0 on the right:

(45) a. Jean n'[est pas]$_{vo}$ arrivé.
         Jean *ne* is not   arrived
         'Jean has not arrived.'
     b. Jean ne [voyait pas]$_{vo}$ Pierre.
         Jean *ne* saw   not   Pierre
         'Jean did not see Pierre.'

Pas as an adverb is restricted to modifying Tense:

(46) *pas*: adv, Tense ——

The constituency of adverbial *pas* is demonstrated by the following cases of VP-fronting (V. Déprez, personal communication):

(47) a. *[Pas rapidement examiné] Pierre ne l'est t.
            not quickly   examined Pierre *ne* it is
     b. [Rapidement examiné] Pierre ne l'est pas t.
           quickly   examined Pierre *ne* it is not
         'Quickly examined, Pierre wasn't.'

In such examples *pas* is clearly joined to the tensed element, and not to the VP.

The constituency is further shown by the following examples, in which *pas* interacts with the S/VP reading of an ambiguous adverb:

(48) a. *Only S-oriented*
         Jean n'[a   [intelligemment pas]] répondu à la question.
         Jean *ne* has intelligently   not   answered to the question
     b. *Only manner*
         Jean n'[a pas] intelligemment répondu à la question.

In (48a) *intelligemment* cannot be adjoined to VP, since it precedes *pas*, which has sentential scope; hence, it has only the subject-oriented interpretation. In (48b) *intelligemment* can be adjoined to the VP, since it follows *pas*; hence, it has the manner interpretation.

The scope of adverbial *pas* is given by a combination of scope rules: the Adjunct Scope Rule, the Head Scope Rule, and the transitivity of scope. The Adjunct Scope Rule says that *pas* has scope over Tense, and the Head Scope Rule says that Tense has scope over the S; hence, *pas* has scope over the S and is perceived as sentential negation. *Ne* is in fact reserved to mark sentential negation.

5.1.2.2.3 Pas *as a Head* As a head, *pas* takes its complement to the right, as the French setting of the directionality of theta role assignment would require. Like English *not*, *pas* is [− tense]:

(49) *pas*:   [+ neg, − tense]

Hence, again like *not*, *pas* cannot precede the tensed verb.

Note that the generalization is that *pas*, either as adverb or as head, cannot precede the tensed verb. This generalizaion would appear to be lost in an analysis that treats *pas* as ambiguous—but in fact, perhaps not. There are actually two independent generalizations. First, as heads, neither *not* nor *pas* can precede the tensed verb; for this reason, we have posited that the negative, when a head, is [− tense] in both languages. Second, as an adverb, negation will behave as adverbs in the language behave: in French it will not occur in pre-Tense position, since no adverb does; and in English *not* does not occur as an adverb. As noted earlier, Pollock's account does not in fact reduce the behavior of *pas* to that of adverbs—the failure of adverbs to occur in pre-Tense position in English and French is a stipulation independent of the differing ability of adverbs in the two languages to appear in the V ____ Direct-Object slot. And the fact that *not* cannot occur in pre-Tense position in English is independent, in Pollock's account, of the fact that *pas* cannot occur in this position in French; in English this prohibition is due to an abstract "LF" *do* movement rule; in French it is due to a syntactic verb movement rule. Hence, the two systems simply capture two different generalizations. In my system, *pas* is ambiguous; when it is an adverb, it is included in a generalization about French adverbs, and when it is a complement-taking head, it presumably will fall under whatever generalization covers the (unambiguous) English word *not*: perhaps universally the negative head is [− tense].

As a head, *pas* takes its complement to its right, and it always has scope strictly over that complement. Like English *not*, *pas* is restricted to apply to predicates and propositions. In the following sentences *pas* takes a predicate as its complement; the absence of *ne* shows that the scope is not sentential:

(50) a. Jean (*n')est arrivé   pas heureux.
        Jean   *ne* is   arrived not happy
     b. Cette histoire (*n')est devenue [pas triste].
        this   story   *ne* is   become   not sad

Like English *not, pas* is devoid of features, and so the phrase [pas XP] is an XP and has the distribution of an XP.

In this account, *ne* is not an instance of negation in itself, but rather a marker of sentential negation. It is in fact omissible in colloquial French. In any case *ne* is not a very sensitive scope marker, as shown by the examples in (48), repeated here:

(51) a. *Only S-oriented*
         Jean n'[a   [intelligemment pas]] répondu à la question.
         Jean *ne* has intelligently   not   answered to the question
     b. *Only manner*
         Jean n'[a pas] intelligemment répondu à la question.

Here, the scope of negation is determined strictly in terms of the interaction of *pas* and *intelligemment*; *ne* precedes in both cases.

The analysis given here of *pas, not,* and *-n't* makes verb movement rules unnecessary. The rules given here are rules governing lexical insertion itself. Any theory, including Pollock's, must have such rules. What form these rules take is an empirical question. I have argued for the particular form of the rules for these words. If these rules are correct, they fully determine, by themselves, the positioning of these elements with respect to the verb and other elements of the clause.

5.2 Larson's Verb Movement, Heavy NP Shift, Precedence, and the Binding Theory

The verb movements proposed by Larson (1988) arise from a problem with the binding theory. The problem in turn arises from the popular assumption that c-command, or some sort of hierarchical organization of the sentence, is what regulates binding theory relations, and that the linear order of elements plays no role. At least, linear precedence is felt to play no role in the "deep" aspects of grammar, including binding and quantifier interpretation, and its effects are felt to be the effects of surface features of syntax that have to do with real-time parsing. I will argue that this is not so—that precedence is a fundamental syntactic notion, as it once was held to be.

As I will illustrate, if precedence is banned, then I see no alternative to Larson's theory; his work develops a serious model of grammar without precedence that is at the same time consistent with other important principles, X-bar theory in particular. I think his theory is carefully enough

worked out that refuting it seriously casts doubt on the notion that precedence is not a part of grammar.

Larson begins with the fact that in the double object construction, the
indirect object can serve as the antecedent of the direct object, but not vice
versa:

(52) a.   Mary assigned John himself.
     b.   *Mary assigned himself John.

Supposing, as Larson does, that the licensing of anaphors depends
solely on the c-command relation, (52) suggests that the indirect object
c-commands the direct object, and not vice versa. The problem is that
X-bar theory does not permit structures in which this is so, if X-bar theory
entails, for example, that every phrase has a lexical head; and it is hard to
imagine what X-bar theory would be if it did not entail this. For (52),
the direct object must be included in a phrase that does not include the
indirect object, as in (53), if the asymmetry is to hold.

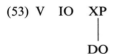

The question is, What is the phrase XP, and what is its head? Larson
supposes that it is a VP and that its head is the trace of the main verb, as
shown in (54).

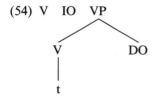

This way, the XP has a head, and the direct object serves as its
D-Structure complement. Sorting out the relation of the verb movement
proposal to the Projection Principle is a little involved, but at least under
this assumption, every argument will be the complement of some predicate at some level. Hence, the Theta Criterion will be satisfied as well.

The obvious alternative to this conclusion is to suppose that (52) illustrates the role of linear precedence, not c-command, in binding, and I will
defend this position later. I believe that if linear precedence is not admit-
ted as a factor in binding theory, then there are really no alternatives to
Larson's proposals that maintain X-bar theory. Thus, it appears that verb

movement is an inescapable consequence of the effort to banish linear precedence from the binding theory.

Larson's analyses all result in right-branching VPs. This in itself is highly suspicious, since it is in right-branching structures that it is difficult to distinguish c-command from precedence.

In general, Larson's analysis differs from standard analyses in positing right-branching binary structures where the standard analysis posits left-branching or ternary-branching structures. For example, the series of arguments and adjuncts following the verb is a strictly right-branching structure, with the verb in the most embedded constituent in D-Structure.

This permits the virtual elimination of the predicate *precedes* from the grammatical rules that Larson considers; given a strictly right-branching structure, *precedes* can always be replaced by *c-commands*. *Precedes* has lost some of its lustre as a theoretical term since S-Structure syntax first began to be modeled on logic in Chomsky 1973, since *precedes* has no analogue in logic. *C-command*, on the other hand, is analogous to the logical notion of scope, as pointed out by J. Blevins (personal communication).

Larson (1988) presents a number of arguments for a strictly right-branching VP. The arguments are based on the behavior of the double object construction, coordination, the behavior of anaphors with VP-internal antecedents, superiority, and the distribution of negative polarity items (NPIs). I will try to show that the standard analyses of these phenomena, which do not require verb movement, are more satisfactory than Larson's alternative.

5.2.1 Binding

Larson's treatment of adjuncts—that they are "innermost" instead of "outermost" constituents of the verb phrase (see section 5.2.5)—gives wrong results for the behavior of pronouns in adjuncts. As Solan (1978) shows, the adjunct acts as though it is not c-commanded by the direct object, whereas the complement of the verb acts as though it is:

(55) a.   Mary shot him$_i$ before John$_i$ could leave.
     b.   *Mary told him$_i$ that John$_i$ could leave.

However, Larson's structures for these two, shown in (56), will be virtually the same.

(56)

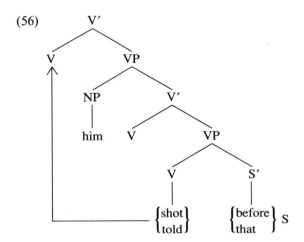

In both cases the pronoun will c-command the embedded clause. Larson's account thus fails to distinguish the two cases, whereas the standard account, as outlined by Solan (1978), clearly does.

5.2.2 Niching

Niching (Ross 1967) also suggests that we be skeptical about the rigid right-branching nature of Larson's structures. These structures predict a larger "break" between the verb and an argument than between the argument and an adjunct. Even leaving aside cases involving the direct object, where Case adjacency may predominate, right branching appears incorrect. (The structure in (57c) corresponds to Larson's structures (13) and (14).)

(57) a. *John talked, I believe, to Bill when Mary was out of the room.
      b. John talked to Bill, I believe, when Mary was out of the room.
      c.

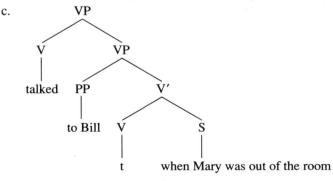

It would appear that the verb, an argument, and an adjunct form a left-branching structure, as the classical theory calls for.

5.2.3 Coordination

Larson (1988) employs a rule of verb movement in the analysis of the English dative constructions. Specifically, the datives are derived from the D-Structure form in (58) (see Larson's (13), (14)) by the application of verb raising.

(58)

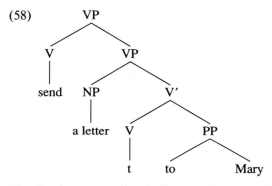

The V raises, according to Larson, to govern the NP *a letter*.

The double object construction is derived by the same verb movement applying to the structure in (59) (see Larson's (25), (26)), accompanied by NP-movement of the NP *Mary* to the Spec of VP.

(59)

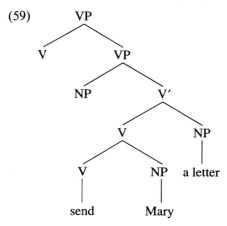

Larson gives two kinds of evidence for these structures. The first is based on the behavior of the double object construction in coordinate structures. The second, derived from proposals by Barss and Lasnik (1986), is based on the way the binding theory treats these structures. I believe that the conclusion drawn from the evidence is mistaken in both cases.

Assuming that only surface constituents can be coordinated, Larson presents the following example (his (17a)) as evidence for the structure (58):

(60) John sent a letter to Mary and a book to Sue.

An example of this kind was given in Williams 1978a to show that coordination of (surface) nonconstituents is possible, and that consequently deletion (of the second occurrence of *send* in this case) must be posited. Larson supposes instead that the structure is (61) (his (18)),

(61) send [a letter t_i to Mary]$_{VP}$ and [a book t_i to Sue]$_{VP}$

where the traces are traces of ATB verb movement. For a more complicated case, like (60) but with an adverb added, Larson proposes the following structure,

(62) I wrote [a letter t to Mary t in the morning]$_{VP}$ and [a note t to Max t during the afternoon]$_{VP}$.

where the traces are the traces of successive-cyclic ATB movement (see 1988:fn. 11). Again, it is assumed that coordination always involves constituents, and no deletion is appealed to, apart from that resulting from ATB movement.

However, Larson's assumptions are not sufficient to generate the full set of coordinations. In particular, nonconstituents are coordinated in the following sentence:

(63) I gave to John everything that he demanded, and to Mary everything that she wanted.

In Larson's view, heavy NP shift is effected not by moving the object to the right, but (as shown in (64)) by moving the PP together with the verb (*gave to John* in a case like this) to the left, after reanalyzing the V and the PP as a complex V.

(64)

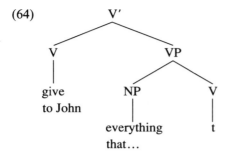

Larson's reasons for positing this structure will be discussed in the next section. Clearly, though, *to John everything that he demanded* is not a constituent in this structure, and so we still must appeal to a rule of coordinate reduction. But if this is so, then there is no longer an argument for the structure in (58), since (60) can just as easily be derived from the more standard D-Structure representation by coordinate reduction.

5.2.4 The Idiom Argument

As evidence for the proposal that "a verb and its outer complements can form a single thematic complex," Larson cites "discontinuous idioms" like *send ... to the showers, take ... to the cleaners* (p. 340). Under his proposal, these idioms are not discontinuous, and his argument for these structures is based on the implicit notion that idioms are never discontinuous. If there were idioms of the form *give x to NP*, where the free position was the *to* NP, then Larson would be forced to accept discontinuous idioms in any case. He dismisses examples like *give hell to NP* and *give one's all to NP* on the grounds that it is not V + *hell* and V + *all* that are idiomatic, but the NPs *hell* and *all*. However, this seems incorrect for examples such as these:

(65) a. pass the baton to X
       b. put the moves on X
       c. give the lie to X

In general, then, there are idioms both of the form *V NP to X* and of the form *V X to NP*, perhaps comparable numbers of each; thus, whatever D-Structure representation is chosen, there will be discontinuous idioms.

5.2.5 Heavy NP Shift

As mentioned earlier, Larson argues that as illustrated in (66), heavy NP constructions are derived by the same verb movement rule, preceded by a reanalysis rule.

(66)

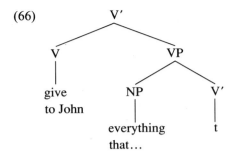

The reanalysis rule applies to predicates that have "one undischarged internal theta role" (p. 348). The reanalysis rule converts a V' (here, *give to John*) into a V that can undergo verb raising. This analysis runs afoul of the treatment of adjuncts that Larson's account of coordination requires.

As discussed earlier, in Larson's view adjuncts are not outer elements, but interior elements. Hence, for the complex case (67a), Larson (pp. 349–50) posits the D-Structure representation (67b).

(67) a. I saw at the conference yesterday everyone who believes in UFOs.

b.

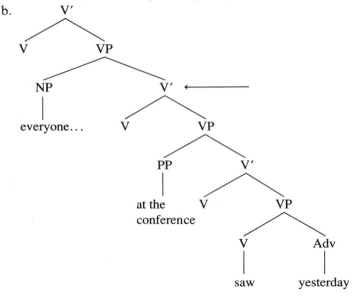

Given the optionality of reanalysis, this will give a good many alternatives, generating shifted Ss and NPs and unshifted Ss and NPs. It will not,
however, generate all needed possibilities. Consider the following sentence, whose complements and adjuncts can appear in six different orders:

(68) I said
$$\left\{\begin{array}{l}\text{that I was leaving to Bill yesterday}\\\text{that I was leaving yesterday to Bill}\\\text{yesterday that I was leaving to Bill}\\\text{to Bill yesterday that I was leaving}\\\text{to Bill that I was leaving yesterday}\\\text{yesterday to Bill that I was leaving}\end{array}\right\}.$$

Making the assumptions that Larson makes about other examples, this
would have the D-Structure form in (69).

(69)

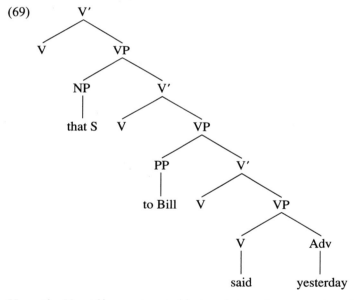

Here, the V *said* is unsaturated in two internal argument positions, corresponding to the *that* clause and the dative PP, and so *said yesterday* cannot undergo reanalysis. But this means that the only versions of (68) that
can be derived are the ones in which *yesterday* follows *to Bill*.

The traditional notion of the order of postverbal constituents, which
goes back to Ross 1967, seems roughly correct for these examples. It holds
that the constituents are ordered with respect to "heaviness," where sheer
length, as well as category, determine heaviness. And in fact, it predicts

that of all the orderings in (68), the first one is probably the worst, since here the elements occur in inverse order of heaviness.

On the other hand, the traditional view leaves unexplained why the double object construction is immune to reordering:

(70) a. I gave John the book.
     b. *I gave the book anyone who wanted it.

It is this limitation that Larson sought to explain by restricting reanalysis to predicates unsaturated in a single position. But we have seen that this restriction prevents the generation of the full set of postverbal orderings. Moreover, it is purely stipulative, and so cannot be said to explain the reordering constraints it was designed to explain.

5.2.6 Reflexives and Negative Polarity Items
The behavior of anaphors and negative polarity items with direct object antecedents is the strongest evidence Larson gives for the strictly right-branching VP. As pointed out by Barss and Lasnik (1986), in the dative and double object constructions, the first NP asymmetrically serves as the antecedent for the second NP:

(71) a. I showed Mary herself.
     b. *I showed herself Mary.
     c. I sent no presents to any of the children.
     d. *I sent any of the packages to none of the children.

This and other facts suggest that the first NP asymmetrically c-commands the second NP, and Larson's structures allow him to use the usual structural notion of c-command. However, the full range of cases resists such treatment, indicating instead that the two positions in the double object construction are mutually c-commanding, but that precedence plays a role in anaphora and other phenomena.

Consider the following examples:

(72) a. ?I gave some some pictures of himself to Bill.
     b. I gave to Bill some pictures of himself.

(72a) accords with Larson's proposals, but (72b) does not; the problem is that *Bill* in (72b) does not c-command the reflexive. The failure of c-command is not simply a matter of the PP that contains *Bill*. Recall that in Larson's treatment of heavy NP shift phenomena, the phrase *gave to Bill* is reanalyzed as a V—hence, the autonomy of lexical items is not observed under Larson's analysis, since the antecedent is a proper part of a V. Larson could change this aspect of his theory (permitting V'-fronting (as well as V-fronting) without reanalysis), but there would still be a problem with c-command (the V' would prevent the antecedent from c-commanding the reflexive). And V' must count for c-command; otherwise, the asymmetry of the double object construction with respect to anaphora is unaccounted for (NP_1 can antecede NP_2, but not vice versa).

How, then, should the difference between (72a) and (72b) be accounted for? I would suggest that the difference is not a matter of grammaticality, since *Bill* c-commands the reflexive in both cases, and is not c-commanded by it in either case. Rather, I believe that examples show a precedence effect. The matter is somewhat involved, since there actually seem to be two overlapping precedence effects, with different theoretical status and with different effects on judgments.

(72b) should be sharply distinguished from the following example, however, which is much worse:

(73) *I recommended himself to John.

The factor determining the difference seems to be whether or not the anaphor c-commands the antecedent. The anaphor is not forbidden from c-commanding the antecedent, but when it does, the antecedent must precede the anaphor. An old idea, really.

If this is correct, then it implies that the direct object NP and the *to* NP c-command each other, and all else being equal, either may antecede the other. In fact, in a number of contexts we find evidence of mutual c-command:

(74) *Passive*
      a. The book was given by John to himself.
      b. The book was given to John by himself.

      Nominalization
      c. the destruction by the city of itself
      d. the destruction of the city by itself
      e. the assignment of Mary to herself

And in all of these cases, the result is degraded if the reflexive precedes its antecedent:

(75) a. ??The book was given to himself by John.
      b. ??The book was given by himself to John.
      c. ??the destruction of itself by the city

    d. ??the destruction by itself of the city
    e. ??the assignment to herself of Mary
    f. ??the assignment of herself to Mary

See Williams 1989 for further discussion.

Even (73) can be improved, if the order is changed:

(76) I recommended to John HIMSELF.

This example requires heavy stress on *himself*, but of course this is because *himself* must count as a heavy NP in order to be shifted, and stress contributes to heaviness.

If this is correct, then the distribution of reflexives comes down to two separate factors: the antecedent must c-command the reflexive, and the antecedent must precede the reflexive if the reflexive c-commands it. The precedence requirement comes in two grades, strong and weak: when the anaphor c-commands the antecedent, there is a strong precedence requirement, and when it does not, there is a weak precedence requirement. The last condition is perhaps a parsing principle, but at least a weaker principle. I believe that these precedence requirements account for the facts that Larson sought to explain.

The antecedent must c-command the reflexive, but it must also be possible for the reflexive to c-command the antecedent. In the dative construction—for example, (72b)—the direct object and the *to* NP c-command each other; this is necessary to allow not only (72b), where the *to* NP c-commands the direct object, but also (77), where the opposite holds.

(77) I introduced John and Mary to each other's parents.

The binding theory will then look something like this:

(78) *Binding theory*
    A. An anaphor must be bound in some domain.
    B. A pronoun must be non-anaphor-free in some domain.
    C. An R-expression is non-anaphor-free.

The term *non-anaphor-free* is used here because in the circumstances just described an anaphor may c-command its antecedent.

The precedence requirement that I am arguing for, at least the strong one, is a grammatical requirement, not a processing requirement. In particular, it seems not to be reducible to a by-product of parsing, at least not in an obvious way. Since it is part of the binding theory, it holds not of S-Structure, but of NP-Structure, under the assumptions entertained here.

So, for example, the relevant precedence relations are calculated before *wh*-movement:

(79) a. To whom did you give pictures of himself?
     b. I gave pictures of himself to Bill.
     c. *To whom did you recommend himself t?
     d. *I recommended himself to Bill.

Fronting the *to* NP in (79a) may make it slightly better than its non-fronted version would be; compare (79a) with (79b). However, I have judged (79b) to be much better than it is ordinarily judged to be—not, for example, as bad as (79c) or (79d). Since (79b) is what we have identified as a violation of the weak precedence requirement, the fact that (79a) is better than (79b) might be taken as evidence for a slight S-Structure precedence preference. And, as mentioned earlier, it may be that this preference is related to parsing, or to on-line antecedent assignment routines.

Note here the reinforcement of the conclusion in chapter 4 that heavy NP shift must be an NP-Structure movement (in other terms, an A-movement): binding conditions apply *after* HNPS in (76), but *before* *wh*-movement (an $\bar{\text{A}}$-movement), as in (79c).

Importantly, though, an example like (79d) is not improved at all by *wh*-movement, as (79c) shows. In the case where the anaphor c-commands the antecedent, the strong precedence requirement holds: linear precedence at S-Structure by itself is not sufficient; instead, precedence must hold before S-Structure. Thus, this precedence requirement is quite different from the one illustrated in (79a–b): first, it is a much stronger effect; and second, it holds at NP-Structure, not at S-Structure.

Negative polarity items (NPIs) present a picture similar to that of anaphors. They are subject to a precedence restriction that is quite inviolable; and this precedence restriction cannot be reduced to c-command:

(80) a. *I gave any indication that something was amiss to no one's parents.
     b. I gave to no one's parents any indication that anything was amiss.

Clearly, the negative item does not c-command the NPI in either of these cases, with or without Larson's assumptions about the structure of VP; yet the one in which it precedes is far better, to the point where the difference could well be one of grammaticality versus ungrammaticality.

The precedence condition seems to apply in a blind fashion in the following cases:

(81) a. Anyone can do that.
    b. *Anyone can't do that.
    c. Can't anyone do that.

(81a) shows that a modal can license an NPI without preceding it; but (81b) shows that if there is a negative, it must precede the NPI, even if the NPI could be licensed by something else. (81c) shows that SAI allows the precedence condition to be met.

5.2.7 Superiority

At first glance, superiority provides strong evidence for the structures that Larson proposes; but in the end these proposals cause as many new problems as they solve. As Barss and Lasnik (1986) show, when two NPs in the double object construction are both *wh*-NPs, only the first can be moved:

(82) a. *What did you give who?
    b. Who did you give what?

If the Superiority Condition forbade the moving of a *wh*-phrase over a c-commanding *wh*-phrase, then these facts would follow from the structure Larson assigns, since here the first NP asymmetrically c-commands the second.

Alternatively, Superiority could be stated in terms of precedence:

(83) *Superiority Condition*
    Only the first of two *wh*-phrases can be moved.

However, this can be shown to be inadequate for the full range of cases. Consider the following, where an adjunct can be moved over a direct object:

(84) a. Where did you see who?
    b. *Where did who go?

Presumably (84a) is good because the direct object does not c-command (the D-Structure position of) the adjunct. In (84b) the subject c-commands the adjunct, and so Superiority is violated. If this is correct, then the pure precedence version of Superiority is not adequate. Incidentally, (84) suggests that adjuncts really do move even in simple sentences; in neither case do the in-situ phrases c-command the S-Structure position of the adjuncts, and so the proper distinction can be drawn only in terms of the D-Structure position.

Still left open is the possibility of a version of Superiority in which both c-command and precedence play a role: "Do not move a *wh*-phrase over another c-commanding and preceding *wh*-phrase." Of course, positive evidence must be given to support this over the simpler, pure "c-command" version. In a sense, we already have that evidence—namely, in the double object construction—but that is the construction in question in the first place. However, if we are correct in concluding that the evidence from anaphora shows that the two positions must c-command each other, then we must include precedence in the Superiority Condition in order to discriminate (82a–b).

Although Larson's account is able to predict the correct behavior of the Superiority Condition in the double object construction, it fails for the cases involving adjuncts. Recall that in his theory an adjunct is an innermost constituent of VP and hence is c-commanded by the direct object; hence, Superiority should prevent the movement of a *wh*-adjunct over a *wh*-direct object. As we have seen, however, this is perfectly possible, and in fact crucially contrasts with the impossibility of moving an adjunct over a *wh*-subject.

It seems likely that superiority is not an isolated phenomenon, but rather an instance of weak crossover (WCO), in which case the analysis of WCO in section 5.2.8.2 will tell us that precedence is a crucial element in superiority.

Chierchia (1992) has argued that the sentences on which May (1985) bases his theory of quantifier scope do not reflect quantifier scope at all, but WCO. May observes that sentences like (85a) are ambiguous, whereas ones like (85b) are not.

(85) a. Who does everybody like?
     b. Who likes everybody?

He argues that the difference is that in (85a), but not (85b), *everybody* can have scope over *who*. Chierchia argues that the scope of *who* is unambiguously broad in both cases, but that it can be interpreted "functionally" in (85a) but not in (85b). He thus analogizes such cases to ones like (86a–b).

(86) a.   Which poem does every poet like best? (Answer: His first.)
     b. *Which poem pleases every poet most? (Answer: His first.)

In (86a) *which poem* is treated "functionally" in that its reference varies under the influence of the quantifier *every poet*. The answer is functional as well; the questioner is asking the hearer to supply a function with the property that for a poet given as input, the function will return what that

poet likes best as output. The lack of a "functional" interpretation for
(86b) is clearly due to WCO, as it is standardly conceived, since the
wh-phrase contains a pronoun. Chierchia's insight is that the same holds
for (85b); the "list" answer that is given is nothing more than a way to
specify a function, by listing input-output pairs, with *every poet* marking
the independent variable. The WCO Condition thus determines not just
what pairs of nodes can be anaphorically related, but rather what nodes
can be functionally related. It says that a dependent item cannot precede
an item it is dependent on.

It seems to me that superiority can be brought under the WCO um-
brella as well, under certain assumptions. Superficially, the superiority
effect is different from the WCO effect, or May's effect:

(87) a. *What did who buy?
     b. What did everybody buy?

In the very same position, *everybody* is ambiguous and *who* is ungrammatical, so the prospects of drawing these together seem remote. However, if we suppose that unmoved *wh*-words must be treated functionally,
and WCO is sorted out at NP-Structure, then we have the following analyses for (87):

(88) a. who(dep. or indep.) bought what(dep.)
     b. what(indep. or dep.) did everybody buy t

What does it mean for one *wh*-phrase to be dependent on another? The
answer to a multiple question is a set of pairs. In this conception, however,
the two elements of the pair are not on a par: the first element is an
individual of the appropriate type for the independent *wh*-phrase, but the
second element is a function that, given the first element, returns an element of an appropriate type for the dependent phrase. Therefore, (88)
really asks, "Give me pairs, $\langle x, f(x)\rangle$, such that x bought $f(x)$."

(87a) is then ruled out on the basis of WCO, since *who*, which must be
dependent, precedes the only thing it could be dependent on, and (87b) is
ambiguous, depending on whether *what* is taken as dependent or not.

A number of researchers have noted that phrases like *which boys* are
immune to the Superiority Condition:

(89) Who did which boys like?

We may explain this by exempting *which boys* from the rule requiring
that unmoved *wh*-words must be dependent; in other words, *which boys*
is allowed to be independent. This is perhaps connected to its being

"discourse-linked" in the sense of Pesetsky (1987), though the link is not a necessary one, since it is possible for a *wh*-word to be neither dependent nor discourse-linked. We might say of the unmoved *wh*-phrases that they must be either discourse-linked or dependent on another *wh*.

A consequence of this theory is that a single *wh*-word cannot remain in situ, unless it is dependent. Perhaps this accounts for the more or less obligatory character of *wh*-movement in matrix questions:

(90) a. *John saw who? (unless it is an echo question)
     b. ?John saw which boy?

If Superiority is an instance of the WCO Condition, then it is essentially a relational condition—that is, a condition that governs relations between items, not the items themselves. The WCO Condition governs the relation between a pronoun and its binder, or, in its extended form, between a dependent and an independent item. The relational nature of the Superiority Condition is revealed by the following examples:

(91) a. *Where did who go?
     b. Who knows where who went?

Under many formulations of Superiority (e.g., Chomsky 1973), (91b) is ruled out, by virtue of containing the sequence ... *where who* ..., just as (91a) is ruled out. In fact, though, (91b) is ruled out only on one interpretation, the one in which the embedded clause is interpreted as a multiple question; on that interpretation, the embedded *who* is dependent on *where*, whose trace is to the right of *who*. But (91b) has a valid interpretation in which the embedded *who* is dependent on the matrix *who*—this dependency is not ruled out by the WCO Condition. Hence, moving one *wh*-element over another is not prohibited in an absolute way—what is prohibited is moving one *wh*-element over another that is dependent on it.

If this approach to Superiority is correct, then it is no surprise that Superiority, which exhibits a strong linear precedence effect, is a subcase of WCO, since we will see in section 5.2.8.1 that WCO is subject to precedence.

5.2.8 Precedence Elsewhere in Grammar
Since Larson's proposals concerning verb movement were made in defense of the notion that precedence plays no deep role in grammar, it would be worthwhile to check on other places where efforts have been made to replace a system involving precedence with a purely hierarchical

system. In all of the cases to be reviewed, I feel that precedence does play a role, and this buttresses the conclusions reached earlier in this section.

5.2.8.1 The Nested Dependency Condition The Nested Dependency Condition (NDC) of Fodor (1978), stated in terms of precedence, has been recast by Pesetsky (1982) purely in terms of domination as the Path Containment Condition (PCC). In Fodor's formulation, the following sequence of *fillers* and *gaps* was forbidden:

(92) filler$_1$ ... filler$_2$ ... gap$_1$ ... gap$_2$

For example, the extent to which (93b) is worse than (93a) can be attributed to this constraint.

(93) a. ?Who did you wonder what John talked about t to t?
     b. *Who did you wonder what John talked to t about t?

In Pesetsky's reformulation, it is not the linear order of fillers and gaps that determines the outcome, but rather the relation of two paths through the tree: the path from filler$_1$ to gap$_1$ and the path from filler$_2$ to gap$_2$. The PCC requires that if these paths touch, then one must properly contain, or nest, the other.

If English is basically right-branching, and binary-branching, these two conditions provide roughly the same coverage. (94) employs the right-branching structure of Larson's analysis of the dative.

(94) *Who did you wonder what John talked [to t [about t]]$_{XP}$?

Path(who, t) = aboutP, XP, VP, S, S', VP, S, S'
Path(what, t) = toP, XP, VP, S

Here the paths do not nest, and the dependencies intersect; in the "opposite" case, (95), the paths nest, and the dependencies do not intersect.

(95) What did you wonder who John talked to about?

However, in the cases where the two theories are not the same, the original NDC seems to be the correct formulation.

First, there is the case of adjuncts, which, if they are not in the VP, permit certain left-branching structures in English:

(96) a. What fruits do you wonder what people Bill [thinks of t] when he eats t?
     b. *What people do you wonder what fruits Bill [thinks of t] when he eats t?

If these structures and judgments are correct, then the NDC is the correct principle, not the PCC, since the paths do not nest in either case, but the linear dependencies nest only in (96a).

However, the structures in these examples are open to question. Although there is evidence in favor of left-branching here (Solan's (1978) evidence cited earlier), Larson's program of reinterpreting everything in terms of hierarchical structure demands that even these examples display right-branching, and this is what he proposes. So, although Pesetsky himself makes no claims about the structure of such sentences, we must nevertheless concede that these examples are not decisive in the context of the questions Larson has raised.

However, there is another sort of case where such doubts cannot arise. Subdeletion provides examples where the existence of left-branching is beyond question:

(97) a. *Donkeys, which I gave elephants to more Republicans than I gave t to [t Democrats], ...
     b. Democrats, who I gave more elephants to Republicans than I gave [t donkeys] to t, ...

Here, subdeletion (deletion of the specifier of an NP in a comparative clause) provides the crossing dependency—it crosses the *wh*-trace dependency in (97b), but not (97a), and as a result (97a) is much worse than (97b), though of course both are marginal. According to the PCC, on the other hand, the difference should be the reverse of what is found. Since the path segment from the deleted determiner to its containing NP uniquely belongs to the comparative path, this path must be the longer one. It is in (97a), but not in (97b), exactly wrong.

These cases therefore provide evidence for the linear-order NDC that is independent of assumptions about the right-branching nature of the VP and the material that follows it.

Pesetsky (1982:274–304) does address the question of empirical evidence distinguishing the PCC from the NDC; he gives two pieces of evidence in favor of the PCC, one from Dutch and one from English. The evidence from Dutch is not decisive for reasons Pesetsky himself cites. The Dutch evidence involves (98),

(98) Amsterdam, waar de auto gemakkilijk is [om [t mee]
     Amsterdam which this auto easy   is to [t with]
     [t naartoe] te gaan], ...
     [t to]   to go
     'Amsterdam, which this auto is easy to go to t with t, ...'

which is judged grammatical, at least relative to the same sentence with the two PPs reversed (just the opposite of English). But this is so under the PCC only on the assumption that the preposition *naartoe* undergoes reanalysis with the verb, in order that the path of its trace will nest the path of the other trace. But, although there is evidence in favor of a reanalysis rule in Dutch, there is evidence against reanalysis for this case —namely, evidence that *naartoe* does not undergo the motivated reanalysis rule:

(99) *Om   [met de auto] [naar Amsterdam toe] te gaan ...
     in order to with the car   to   Amsterdam   to go
     (Pesetsky 1982:(83))

Pesetsky therefore posits a "reanalyis rule applying late ...," different from the motivated reanalysis rule. Only by appeal to this rule can the structure be ruled out by the PCC; and since this rule is otherwise not required, no explanation is afforded.

5.2.8.2 Weak Crossover   In earlier theories, the weak crossover (WCO) phenomenon was described in terms of precedence: a pronoun cannot precede a variable on which it is dependent. Koopman and Sportiche (1988) (K&S) reconstrued the principle in terms of pure hierarchical domination, furthering the program—begun by Chomsky (1973) and canonized by Reinhart (1983)—of logicizing the principles of grammar.

I will use the term *WCO* to refer to the phenomena illustrated in (100); the term *WCO Condition* to refer to the condition, whatever it is, that governs the WCO phenomena; and the term *Leftness Condition*, especially in chapter 6, to refer to the WCO Condition that incorporates a linear order, or precedence, condition.

In K&S's theory, a *variable* is an element (pronoun or trace) whose closest binder is in an $\overline{A}$-position, and the binder must c-command. A WCO case will then have two variables:

(100) a. ?Who does his$_i$ mother love t$_i$?
      b. Who t$_i$ loves his$_i$ mother?

If *his* does not c-command *t* in (100a), then the nearest binder to each is *who*, in $\overline{A}$-position, and so both are variables. In (100b) *t* binds *his*, so *his* is not a variable (in this technical sense). We may then discriminate the two cases by requiring that an operator (here, *wh*-word) bind only a single variable (the Bijection Principle).

The traditional account of WCO (deriving ultimately from Postal 1971) would rule out (100a) on the grounds that the pronoun precedes the variable (*t*) that it is dependent on.

Two types of cases would tend to favor the traditional account. First, there are the cases where the pronoun is in an adjunct, and the variable is in direct object position:

(101) Who did you [see t] before he died?

If the direct object does not c-command the trace, then this should violate the Bijection Principle; but it is good.

Again, in the present context these sentences are not decisive and should be put aside, for although there is evidence to the contrary, Larson has proposed that the direct object does c-command adjuncts.

There is another sort of consideration, however. Consider the following pair:

(102) a.   Whose mother t likes his father?
       b.   *Whose mother does his father like t?

Under a "Leftness" treatment, these are straightforward. But is there a consistent treatment for them under the Bijection Principle?

The crucial question is, Does the trace of *whose* c-command *his* in (102b)? Let us assume not, for only if it does not can (102b) be ruled out by the Bijection Principle. Now, why does *whose* not c-command *his*? Suppose that the relevant structure is either one of the following, where the trace of *whose* is properly contained in the object NP:

(103) a.   whose [t mother]$_{NP}$ does his father like (no reconstruction)
       b.   whose does his father like [t mother]$_{NP}$ (reconstruction)

In either case the Bijection Principle is violated. However, under the assumptions that work to rule out (102b), (102a) will also be ruled out, in this case incorrectly. The structure of (102a) will be as follows:

(104) a.   whose [t mother] t likes his father (no reconstruction)
       b.   whose [t mother] likes his father (reconstruction)

Both of these structures violate the Bijection Principle, since *t* inside the subject NP does not c-command anything outside. Of course, if the position occupied by *t* here *does* c-command outside the NP, then it will also do so in (103a–b), wrongly predicting them grammatical.

Thus, it seems that there is no consistent set of assumptions about c-command that will account correctly for both (103) and (104) under the Bijection Principle.

We will return to the issue of precedence and WCO in section 6.4.

5.3   Verb Movements

There are indisputable verb movements, such as subject-aux inversion (SAI) in English and verb second (V2) in German. What is the difference between these cases and the verb movements we have previously argued against? More to the point, how is a child to know whether the ambient language is a verb movement language or not?

One way to distinguish real from false verb movements is in terms of the target of movement. Empty functional projections serve no other purpose than to host landing sites for movement; if we simply bar empty functional projections (functional projections for which the lexicon contains no items that can serve as heads), then these movements cannot exist. English SAI and German V2 will not be eliminated, since the landing site, the head of CP, is lexical.

Surely the burden is on the proponents of empty projections to provide a plausible account of how these empty projections are learned. One proposal is that they are universal; but this seems unlikely, since languages differ in what categories are relevant.

I think the real key to distinguishing real from false verb movements is the theta role assignment configuration (TRAC). If a sentence does not appear to obey the TRAC, then movement has taken place; otherwise, not. SAI sentences, for example, clearly involve moving a verb away from its complement:

(105)   Must [John come with all his relatives]$_{IP}$?

The complement of *must*, the VP, is not sister to *must*, so the TRAC has been violated.

Another example of TRAC violation is German V2, where the verb is moved over its arguments:

(106)   Adolf sah Peter t.
        Adolf saw Peter

The notion of TRAC includes directionality, and the direction of theta role assignment in German is leftward, so only the input to V2 satisfies the TRAC. Presumably, the child knows that although the theta directionality parameter might vary across categories within one language, it must have a consistent value for any given category. So, (106) alongside of (107) would be sufficient to trigger the V2 hypothesis.

(107) Adolf hat Peter gesehen.
       Adolf has Peter seen
       'Adolf has seen Peter.'

Thus, the child would use the following conservative hypothesis: if there is no evidence of verb movement (that is, if the TRAC is observed), then verb movement is not posited. The intervention of adverbs between the direct object and the verb will not be sufficient evidence of verb movement, for the theory of adverbial modification proposed here will respect the TRAC, as we have seen in the case of French $[V\ Adv\ NP]_{VP}$ constructions.

We will consider two case studies in the literature in light of TRAC: Koopman's (1984) analysis of the short verb movement phenomena in Vata, and Holmberg's (1986) analysis of verb movement in Scandinavian.

5.3.1 Vata

Koopman (1984) presents three arguments that Vata is basically head-final, even though simple SVO sentences are verb-medial. She shows that there are three generalizations whose exceptions can all be explained if the verb is generated finally, but moved to medial position when it is the only tensed element.

The generalizations all concern processes that require adjacency of some element to the verb. Clause restructuring requires the clause that is restructured to be adjacent to the verb. Particle constructions have idiomatic meanings only when the particle is next to the verb. And P-stranding is allowed only when the P to be stranded is next to the verb.

The systematic set of exceptions occur when verb movement has taken place. For example, stranding is possible in the first two of the following contexts, but not in the third:

(108) a. $NP_i \ldots NP\ [t\ P]\ V$
       b. $NP_i \ldots V \ldots XP\ [t\ P]\ V$
       c.   *$NP_i \ldots [t\ P]\ XP\ V$

One might argue that these generalizations do not really involve adjacency. It seems incontrovertible, for example, that P-stranding in English is not dependent on adjacency of the P to the V, and that it does not involve reanalysis, as Van Riemsdijk (1978) has established. One might argue that it is finality, rather than adjacency to V (or its trace), that governs strandability; something like finality seems to hold in English (see

Kuno's (1976) Clause Nonfinal Incomplete Constituent Constraint). It also seems likely, given the assumptions of this book, that idioms are not D-Structure constituents; this is surely true in general, and may in fact be true of such VP idioms as *take to task*, and even verb + particle idioms in English. However, let us suppose that Koopman's conclusion is correct: that Vata is verb-final, and that the language does have verb movement. What are the cues that there is movement in this case?

It must be simply that there are two orders with respect to the verb and its arguments; so the TRAC requires that one be basic, and the other derived.

The situation is similar to that in German, but different. In German the surface order is (109),

(109) XP V ... t$_V$

where XP can be any constituent. In Vata the preverbal constituent can only be the subject. There seems to be an irreducible difference between the two languages, both in the account given here and in Koopman's (in Koopman's account the difference reduces to different positionings of Infl in the two languages, a difference with no other consequences).

5.3.2 Icelandic and Swedish
We may contrast this situation with the situation in Scandinavian and Icelandic. I think that in these languages the arguments for verb movement, and also for object movement, do not stand up to the above test. In particular, both the purported rules of object movement and verb movement in these languages respect (that is, do not alter) the TRAC, and so their role is suspect. We postulate that the child will not look for verb movement in these circumstances.

Holmberg (1986) notes that the following generalizations hold for Icelandic and Swedish: (1) In Swedish the verb moves leftward in matrix but not in embedded contexts (this is shown by the different positioning of the verb with respect to a class of adverbs that includes negation, as in (110)–(111)), (2) Icelandic, which is like Swedish in matrix clauses, is the reverse in embedded clauses.

(110) *Swedish main clause*
    Johan kopte inte den.
    Johan bought not it
    Johan kopte den inte.
    *Johan inte kopte den.

(111) *Swedish embedded clause*
　　　*att Johan kopte inte den
　　　that
　　　*att Johan kopte den inte
　　　att Johan inte kopte den

(112) *Icelandic main clause*
　　　Jón keypti ekki hann.
　　　Jon bought not it
　　　Jón keypti hann ekki.
　　　*Jón ekki keypti hann.

(113) *Icelandic embedded clause*
　　　að Jón keypti ekki hann
　　　that
　　　að Jón keypti hann ekki
　　　*að Jón ekki keypti hann

At stake in these paradigms is the relative order of negation and the verb.
Assuming a fixed base order, that order must be established, and some
account must be given of the alternate orders.

Holmberg assumes two differences between the languages to account
for the contrast. First, he assumes a different positioning of negation:

(114) *Swedish*　　　　　*Icelandic*
　　　C [Neg IP]　　　　C [I [Neg VP]]
　　　 ‾‾‾‾‾‾‾‾‾　　　　 ‾‾‾‾‾‾‾‾‾

Second, he assumes that V moves to C in main clauses in Swedish, but not
in Icelandic. He assumes that both languages have V-to-I movement in
both main and subordinate clauses. Thus, the V will appear to the left of
Neg in Swedish main clauses, but to the right in all others.

Other facts of interest involve the positioning of the direct object and
the negative, when both are present. In Swedish (and Danish and Norwe-
gian), the positioning of the direct object and the negative depends on
whether the direct object is a pronoun or not:

(115) a.　Vafor laste studenterna inte alla den?
　　　　　why　read the students not　　them
　　　　　Vafor laste studenterna den inte alla?

　　　b.　Vafor laste studenterna inte alla artikeln?
　　　　　why　read the students not　　the articles

*Vafor laste studenterna artikeln inte alla?

(Holmberg 1986:chap. 6, (7a))

When the direct object is a pronoun, either order is possible; when it is not, the negative must precede. Holmberg accounts for this by positing a rule of object movement: when the object is a pronoun, it may move to the left, but not otherwise.

By contrast, Icelandic permits either order regardless of the nature of the direct object.

Holmberg accounts for the difference by supposing that Swedish pronouns are endowed with "m-case," an intrinsic, nonlicensed feature that permits them to appear in positions not governed by a Case assigner; further, all Icelandic nouns have this property.

In addition, there is a requirement that when the NP is a pronoun in Icelandic, it must move to the left.

In sum, then, the permissible orders of V, Neg, and direct object in Swedish and Icelandic are displayed in table 5.2.

Now, in all of these languages, the underlying and all surface orders are head-initial (VO); hence, there is every reason to think that the TRAC is obeyed in all of these structures. Since the TRAC is respected, we suspect that there is no verb movement in these cases. But then what sort of description is available when verb movement is not a part of the account?

Any account will need to distinguish main and subordinate clauses. Let us suppose that there is a distinction between main and subordinate Tense ([$\pm$main]), a difference that in these languages is not marked morphologically.

If we were to think in combinatorial terms, we might reason this way. The Neg in Swedish attaches to some projection of V, call it X. Now, [V NP]$_{VP}$ is too "large" to be X; however, V + pro is not too large. Hence, there is some difference in the projection at which NP and pro are at-

Table 5.2
Permissible orders of V, Neg, and direct object in Swedish and Icelandic

	Embedded	Main
Swedish	Neg V NP	V Neg NP
		V pro Neg
Icelandic	V Neg NP	V Neg NP
	V NP Neg	V NP Neg
	V pro Neg	V pro Neg

tached. We might imagine that a pro could attach at the X^0 level—this is the common assumption for clitics, and in fact the phenomenon illustrated here is attested only for stressless pronouns, making this conclusion quite attractive. We may then suppose that negation attaches to the V^0 level, as in (116).

(116)

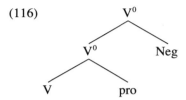

Now, one thing this should *not* commit us to is the lexical atomicity of V^0. Although X^0 is the output category of the word formation rules, and the internal structure of words formed by word formation rules is inaccessible to syntax, X^0 is also a category in syntax, and apparently a recursive category, if our account of French adverbs is correct (section 5.1.2.2.1). In fact, V-to-C movement, and some other phenomena, show that the internal V is accessible in syntax.

There is the further restriction in Swedish that negation appears suffixally only with main clause tense. Hence, the negative particle is subcategorized as follows:

(117) *inte*: V_{MCT^0} ———   (lexical adjunction)
              ——— VP_{MCT} (phrasal adjunction)

And what holds for negation holds as well for sentence adverbs.

This is a familiar pattern—lexical adjunction on one side, phrasal adjunction on the other. As noted in the discussion of French, not only can the direction of adjunction differ from the direction of complementation; it can be different at these two different levels as well.

Icelandic has no main/subordinate distinction, no distinction between main and subordinate clauses, and no distinction between pronouns and full NPs. Pursuing the logic above, we imagine that adjunction can be either lexical or phrasal, but is always to the right. When it is phrasal, the order V NP Neg results; when it is lexical, V Neg NP.

Hence, the description of Swedish and Icelandic fits well within the parameters of variation already proposed.

Further ordering is required for a range of facts described by Vikner (1990), who gives the following paradigm for double object constructions in Icelandic (his (52)–(55) in chapter 4):

(118) a. Petur syndi   oft   Maríu bokina.
          Peter gives   often Maria book
      b. Petur syndi Maríu   oft   bokina.
      c. Petur syndi Maríu bokina oft.
      d. *Petur syndi   bokina oft   Maríu.
      e. *Petur syndi   oft   henni bokina.
                                               her
      f. Petur syndi henni bokina oft.
      g. *Petur syndi   oft   Maríu hana.
                                               it
      h. Petur syndi Maríu hana   oft.
      i. ?Petur syndi   hana oft   Maríu.

The clear generalizations here are first, that the pronoun must precede the adverb, and second, that the two NPs cannot be exchanged.

Taking the second generalization first, we may consider it to be a special case of TRAC. English exhibits a similar phenomenon, in the double object construction:

(119) *I gave the book Bill.

The extent of the phenomenon is not clear—in English the restriction is limited to the double object construction. All other arguments can be reordered in English, subject to heaviness restrictions. Even predicate nominals can be reordered:

(120) I called an idiot the man who came here yesterday.

Order in this case is perhaps part of the TRAC for English: an NP is assigned the Goal argument only when it precedes another NP.

The second generalization is the requirement, in (118), for the pronoun to precede the adverb. Again, we can observe similar restrictions in English, when a particle occurs with a double object construction:

(121) a. ??I gave Bill it back.
       b. *I gave Bill back it.

The restriction is reminiscent of the English heaviness restriction on heavy NP shift. A pronoun is intrinsically lighter than a member of a lexical category and, unless the "normal theta order" dictates otherwise, should precede that category; hence, the pronoun should precede the adverb in (118g). Similar reasoning applies to (121b).

Chapter 6
Binding Theory and
Theta Theory

Here I will argue that binding theory is really a chapter in theta theory —that the subject matter of binding theory is theta roles, and that the subject matter of theta theory (the "argument of" relation) is a binding relation.

Leaving aside this rather strong claim for the moment, it appears at the very least that theta theory is relevant for determining the operation of the binding theory. This is true classically to a small extent—after all, "complete functional complex" is a theta-theoretic notion. But the truth of this is deeper than that. In chapter 2 I argued that the locality effects usually attributed to subjects under "Condition A" are better understood as due to a condition on the opacity of predicates: specifically, I proposed that maximal projections interpreted as predicates are opaque to binding. This conclusion by itself places theta theory at the heart of binding theory, since the notion "predicate" is theta-theoretic.

First we should ask, What does the binding theory hold of? It is ordinarily construed as a set of laws regulating coreference relations among NPs. We might instead construe it as a set of laws regulating relations among *theta roles*. We would then regard theta roles as the entities with the property of "reference," and the NPs to which theta roles were assigned would simply provide conditions on the reference of the theta roles. Given this construal, it is not surprising that theta-theoretic elements turn up in the statement of the binding conditions; binding conditions are part of theta theory in the first place.

I will argue this point from both directions. First, I will argue that unassigned theta roles (implicit arguments) act just like overt NPs with respect to binding theory. At least for those, then, the binding theory must refer directly to theta roles (but then, why only for those?). This will tend to show that binding theory refers to theta theory.

Second, I will argue that the theta role assignment relation itself is a binding relation, and that it chains together with other binding relations to define the domains for binding and for reconstruction. This will tend to show that theta theory refers to binding theory. All in all, the relation between the two is intimate at least.

In the last section I will argue that in fact two quite different conditions govern anaphoric possibilities: the binding theory, which operates in terms of command and determines the coreference possibilities of theta roles; and the Leftness Condition, which operates in terms of precedence and determines the conditions of anaphoric dependence, a relation only incidentally related to coreference.

6.1 The Subject Matter of the Binding Theory

6.1.1 Implicit Arguments Are Unassigned Theta Roles

If the binding theory regulates relations among theta roles, and not (directly) among NP positions, and if theta role assignment is optional, then we might expect to find instances in which the binding theory applies to an unassigned theta role, and assigns it coreference with or disjointness from some other theta role.

Suppose that the noun *attempt* has two arguments, the *attempter* argument and the *thing attempted* argument, and suppose similarly that *respect* has two arguments. Then in the following NPs we find binding and control by an inaudible antecedent, the *attempter* argument of the head noun in (1a), the *respecter* argument in (1b):

(1) a. *Control*
       the attempt to leave
       (attempter = leaver)
    b. *Binding*
       Respect for oneself is important.
       (respecter = respectee)
       (Williams 1985a)

In addition, Conditions B and C of the binding theory, the disjoint reference rules for pronouns and NPs, can "see" these missing arguments:

(2) a. *Condition B*
       admiration of him
       (admirer = admiree)
       (Williams 1985a)

b. *Condition C*
the realization that John was unpopular
(realizer = John)
(Ross 1969)

c. the [e] realization that John was unpopular

One way to assimilate these cases to the binding theory as usually understood would be to supply a phonologically null NP in the determiner of the NP (as in (2c)); this NP could then serve as antecedent for various applications of the binding theory principles. This solution will not work in general; see Williams 1987 for arguments against it. A simple sort of argument is provided by the following example:

(3) Yesterday's realization that John was unpopular ...

The facts of (3) are the same as those of (2c), but the determiner of (3) is filled, precluding the sort of solution just alluded to.

In light of these facts, we could construct a sort of hybrid binding theory that counted unassigned theta roles among the things it applied to, along with NPs. But a simpler, more radical theory is at hand: suppose that the binding theory applies *only* to theta roles, never to the NPs that they are assigned to. This will make implicit arguments the "central" case, not a peripheral phenomenon. Such a theory will say of a pair of theta roles in a sentence whether they are necessarily coreferential, necessarily distinct in reference, and so on. What role will NPs play in such a theory? We might think of them as "conditions on the reference" of a theta role:

(4) John$_i$ left.
     (Th$_i$)

It is the Theme argument that refers; the NP *John* conditions the reference, in that the referent must satisfy the NP description "John(x)."

6.1.2 The Recasting of the Binding Theory
Now, some theta roles are assigned to anaphors, and this of course determines how the binding theory will apply to them. We will want to distinguish theta roles assigned to anaphors, from theta roles assigned to pronouns, from theta roles assigned to R-expressions. We may then define the binding theory along the following lines:

(5) X is *th-bound* if there is a theta role c-commanding X and coindexed with X.

And suppose that we define the objects that the theta binding theory will apply to—th(eta)-anaphor, th-pronoun, and th-R-expression—in the following way:

(6) A *th-anaphor* is a theta role assigned to an anaphor.
    A *th-pronoun* is a theta role assigned to a pronoun.
    A *th-R-expression* is a theta role assigned to an R-expression.

We may then rewrite the binding theory as follows:

(7) *The th-binding theory*
    A. A th-anaphor must be th-bound in some domain.
    B. A th-pronoun must be th-free in some domain.
    C. A th-R-expression must be th-free.

Consider how this will work for some simple cases:

(8) a. *John_i likes him_i.
           (a_i, b_i)
   b. $[\text{John}_i\text{'s mother}]$ likes him_i.
             (a_j, b_i)

In (8a) *him* is a th-pronoun, so it must be th-free in some domain, but there is a th-commanding argument, a_i, that binds it. In (8b) there is no theta role that th-commands b_i, so the coreference is permitted.

Evidently, this theory mimics the action of the standard binding theory, and this is not a surprise: the relation between theta roles and the NPs they are assigned to is so close that it will be difficult to distinguish a theory of one from a theory about the other. In fact, though, one difference is already apparent: as we have seen from (1) and (2), the laws of the theta binding theory, unlike the standard theory, will apply even when one of the theta roles is not realized.

Let us consider another sort of case that I think distinguishes the two theories:

(9) *John_i took his_i picture.

(10) John found his wallet.

Although (9) and (10) are structurally identical, coreference is allowed in (9) but not in (10). The difference is that the verb *take* has the special property that its Agent argument controls the Agent argument of its complement:

(11) *John_i took his_i picture.
          (A_i, Th) (A_i, Th_i)

Given this, it will now be impossible to bind the Theme argument of *picture* to *his*, for this would result in the argument structure (12),

(12) picture
     (A_i, Th_i)

which is illicit unless Theme is bound to an anaphor. If we replace *his* by an anaphor, *his own*, then the structure becomes good:

(13) John$_i$ took his own$_i$ picture.
     (A_i, Th) (A_i, Th)

The standard binding theory has no way to account for the difference between (9) and (10), because it holds of NP positions, and there is no difference in the NP positions in (9) and (10).

As (14) illustrates, the fact that *his* cannot refer to *John* in (9) has nothing to do with its structural position, and everything to do with what theta role it is assigned.

(14) *John took Mary's pictures of him.
                    (A, Th)

Here, *him* even appears across a "subject" from *John*, and still cannot corefer with *John*, so long as *John* is understood as the Agent argument of *picture*, and *him* as the Theme argument.

Very similar remarks apply to Higginbotham's (1983) example, discussed in chapter 3:

(15) a. John$_i$ is his$_j$ cook.   *$i = j$
                   (R_i, X_j)
     b. John$_i$ is his own$_j$ cook. $i = j$
                   (R_i, X_j)

In (15a) *John* is bound to the R theta role, which makes coreference with *his* impossible, if *his* is bound to the X theta role.

That it is not the structural configuration of NPs that governs coreference, but rather the control relations holding between theta roles themselves (the elements of argument structures), is made even clearer by the following examples:

(16) John performed his first operation in 1948.
          (A_i, Th) (A_i, Th)

Parallel to (9), this cannot mean 'John performed the first operation on himself in 1948', and the reason here is the same: *John* controls the Agent role of *operation*, in accordance with the control specification of the verb

perform, and Condition B says that if the Theme of *operation* is linked to
a pronominal, then it must be made distinct from the Agent.

What is surprising about (16), though, is that it has a good interpretation in which *his* refers to *John* but is linked to the Agent role of *operation*,
not the Theme role. Under this interpretation, the Agent role of *perform*
is then both assigned (to *his*) and controlled (by the Agent of *perform*).
Why should this be permitted? Because nothing prevents it. First, the
Theta Criterion is not violated, since both *John* and *his* have independent
theta roles. Second, if the binding theory holds of theta roles, then it too
must be satisfied by (16)—we know from (13) that Condition B cannot
assign disjointness between the two Agent arguments, since in general
these arguments can be coreferential, so no conflict of reference arises.
Thus, (16) satisfies both the Theta Criterion and the binding theory. The
importance of this example for our present concern is that it is difficult to
see how structural conditions alone could distinguish its good and bad
interpretations since the relevant structure is the same for both.

6.1.3 Asymmetries of Binding

The binding theory presented so far implies a symmetry among coarguments. In many languages, including English, this symmetry is valid:

(17) a. John was given a book by himself.
     b. A book was given to himself by John.
     c. A book was given to John by himself.

However, there is one relation that will always thwart complete symmetry
—namely, the external argument/internal argument distinction:

(18) a.   John saw himself.
     b. *Himself saw John.

The structure of (18b) is shown in (19).

(19)

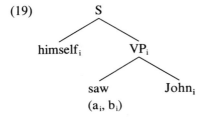

This structure is illicit: the VP$_i$ binds *John$_i$*, which is not allowed, under
Condition C. Note that the violation is *not* internal to the argument struc-

ture of *see*—it is the configuration where a referential expression is vertically bound to a predicate that is illicit.

6.2 The Binding-Theoretic Nature of the "Argument Of" Relation

6.2.1 Defining Th-Command

In the preceding section we did not define th-command, the structural relation between theta roles that is the analogue of the syntactic relation of c-command that holds between syntactic positions.[1] One way to define th-command would be to make it parasitic on a structural relation:

(20) Theta role 1 *th(eta)-commands* theta role 2 if the predicate of which theta role 1 is an argument c-commands the predicate of which theta role 2 is an argument. (Also, a predicate must c-command itself.)

An alternative sort of definition of th-command defines it in terms of the theta role assignment relation itself. The definition is recursive.

In the notation for theta role assignment introduced in chapter 2, theta role assignment always results in the coindexation (or linking) of two theta roles: the theta role being assigned, and the external theta role of the NP it is assigned to. We may capitalize on this to define th-command in the following way:

(21) For two theta roles X and Y, X *th-commands* Y if X is a coargument of Y; or, if X th-commands B, B is assigned to Z, and Z th-commands Y.

Two theta roles are coarguments if they are different arguments of the same predicate. To see how this definition works, consider (22).

(22)
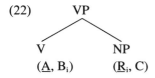

In this tree, B is assigned to $\underline{R}$, $\underline{A}$ and B are coarguments, and $\underline{R}$ and C are coarguments. $\underline{A}$ th-commands B and $\underline{R}$ th-commands C by the first clause of (21); but since B is assigned to $\underline{R}$ by theta role assignment, $\underline{A}$ th-commands C as well, $\underline{R}$ serving as the Z in the definition. C does not th-command $\underline{A}$, for reasons we will discuss in the next section.

1. Sections 6.2 and 6.3 are based on Williams 1989.

The reason for the recursive part of the definition is cases like the following:

(23) John saw a picture of himself.

Here, *John* and *himself* are not coarguments. However, by the definition just given *John* nevertheless th-commands *himself*; or, more properly speaking, the theta role assigned to *John* th-commands the theta role assigned to *himself*. To see why, consider (24).

(24)

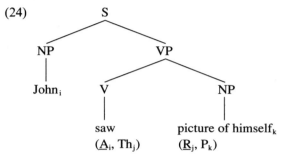

Ordinarily, we would speak of *John* commanding *himself*. But in the scheme being developed here, it is more proper to speak of the theta role assigned to *John* as (th-)commanding the theta role assigned to *himself*. In (24) the Agent argument of *see* is assigned to *John*, and that argument th-commands the Theme argument of *see*; since that Theme argument is assigned to the $\underline{R}$ argument of *picture*, the Agent argument th-commands all of the arguments of *picture*, by the recursive part of the definition, and so th-commands the P argument of *picture*, which is assigned to *himself*.

6.2.2 Linking or Coindexation
As in other contexts, such as pronominal binding, we may ask whether the correct representation of the relation of the two items (verbal theta role, NP) is a symmetric one, for which we may take coindexation as the correct notation, or an asymmetric one. The definition of th-command given in (21) implicitly assumes that the relation is asymmetric—the phrase *is assigned to* is intrinsically asymmetric. However, nothing considered so far would prevent us from substituting *is coindexed with* for this expression.

An empirical advantage of this definition as given in its asymmetric form is that it will allow the internal arguments of a verb to th-command positions inside the subject NP, but not vice versa, as illustrated in (25).

(25)

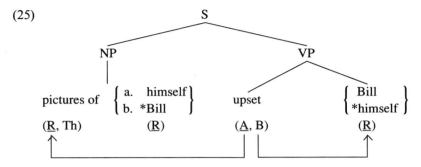

c. *Pictures of himself upset John's sister.

In (25a) B (assigned to *Bill*) th-commands Theme because it is a coargument of $\underline{A}$ and $\underline{A}$ is assigned to the (external) theta role $\underline{R}$ of *pictures* (by theta role assignment), which is a coargument of Theme. Hence, the possibility of backward anaphora is a consequence of the definition.

For many speakers, backward anaphora is restricted to the context of psych predicates, such as *upset* and *surprise*. This restriction does not follow from the definition of th-command.

When anaphor and antecedent are reversed, as in (25b), anaphora is impossible. This is because B is assigned to $\underline{R}$, not $\underline{R}$ to B—that is, the theta role assignment relation is not symmetric. And if the antecedent is embedded lower than the VP, as in (25c), anaphora is again impossible, because the theta role assigned to *John* does not th-command the theta role assigned to *himself*.

Quite parallel to the backward anaphora cases are the cases of "connectedness" without *wh*-movement cited by Higgins (1972):

(26) a.   John's greatest problem is a fear of himself.
               ($\underline{R}$, A)   ($\underline{R}$, Th)
       b.   I consider a fear of each other John and Mary's greatest problem.
       c.   *I consider a fear of John and Mary each other's greatest problem.

(26a) differs from (25a) only in that the predicative phrase (*John's greatest problem*) is an NP instead of a VP, and it precedes the subject here instead of following it. The th-command relations are exactly the same—with an asymmetric link from the subject phrase to the predicate phrase. (26b) and (26c), in which the subject NP rigidly precedes the predicative nominal, simply emphasize that it is the direction of theta role assignment, and not the nature of the dominating categories involved, that makes the difference—in both cases the categories dominating both the anaphor and its antecedent are NP.

These examples show that theta role assignment is not best represented as coindexation, because coindexation is a symmetric relation. Rather, theta role assignment sets up an asymmetric linking relationship, in the sense of Higginbotham (1983): the theta role of the predicate is "linked to" the external theta role of some NP.

The verbal theta role is like a pronoun (or anaphor), and it takes the NP it is assigned to under theta role assignment as its antecedent.

Given that the relation of theta role assignment is asymmetric, why does it hold in the direction that it does, rather than the reverse? Semantically, we might say that the reference of the verbal theta role is determined by the NP it is linked to; this certainly accords with our intuitions about what the syntactic expression of arguments is for.

Given this, we will reject the use of coindexation to represent the theta role assignment relation and will instead use the "linking" representation, in which an arrow is drawn from the anaphor (the verbal theta role in this case) to the antecedent (the external theta role of the NP that the verbal theta role is being assigned to). For example, the relation between a verb that takes a Patient argument and its direct object will be as shown in (27).

(27)

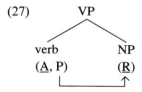

As in Higginbotham's (1983) notation, the arrow begins at the anaphorically dependent item, and its head points to the anaphorically independent one. In fact, though, wherever it doesn't matter, I will continue to use the easier coindexation notation.

I will represent the relation of a theta role to the NP it is assigned to as a linking relation. However, the relation that holds between a head and the phrase it projects, insofar as it involves theta roles, I will still regard as a symmetric relation, one for which coindexation, or perhaps a double-headed arrow, is fully justified. In fact, this is implicit in the discussion of (25). The full "chain" of links that licenses the anaphor in (25) is as follows:

(28) B to A,   (coargument)
     A to V,   (head of argument structure)

V to VP,   (head of phrase)
VP to NP,   (predication)
NP to N,   (head of phrase)
N to R,   (head of argument structure)
R to Th   (coargument)

Observe here that the "head of" relations run sometimes one way (V to VP) and sometimes the other way (NP to N), so, in general, we must allow them to run both ways. The predication link, on the other hand, runs only one way, from predicate to subject.

Reinhart and Reuland (1991) have argued that "picture noun" reflexives of the sort discussed here are not really anaphors, but pronouns whose antecedents are determined under the canons of logophoricity. Their arguments are compelling, and if their conclusions are accepted in full, then the "backward" reflexive cases just discussed do not constitute grounds for the amendments to binding theory just outlined. However, some suspicion must remain that binding theory adjudicates these relations, since the same paradigm holds for reciprocals:

(29) a. Pictures of each other upset John and Mary.
    b. Pictures of each other$_i$ upset [John and Mary]$_i$'s mothers.

It seems highly unlikely that reciprocal pronouns can be reconstrued as logophoric. If not, then our conclusion remains.

Another obstacle to our proposal is found in work by Belletti and Rizzi (1986), who propose that backward reflexivization occurs when and only when the matrix verb is "unaccusative," that is, when it has no external argument in D-Structure; in fact, they propose that the binding of the reflexive occurs in D-Structure. Their structure for a case like (29a) is (30),

(30) e [upset pictures of each other] John and Mary

where *John and Mary* binds *each other* and then moves to subject position. I think this is wrong, for two reasons. First, and most importantly, the ordering of binding before NP-movement is unattested elsewhere, and is not in fact available in the model under examination, since, of course, there is no pre-NP-movement structure. Second, I believe that Belletti and Rizzi are mistaken in identifying these verbs as unaccusative, since they have passives, and lack of a passive is the hallmark of an unaccusative verb:

(31) John and Mary were upset by pictures of each other.

Our conclusion is then clear: the theta role assignment relation is a binding relationship, and in fact, like other cases of binding, it is an instance of asymmetric linking.

6.2.3 Novelty

Some insight into the binding nature of theta role assignment, and its asymmetric linking character, comes from Wasow's (1972) Novelty Condition.

The Novelty Condition is the most fundamental nonstructural property of anaphoric and coreference relations. It says that an anaphorically dependent element cannot have more determinate reference than its antecedent. In its most general form, it applies to any pair of NPs that corefer, even where both are lexical. For example, it regulates the following cases:

(32) a.   A captain$_i$ walked into the room. The officer$_i$ at first said
          nothing.
     b.   *An officer$_i$ walked into the room. The captain$_i$ at first said
          nothing.

In these examples the second NP in each case is dependent on the first for its reference—hence, we call the first the antecedent, and the second the dependent. Assuming that the set of officers properly includes the set of captains, *captain* is more determinate in reference than *officer*—that is, it picks out a smaller set of possible referents. Hence the oddness of (32b), but not (32a), under the Novelty Condition.

The Novelty Condition applies in the case of ordinary pronominal anaphora as well. For example, in *John thinks he is sick* the set of *John*'s is a subset of the set of *he*'s (the set of singular male entities), and so the condition is satisfied.

The Novelty Condition can be observed in the case of theta role assignment as well. This constitutes evidence that the theta role assignment relation is a linking relation, and gives further evidence that the direction of linking is from theta role to NP, and not the reverse.

This is most easily observed in the case of noun-incorporating languages. These languages have a rule that, according to the lexicalist hypothesis, involves a compounding of a noun with a verb, in such a way that the noun "qualifies" one of the theta roles of the verb. Consider the following example from Mohawk (Baker 1983:6):

(33) a.   i?i ye-k-hreks ne   yeokar
          I t1-1s-push prefix bark
          'I push the bark.'

    b. i?i ye-k-kar-hreks-s
       I   t1-1s-bark-push
       'I bark push.'

Here, the noun 'bark' has been compounded with the verb 'push', and the resulting verb means 'to push bark'—in other words, 'bark' has been added as a qualification to the reference of the Patient theta role.

In general, "incorporated" nouns do not "satisfy" the theta role that they qualify; thus, for example, Mithun (1983) cites the following examples from Mohawk (her (106) and (105), respectively):

(34) a. kanekwarunyu wa'-k-akyatawi'tsher-u:ni
         it.dotted.DIST PAST-I-dress-make
         'I dress-made a polka-dotted one.'
     b. sha'te:ku niku:ti   rabahbot wahu-tsy-ahni:nu ki ...
         eight   of.them bullhead he-fish-bought ...
         '[He] bought eight bullheads.'

In each of these, the argument is "qualified" by the incorporated noun, and then it is "satisfied" by the direct object NP.

Now, the qualification sets some limits on the referent of the theta role, and the NP that satisfies the theta role sets others. From the point of view of syntax, the limits set by the incorporated noun are "prior" to the limits set by the NP argument, because they are set in the presyntactic morphology. From the point of view of theta role assignment, then, the limits set by the incorporated noun are a part of the "pronominal" theta role to be assigned. Consequently, the Novelty Condition will require that the NP to which the theta role is assigned be at least as determinate in reference as the incorporated noun. All cases that I have seen conform to this. In most cases, as in (34b), the incorporated noun ('fish') is less determinate than the external NP ('bullhead')—a bullhead is a kind of fish, and hence more determinate in reference. In one type of case the incorporated noun and the external NP are equivalent in determinateness—namely, when they are identical:

(35) ka-nuhs-raku   thiku ka-nuhs-a
     3n-house-white this   pref-house-suf
     (Baker 1983)

This is consistent with the Novelty Condition, which permits, for example, one pronoun to take as its antecedent another instance of the same pronoun. But I have seen no examples that are the reverse of (34b), which would be translated as (36).

(36) *He fish bullhead-caught.

Such examples would violate the Novelty Condition, since the "pronominal" theta role (the Patient theta role of 'caught' qualified by the predicate 'bullhead') is more determinate in reference than the NP it is linked to ('fish').

The absence of such examples strongly confirms the applicability of the Novelty Condition to theta role assignment, and hence also the anaphoric nature of theta role assignment. It also strongly confirms the direction of the anaphoric relation involved: the theta role to be assigned is the anaphorically dependent element, and the NP it is assigned to is the antecedent.

6.2.4 Prepositional Phrases

In chapter 2 we discussed the relation of "function composition," which obtains when the head of a complement juncture does not have an external argument: the external argument of the complement becomes the external argument of the whole juncture. This concept, combined with the two ideas of this chapter that it is theta roles that corefer and that the theta role assignment relation is a binding relation, permit a solution to a problem with PP arguments, a solution that has interesting implications for the binding theory.

The following sort of fact is often cited in favor of a hierarchy of theta roles governing anaphoric binding:

(37) a.   I talked to Bill about himself.
     b. *I talked about Bill to himself.

The *about* theta role is said to be lower on the hierarchy than the dative role, and in general the antecedent must be higher than the anaphor, so (37b) is bad.

I would suggest instead an explanation along the lines of chapter 2. Suppose that the preposition *to* does not have an external theta role, but that the preposition *about* does. Given this distinction, then (37a–b) will have the following representation:

(38) a.   I talked [to Bill$_i$]$_{PP_i}$ [about himself]$_j$.
       (... Th$_i$, G$_j$)   ($\underline{X}_j$)
     b. *I talked   [about Bill$_i$]$_{PP_j}$ to himself.
       (... Th$_i$, G$_j$) ($\underline{X}_j$)

The crucial difference is the index on the PPs: in the case of *to*P, the index is the index of the NP object of *to*, by the principle of relativized head; but in the case of *about*P, the index is the external argument of *about*, by the same principle. As a result, the object of *to* is linked to the G argument of *talked*, whereas the object of *about* is not, and therefore, the object of *to* th-commands the argument structure of *talked*, but the object of *about* does not. Hence the difference in binding possibilities.

We have encoded the intuition that some prepositions are "semantic," whereas others are merely "grammatical," or "Case-marking," in terms of whether or not the preposition has its own external theta role. If it does not, it will be "transparent" for the object—the object will act as though it c-commands material outside the PP and can serve as an antecedent for material outside, though of course in our terms the relation is really th-command.

It should not be too difficult to distinguish these two views, for where the hierarchy gives an *n*-way distinction, the alternative just mentioned— call it the binary theory—gives only a two-way distinction.

One prediction made by the binary theory but not by the hierarchy theory is that if (A) there are two prepositions neither of which can contain an antecedent for a third, then (B) neither can contain an antecedent for the other, either. Under the binary theory, for (A) to hold, the two prepositions must both be semantic; but if they are, (B) will hold as well, for a semantic preposition cannot contain an antecedent for any other PP. The hierarchy theory does not make this prediction. For (A) to hold, the two prepositions must both be lower in the hierarchy than the third; but (B) does not follow, for even if they are both lower than the third, one of them will be ranked above the other and should be able to antecede the other.

The following cases seem to bear out the binary theory:

(39) a. *I spoke about Bill to himself.
    b. *I spoke on behalf of Bill to himself.
    c. *I spoke about Bill on behalf of himself.
    d. *I spoke on behalf of Bill about himself.

(39a–b) show that (A) holds, but (39c–d) show that (B) holds as well, confirming the binary theory and setting a problem for the hierarchy theory.

A large class of facts will force any hierarchy that governs anaphora to be very flat. As noted earlier, the internal Agent and Goal are each able to antecede the other, and to these two could be added the Theme:

(40) a. The book was given to John by himself. (G > A)
    b. The book was given by John to himself. (A > G)
    c. the destruction by the city of itself   (A > Th)

    d. the destruction of the city by itself   (Th > A)
    e. the assignment of Mary to herself   (Th > G)
    f. the assignment to Mary of herself   (G > Th)

In the hierarchy theory, this would mean that all of these roles occupy the same position in the hierarchy, a circumstance that vitiates that theory, reducing it virtually to the binary theory.

What is missing is a case of three theta roles A, B, C, such that A must strictly precede B and B, C. This of course would be crucial evidence for the hierarchy theory over the binary theory.

The problem deepens somewhat when we consider predicative uses of PPs projected from semantic Ps. A prepositional phrase headed by a grammatical preposition does not project a PP that can have a predicative use, since the P has no external argument, whereas a semantic preposition does project a predicative PP. If *of* (in nominalizations) is grammatical and *about*, as mentioned above, semantic, then we expect the following judgments:

(41) a. *The destruction was of the city.
      b. The book was about Mary.

In (41a) a nonsemantic P projects a PP in a predicative position, which is illicit; (41b) on the other hand is fine.

This is a nice result, since it correlates the inability to stand after the copula with the ability to contain an antecedent (and vice versa), a surprising correlation in the absence of theory. However, in general we are forced to posit massive ambiguity to make this work:

(42) a. the letter to John by himself
      b. The letter was to John.

(42a) shows that *to* is grammatical, and (42b), that it is semantic. There is really no contradiction here as long as we allow *to* to be ambiguously grammatical or semantic.

Some prepositions are not ambiguous—for example, the *of* Theme marker (41a) and the *by* Agent marker:

(43) *The destruction of the city was by the enemy.

However, there is a related *by*, called the "authorship" *by* in Williams 1987, which is semantic and can appear in postcopular position:

(44) The book was by Harry.

And the following sentence is ungrammatical because contradictory demands are placed on *by*:

(45) *The book about himself was by Harry.

The postcopular position requires a semantic preposition, but the use of *Harry* as antecedent requires a grammatical preposition.

An alternative view of these postcopular PPs would claim that they are extraposed from theta-marked positions inside the precopular PP; something like this is suggested in Chomsky 1970. A problem for this view is the following sentence:

(46) John's favorite picture of a male is of Bill.

Here the Theme role of *picture* is already saturated internally and so cannot be assigned to *of Bill*.

Contrary to all expectations (except probably those deriving from the account in Higgins 1972), an anaphor can appear in the postcopular PP of (46):

(47) John's favorite picture of a male is of himself.

If *of himself* is a predicative use of a PP, then the theory espoused here will not allow the reflexive in (47) (because the link from predicate to subject goes in the wrong direction). Perhaps the postcopular PP is really part of a reduced postcopular NP:

(48) John's favorite picture of a male is a picture of himself.

Perhaps this is an "inverted" copular sentence, in which case the anaphora is a case of the "backward" anaphora considered earlier. Because of this possibility of inversion, the copula itself is not a good guide to sorting out the subject NP from the predicate NP. However, other predicative environments do so clearly:

(49) a. *I consider John's favorite picture a picture of himself.
      b. I consider a picture of himself John's favorite picture.

However, if the kind of NP-ellipsis that is needed to derive (47) is allowed, then what is wrong with (43), where the postcopular grammatical PP could be construed as the remnant of a reduced NP? Perhaps such cases do exist:

(50) The most thorough destruction of a city by an army ever was (the destruction) of Carthage.

What is wrong with (43), then, is that the unreduced source is itself ungrammatical:

(51) *The destruction of the city by the army was (the destruction (of the city)) by the Roman army.

The good examples of this (like (50)) seem to require indefinite arguments in the precopular NP and the presence of something like the superlative; this may be to buttress the predicational interpretation of the precopular NP, which by virtue of its position would normally be interpreted referentially.

If this line of reasoning is correct, the correlation between being able to appear in postcopular position and being headed by a semantic PP will no longer hold in a simple way. What will hold still is the proposition that only semantic PPs can appear in postcopular position when the precopular NP is not interpreted predicatively—the difference between (40a) and (40b). And of course, the support for the grammatical/semantic distinction for Ps derived from the facts of coargument anaphora discussed at the beginning of this section remains unaffected. Overall, the results of this section, if correct, tend to support the identification of the theta role assignment relation as a binding relation. What we have seen is that absence of a theta role on the head of a PP makes the PP transparent for binding by the object of the PP. The mechanism of transparency is the inheritance, by the PP, of the external argument index of the object, under the definition of relativized head.

6.3 General Reconstruction Effects

In (21), repeated here, we defined th-command with the relation "x is assigned to y" in the recursive step of the definition:

(52) For two theta roles X and Y, X *th-commands* Y if X is a
     coargument of Y; or, if X th-commands B, B is assigned to Z, and
     Z th-commands Y.

And we assume further that the antecedent of an anaphor must th-command it.

Now, how does *wh*-movement fit into this picture? Specifically, we seek to understand reconstruction effects, as in (53), where a reflexive is c-commanded by its antecedent before *wh*-movement, but not after.

(53) Which picture of himself$_i$ does George$_i$ like t?

I think that (52) already answers the question rather adequately. (52) is stated in terms of the theta-theoretic notion "is assigned to." This relation is not altered by the application of *wh*-movement. That is, in (53), for example, the object theta role of *like* "is assigned to" the NP *which picture of himself*, and the fact that *wh*-movement has moved this phrase does not alter this. Hence, *wh*-movement should have no effect on antecedent-anaphor relations. Reconstruction effects are thus understood to arise from the "theta-theoretic neutrality" of *wh*-movement. From this it follows that there will be reconstruction effects for phenomena involving theta roles—binding theory, for example—and for nothing else.

This account is satisfactory for a wide range of cases, and is theoretically unimpeachable as well, since the definition in (52) is needed independently of considerations of *wh*-movement. However, for reasons that will be discussed I think another avenue should be explored.

We might instead take advantage of the insight just gained in section 6.2 and redefine th-command in terms of *linking*, since "is assigned to" is a special case of "is linked to":

(54) For two theta roles X and Y, X *th-commands* Y if X is a coargument of Y; or, if X th-commands B, B is linked to Z, and Z th-commands Y.

But this new definition applies much more widely than just to the cases we have been considering—it applies not only where the theta assignment relation is involved, but where any anaphoric dependence is involved. Hence, (54) is a nontrivial generalization of the original definition, and in fact it has the possibility of deriving the full set of reconstruction effects. If this is so, we must count this as a further piece of evidence in favor of the proposition that theta role assignment is a special case of linking.

Already, we have seen how (52), and so now (54), derives backward anaphora cases, which we take to be one kind of reconstruction, as well as Higgins's (1972) "NP *be* NP" cases (26). We will now explore how (54) covers the full set, including of course the central *wh*-movement cases.

Consider, for example, relative clauses. What is the relation of a relative to the head it modifies, and how does that relation fit into theta theory? Certainly, the relative is not an argument of the head noun. Plausibly, the relative is a one-place predicate and takes the head noun as its sole argument. The noun-relative relation then is something like the NP VP relation: the head noun is the "subject" and the relative is the "predicate." The noun is then the "antecedent" of the noun-relative relation, and the relative is (or contains), in some sense, the anaphorically dependent element. We will assume that the relative is linked to the head noun; further, we will assume a linking between the relative and its head, just as in the case of a predicative expression. The head of the relative will be the *wh*-phrase.

Therefore, arguments of the head will not th-command elements of the relative, but it should be possible for elements within the relative to th-command the head. Suppose that it is the *wh*-word that is the anaphorically dependent element in a relative—then anything that th-commands it will th-command the head. And, since the trace bound by the *wh*-phrase is anaphorically dependent on the *wh*-phrase (that is, as Higginbotham proposes, a *wh*-trace is linked to the moved phrase that gave rise to it), anything that th-commands the *wh*-trace also th-commands the head. But this is exactly the result we need to account for a certain class of reconstruction effects:

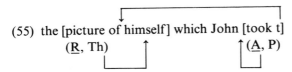

(55) the [picture of himself] which John [took t]
      (R, Th)   (A, P)

Here, *John* th-commands P, P is dependent on *t*, *t* on *wh*, and *wh* on the external argument of *picture of himself*, which th-commands *himself*. Hence, *John* th-commands *himself*, and binding is possible.

In general, reconstruction effects can be derived via "linking" and th-command in this way. In Williams 1983 it was shown that reconstruction effects all run in a particular direction: the "predicate" contains an antecedent for something in the "subject" of that predicate, but not the reverse. This result is now rationalized in terms of "th-command" defined in terms of linking: the predicate is linked to the subject, not vice versa, so elements in the predicate will th-command elements in the subject, and not vice versa.

Thus, for example, it is possible to rationalize the distinction between the two cases of the pseudocleft construction distinguished by Higgins (1972):

(56) a. *Predicational*
         What John is is important to him.
      b. *Specificational*
         What John is is important to himself.

The specificational pseudocleft, but not the predicational, shows reconstruction effects. The reason is that the real subject of the predicational pseudocleft is the clefted clause, with the AP *important to him* predicated of it, whereas the real subject of the specificational pseudocleft is the clefted constituent *important to himself*, and the clefted clause is (a free relative NP) predicated of that constituent.

The surface forms of the pseudoclefts do not show what the real subject is, since there is free inversion around the copula. However, various processes distinguish the real from the apparent subject; for example, raising only raises the real subject:

(57) a. *Predicational*
　　　　What John is seems to be important to him.
　　　　*Important to him seems to be what John is.
　　 b. *Specificational*
　　　　*What John is seems to be important to himself.
　　　　Important to himself seems to be what John is.

See Williams 1983 for further discussion along these lines.

In general, then, we see that reconstruction effects run from predicate to subject, and not vice versa, in the sense that the subject can contain an anaphor bound by something in the predicate, but not vice versa. See also the discussion in chapter 4.

Note that the general case of reconstruction, as in (55) and (56), is accounted for in exactly the same way (by the definition of th-command) as backward reflexivization, (25), and, for that matter, Higgins's recalcitrant case, (26). This theoretical identification of backward reflexivization and reconstruction effects means that if a language does not for some reason have one of these, it will not have the other. W. Wilkins (personal communication) notes that Spanish is such a language.

There is one further important difference between the account of reconstruction just given, and literal "reconstruction," a difference that again has to do with the asymmetry of linking. We have already seen (example (25)) that it is possible for a predicative expression to contain the antecedent of an anaphor in the subject:

(58) Pictures of each other were upsetting to John and Mary.

And we have just seen (example (55)) that *wh*-moving a phrase that contains an anaphor does not affect binding possibilities—this is the fundamental reconstruction effect:

(59) Which pictures of each other do you think were upsetting to John and Mary?

However, if it is the predicative phrase in (58) that is *wh*-moved, then the result is ungrammatical:

(60) *How upsetting to John and Mary do you think pictures of each
        other would be t?

Clearly, literal reconstruction (or equivalently, applying binding theory
before *wh*-movement) will not discriminate between (59) and (60), since
they have the same reconstructed (deep) structure. However, the definition of th-command will: (59) will work essentially like (55), but (60) will
look like (61).

(61)
[How upsetting to J&M]$_i$ do you think [pictures of each other]$_j$ will be t?
        ($\underline{A}_i$, B)   ($\underline{R}_j$, D)

There is no path of arrows from the theta role assigned to *J&M* (B)
to the theta role assigned to *each other* (D), essentially because the *wh*-
movement link goes in the wrong direction: the trace is asymmetrically
linked to the phrase that binds it. As before, coindexed items are by definition connected by double-headed arrows; see (25), (28), and surrounding discussion. The general theorem of the system is that *wh*-movement
can give rise to reconstruction effects only when nonpredicative expressions are moved, and this is because the link established by *wh*-movement
is unidirectional. This would be quite surprising in the absence of the
connection between theta role assignment and linking that the theory of
th-command gives.

The generalization achieved in the extension of th-command in (54) is
of course far too broad in one respect, predicting, for example, that the
linking of an ordinary pronoun to its antecedent will provide a path for
reconstruction effects. The class of links that th-command works on must
clearly be restricted in some way—not every anaphoric link gives reconstruction effects. The ones that do—theta role assignment and *wh*-bind-
ing—are grammatically determined links, as opposed to the linking of an
ordinary pronoun to its antecedent, which we may consider not to be
grammatically determined, even though there are grammatical restrictions on it.

A further difference between the standard treatment of reconstruction
and the treatment proposed here is found in the "anticrossover" cases.
In Van Riemsdijk and Williams 1981 cases of the following sort are
discussed:

(62) Which picture of John$_i$ did he$_i$ like best t?

We dubbed these cases *anticrossover*, since the coreference that is permitted here should not be allowed under reconstruction—the non-*wh*-moved version of this sentence does not permit coreference:

(63) *He$_i$ did like which picture of John$_i$ best?

In the theory proposed in Van Riemsdijk and Williams 1981, the binding theory applied to the premovement NP-Structure, and for these cases we suggested that there was an S-Structure relaxation of the binding theory for pronouns with definite antecedents. In the present context, a different view suggests itself, since there is no NP-Structure/S-Structure distinction that can be relevant.

Note first that the structure in which anticrossover effects hold is exactly parallel to the structure in which backward anaphora is possible:

(64) Which picture of himself$_i$ do you think John$_i$ likes best?

Thus, it is pointless to deny that the matrix subject th-commands the contents of the moved phrase.

We in fact want it both ways: to th-command in (64), but not in (62). We may achieve this by introducing a nondeterministic branch in the definition of th-command, which will permit *wh*-links to count for some cases, but not for others:

(65) For two theta roles X and Y, X *th-commands* Y if X is a
     coargument of Y; or, if X th-commands B, B is (theta-)linked to Z,
     and Z th-commands Y.

The change in the definition is in the notion of linking it employs. The definition has two versions now, one stated in terms of "theta linking" and the other in terms of the general notion of linking. "Theta linking" differs from "general linking" in not including links generated by *wh*-movement. Thus, only the linkings established by theta role assignment will count for the version based on "theta linking."

We actually have two notions of th-command, and any process can avail itself of either definition, so no stipulation is required. To generate (62), then, we will take the version based on theta linking; since there is no path of arrows from the pronoun to the antecedent that consists purely of theta role assignment arrows, th-command does not hold between the pronoun and the antecedent, and so coreference is allowed. To generate (64), we simply use the version of th-command based on general linking, as before.

Quite parallel to the anticrossever cases is the following:

(66) John's mother$_i$ [likes him$_j$]$_{VP_i}$.
          ($\underline{A}_i$, B$_j$)

Coreference between *John* and *him* should not be permitted here, because
him th-commands *John*. And as in the anticrossover cases, it is impossible
to deny that th-command holds here, because backward anaphora occurs
in exactly this structural configuration:

(67) Each other's mother pleased John and Mary.

Again, we want a variable definition, which permits us to have or not have
th-command depending on circumstances. (66) and (67) do not have *wh*-
links, so the definition in (65) will not distinguish them.

   The linking chains in (66) and (67) both crucially involve the predication link, that is, the link between subject and VP. Although not a
wh-link, the predication link still differs from other theta links in not
involving a lexical item—it is a phrase-to-phrase link. Let us refer to the
predication link as a *nonlexical* link, and to theta links as *lexical* links.

   Now, *wh*-movement links are also nonlexical, in that *wh*-movement
relates two phrasal positions. We may therefore rephrase (65) as follows:

(68) For two theta roles X and Y, X *th-commands* Y if X is a
          coargument of Y; or, if X th-commands B, B is (lexically) linked to
          Z, and Z th-commands Y.

This definition will now cover both sorts of anticrossover cases, (62)
and (66), and still permit backward anaphora in parallel cases like (67).
Moreover, Conditions B and C still hold where they should, as in (69).

(69) He$_i$ [likes John's mother].
          ($\underline{A}_i$, B)

Here, the linking chain is B to *John's mother* (theta role assignment),
John's mother to *John* ("head of" relation), and *mother* to *John*. Each of
these is a lexical relation, and so th-command holds under either variant.
Note that the relevant relation is between theta role $\underline{A}$ and the theta role
assigned to *John*, not between the subject *he* and *John*; this is why the
subject-predicate relation is not involved in this case.

6.4 The Hybrid Binding Theory

In different parts of the book we have arrived at different conclusions
about what relations the binding theory is based on. In this chapter I have

presented the view that the binding theory is less "structural" and more based on "argument of" relations, which have an imperfect relation to S-Structure, than is assumed in standard accounts. But in chapter 4 I argued that the binding theory incorporates the "precedence" relation as an indispensable grammatical term, and hence that binding theory is very much tied to the particulars of S-Structure. However, if we were to write a binding rule like (70),

(70) An NP is disjoint in reference from any NP that it precedes and th-commands.

one would rightly ask, Why are these two relations involved?

They are of course not technically incompatible, but precedence and th-command seem so fundamentally different that one wonders why they occur together in (70). Burzio's generalization provokes the same puzzle-ment—"What do these two things, Case on the object and theta role on the subject, have to do with each other?"—and that is why there seems to be a consensus that Burzio's generalization, despite its widespread utility, is not a fundamental law.

I will argue that th-command and precedence are not terms of a single law that governs all relations—that in fact there are two sorts of relations, one governed by precedence and the other not.

In brief, th-command is relevant to any relation that relates two theta roles, or two theta positions. This includes Conditions A, B, and C, which govern equality of reference among theta roles and the theta role assign-ment relation itself.

Precedence, on the other hand, will be seen to be relevant whenever referential dependence (a relation different from referential equality) be-tween theta roles is involved.

In section 6.4.1 I will take up the question of th-command—specifi-cally, its role in the general theory of syntax. Th-command will be seen to characterize exactly what Van Riemsdijk and Williams (1981) call the "NP-Structure" of a sentence; another relation, one closer to c-command, will characterize "S-Structure." The existence of reconstruction effects will be seen to be an inescapable consequence of the terms of the theory.

In section 6.4.2 I will examine further the nature of the precedence condition. In particular, I will argue that as a precedence condition, the WCO Condition is a special case of a Leftness Condition that holds for anaphora in general. This condition governs not equality of reference, as Conditions A, B, and C do, but rather referential dependence.

Thus, th-command and precedence are not simply two conjoined terms in a weird binding theory law. Rather, th-command is relevant to binding theory simply because th-command is relevant to any theta-to-theta relation, and the binding relations are one such relation. And precedence is not really a term in Conditions A, B, and C, but is a term in a separate principle governing anaphoric *dependence*, a relation that is irrelevant to the binding conditions. So one might say that the theory is modular, and that the modularization is rationalized.

6.4.1 Th-Command and NP-Structure

What relations is th-command relevant for? Exactly the bindings and binding prohibitions regulated by the binding theory, including the theta role assignment relation, which I have argued to be a binding relation. In short, it is relevant in relations of theta roles to theta roles, or theta roles to theta positions; I will refer to the set of all these relations as *theta relations*. On the other hand, it is not relevant for determining *wh*-trace bindings, or quantifier scope, since these do not relate theta roles to theta roles, or theta roles to theta positions.

So, for example, a quantifier can have scope over NPs that it does not th-command (or c-command), and so can a *wh*-phrase:

(71) a. At least one photographer has taken a picture of each of the candidates.
   b. Who do you think left?

Clearly, th-command is not relevant for this kind of relation. On the other hand, the case that th-command is relevant for the binding theory has already been made in this chapter.

Consequently, we will find reconstruction effects for all of the theta relations, but not for other types of relation. This is because the relation *th-commands* is defined in terms of *coargument of* and *is assigned to* or *theta-linked to*, relations that are unaffected by *wh*-movement. For example, earlier we considered definition (65), repeated here:

(72) For two theta roles X and Y, X *th-commands* Y if X is a coargument of Y; or, if X th-commands B, B is (theta-)linked to Z, and Z th-commands Y.

Now, since *wh*-movement simply does not change theta relations, it will not change any relations based on theta relations. In (73), for example,

(73) Whose mother do you think he saw t?

the fact that *whose mother* has *wh*-moved to the front does not change the fact that the internal argument of *see* is linked to, and satisfied by, the external argument of *mother*. As long as this is true, it cannot be that *wh*-movement has altered any th-command relations, since those relations are determined purely by the coargument and "assigned to" relations.

As concluded in Williams 1986b, although we will find reconstruction effects for anaphor binding, NP-trace binding, bound anaphor relations, and theta role assignment, we will not find reconstruction effects involving *wh*-trace.

The first set of expectations is illustrated by the following questions:

(74) a. Who do I like t?
     b. Which pictures of each other do John and Mary like t?
     c. Which of his pictures does everyone like best?
     d. How certain to win do you think John is?
     e. *Which picture of everyone does he like t?

These examples illustrate the reconstruction effect for theta role assignment (74a), anaphor binding (74b), bound anaphora (74c), NP-movement (74d), and Condition C (74e). In each case the moved constituent acts as though it occupied the position of the trace.

However, "$\bar{A}$" relations do not show reconstruction effects. For example, it is impossible to raise a phrase above a Comp that binds something inside that phrase:

(75) a. *Which pictures of t_i did you wonder who$_i$ I saw t?
     b. ?Who$_i$ did you wonder which pictures of t_i I saw t?

In (75a) the NP containing the trace of *who* has been raised above *who*; if reconstruction worked here, this should not matter, but it renders the sentence sharply ungrammatical. (75b) is provided for contrast: exactly the same constituents have moved in (75b) as in (75a), but in reverse order, so that (75b) is only marginally bad.

The difference between raising constructions and *wh*-constructions is this: the raising relation is a theta relation, that is, a relation of theta role assignment; hence, th-command is relevant for it, and reconstruction therefore "feeds" the licensing of the raising relation. Not so for the *wh*-trace binding relation. Not being a theta relation, this relation is governed not by th-command, but by some other relation, and this other relation (probably something like traditional c-command) is not preserved by *wh*-movement.

6.4.2 Precedence and Weak Crossover

Now, what is the domain of the precedence relation? What does it govern? I believe that it governs *anaphoric dependence*, by the following law, the *Leftness Condition*:

(76) *Leftness Condition*
   If NP_i precedes NP_j, NP_i cannot referentially depend on NP_j.

I propose that the Leftness Condition is the condition that governs weak crossover (WCO) phenomena, though its coverage, as I will show, goes well beyond WCO. (I use the term *WCO* here to refer to the phenomena illustrated in (77), for example.)

Here, I concentrate on the role of precedence in bound anaphora, that is, the binding of a pronoun by a quantified NP antecedent:

(77) Everyone$_i$ likes his$_i$ mother.

Bound anaphora is governed by the binding theory first, and then, in addition, by the Leftness Condition (76).

The first question to address is, Is there a specific licensing of bound anaphora? In this chapter I will use the term *anaphoric pronoun* to mean a pronoun with a linguistic antecedent. The antecedent might be in a previous utterance, in previous discourse, and so on, but it is some linguistic phrase. I will use the term *bound pronoun* to refer to a pronoun that is both in the scope of a quantifier and dependent on it. Reinhart (1983:122, 139) proposes that bound pronouns are specifically licensed by the binding theory, in fact as a subcase of Condition A. I disagree; I believe instead that bound pronouns are not specifically licensed, apart from the licensing of anaphoric pronouns in general, a licensing that is not part of sentence grammar, to say the least. I will argue that bound anaphora is not specifically licensed by the binding theory, but that like definite anaphora, it is permitted in all those instances where the binding theory does not forbid it. In other words, the environment of bound anaphora is not an entity defined by the theory directly; rather, it is the complement of the environment(s) in which the theory forbids dependence and equality of reference.

Reinhart proposes that bound anaphora (the only kind of anaphora that can hold between a pronoun and a quantified NP) holds only when the antecedent c-commands the pronoun (pp. 122, 139), the same condition that holds for reflexive binding. But there are two irreducible differences between the two. The first is illustrated by the following sentences:

(78) a. *Everyone$_i$'s mother likes himself$_i$.
     b. Everyone$_i$'s mother likes him$_i$.

Reinhart is aware of the problem caused by this contrast. She discusses examples like (78b) in a chapter entitled "Unsolved Problems of Anaphora" and says of (78b) that such examples are "permitted . . . for many speakers" (p. 127). I think this is incorrect; every speaker of English accepts (78b), and every speaker of English distinguishes (78a) and (78b).

The second difference is illustrated by the fact that bound pronouns can exhibit "split" antecedence, whereas reflexives cannot:

(79) a.   John told Mary that they should get married.
     b.   John told every girl that they should get married.
     c.   Every boy told every girl that they should get married.
     d.   *John told Mary about themselves.
     e.   *John told every girl about themselves.
     f.   *Every boy told every girl about themselves.
     g.   That John inherited a fortune caused every girl to imagine that
          they would make a nice couple.

(In these examples *they* is meant to be understood as bound to both subject and object.) (79a) shows split antecedence with definite anaphora; (79b), that bound anaphora can share a pronoun with a definite antecedent; and (79c), that a bound pronoun can be simultaneously bound to two quantified antecedents. (79d–f), which are the corresponding cases for reflexives, show that the reflexive is not simply the "local" version of bound anaphora, but is fundamentally different. The difference is, I believe, that reflexives are specifically licensed by the binding theory, whereas bound pronouns are not—they occupy the niches that the binding theory fails to forbid.

Another way to put this is to say that a bound pronoun is nothing more than an anaphoric pronoun dependent on and in the scope of a quantifier —there is no reason to distinguish them. Deictic pronouns, on the other hand, are different:

(80) *Every girl$_i$ thinks that they$_i$ would make a nice couple.
     (said while pointing to *John*, intending that *they* = her$_i$ and *John*)

In sum, then, a bound anaphoric relation is allowed whenever the following conditions obtain:

(81) a.   Conditions B and C of the binding theory do not specifically
          forbid a dependence between a pronoun and its antecedent; and
     b.   The pronoun is in the scope of the antecedent.

This is surely the minimal theory of bound anaphora phenomena. If there is anything beyond this, it remains to be demonstrated.

In fact, though, there is a further condition, the Leftness Condition, illustrated here:

(82) *His$_i$ mother likes everyone$_i$.

I argued in chapter 4 that the phenomenon illustrated in (82), the WCO phenomenon, exhibits a precedence effect. I will not repeat those arguments here, but will argue against the one extended effort—by Reinhart (1983)—to show that precedence plays no role in WCO cases. Reinhart argues that c-command alone governs WCO. In my opinion, however, many of her examples that are meant to show that c-command alone is the relevant notion are simply incorrectly judged. (83) gives a sampling of her sentences that are meant to show that preceding but not c-commanding antecedents for indefinite anaphora are insufficient. (These are Reinhart's (5.45b–c), (5.46b–c), respectively.)

(83) a. The actress who$_i$ Brando kissed t in her$_i$ latest film will win the Oscar.
      b. What actress did Brando kiss t$_i$ in her$_i$ latest film?
      c. Who did the police arrest t$_i$ in spite of his$_i$ alibi?
      d. The guy who$_i$ the police arrested t in spite of his$_i$ alibi has filed a complaint.

According to Reinhart's assumption, the structure of these examples is as follows,

(84) [... antecedent ...]$_{VP}$ [... prounoun ...]$_{Adjunct}$

and so the pronoun does not c-command the antecedent. Reinhart judges each of these sentences ungrammatical—mistakenly, in my view—and concludes on this basis that it is not sufficient that the antecedent precede the pronoun.

Another of Reinhart's examples (her (5.48b)) truly is ungrammatical, but for a reason different from the one Reinhart suggests:

(85) *So many people interviewed each of the candidates$_i$ that he$_i$ could not remember them all.

This is ungrammatical on the most obvious reading, where *so many people* has widest scope; but in that case the pronoun, being located in the complement to *so many*, is not even in the scope of the antecedent, and so coreference is simply not coherent. "Being in the scope of" is not the same as "being in the c-command domain of," and it is the latter property that Reinhart is advocating. We will assume, as Reinhart certainly does and all others at least implicitly do, that the pronoun must be in the (semantic) scope of its (quantified) antecedent.

If we alter this example so that the obvious reading is one in which *each of the candidates* has widest scope, then the binding becomes valid, despite the fact that the c-command relations are the same as in Reinhart's example:

(86) So many things happened to each of the candidates$_i$ that he$_i$ couldn't remember them all.

But if these observations, and the observations of chapter 4, show that Reinhart is wrong in pinning everything on c-command, they nevertheless fail to give a rationale for the role that precedence seems to be playing.

If the WCO Condition is the Leftness Condition, then we may understand it as a requirement that an antecedent must precede a coreferential pronoun, a requirement implicit in the word *antecedent*. Apparently, however, this is not always true; the following contrast has been taken to suggest that the Leftness Condition, or whatever the WCO Condition is, is not enforced for definite antecedents:

(87) a. His boss saw John.
   b. *His boss ridiculed everyone.

Only in (87a) is coreference possible.

However, there is actually something special about (87a)—namely, coreference is possible only if *John* is not stressed:

(88) *His boss saw JOHN.

The destressing of *John* indicates that there has been a previous occurrence of *John* in the discourse; on the first mention of *John*, it must be stressed. But if there is a previous mention, then that previous mention could serve as the antecedent of the pronoun. Therefore, we might continue to suppose that antecedents must precede.

If antecedents must precede, then it follows that a pronoun bound by a quantifier must always follow the quantifier, since there could be no possible antecedent other than the quantifier that could have preceded the pronoun in the discourse:

(89) *His mother likes everyone.

Since *his* in (89) takes a different referent for each instance of *everyone*, there of course can be no question of a previous antecedent for it. Could this be the source of the WCO phenomena in the first place? If it is, we could enforce WCO for all relations of antecedence and explain the special case of quantified antecedents in terms of the unavailability of previous or presupposed antecedents other than the quantified antecedent.

Now, there is a systematic source of counterexamples to the notion that pronouns without preceding intra-utterance antecedents depend on previous discourse antecedents. In fact, the literature contains two sorts of accounts of when backward pronouns are possible. According to one, it is when there is a previous discourse topic. According to the other, it is when the pronoun appears in a subordinate clause with respect to the antecedent. In fact, both are probably right. We have already seen examples of the former; (90b) illustrates the latter.

(90) [That company operates like a well-oiled machine.]
   a.   That he had been given no assignments upset THE NEW VICE PRESIDENT.
   b.   *His boss upset THE NEW VICE PRESIDENT. (odd if a new referent)

The context, in brackets, sets up no antecedent of any kind for the capitalized NP. Apparently, when the pronoun is embedded in a subordinate clause, as in (90a), the need for a preceding antecedent, even one in previous discourse, is suspended; not so, however, when the pronoun is simply a genitive on the subject, as in (90b).

This suspension, however, even applies when the antecedent is quantificational—that is, in a typical WCO situation:

(91) [That he might not survive the first year] worries every beginning medical student.

Although the exceptionality of subordinate clause environments is not explained, the fact that it holds both for pronouns with definite (following) antecedents and for pronouns with quantified (following) antecedents supports the idea that the two cases are not really dissimilar.

I do not understand why subordinate clauses make the difference that they do. The following examples cast doubt on whether the subordinate effect can be understood as a consequence of "depth of embedding" or of a failure of c-command:

(92) a.   *His$_i$ mother came to the track and a friend of mine$_i$ won the derby.
   b.   That he might someday meet the Queen inspired every British soldier.
   c.   *The girl that he met in front of him in the registration line eventually married every incoming student.

In (92a) *his* is embedded in the first of two conjoined clauses and hence is as deeply embedded as *he* in (92b), yet (92a) is bad. Llkewise, in (92c) *he* is embedded in a relative clause, making it at least as deeply embedded as *he* in (92a), and again it is bad. These examples suggest that the subordinate clause effect is not structural, at least not in the structural terms we have been considering. I feel that the semantics of subordinate clauses would unravel this mystery, but I have nothing to say about it here.

There is one other context worth mentioning in which a subordinate clause provides an exceptional backward licensing, namely, the context of negative polarity items (NPIs):

(93) a. *Any dogs wasn't there.
   b. *Anyone's brother wasn't there.
   c. [That anyone might doubt him] did not disturb John.
   d. *John denied any accusations.
   e. John denied that he had any connection to Bill.
   f. John denied any connection to Bill.
   g. Any connection to Bill was denied.

The difference between NPs and Ss illustrated in (93a–c) is probably not syntactic but semantic.

Laka (1990) has argued otherwise: she proposes that an NPI in a subordinate clause must be licensed by a negative complementizer. Examples like (93d–e) seem to support her proposal—the negative verbs would not be licensers themselves, but would select a licensing complementizer.

We might take (93f–g) to show that exactly when the NP can be interpreted "propositionally," it can host an NPI. (93f) can be paraphrased as *John denied that there was any connection to Bill.*

Laka dismisses some examples of this sort (pp. 181ff.) by claiming that these cases are "free choice" *any* and hence not subject to the same constraints as NPI *any*. She claims that the cases all involve "action" nouns. I believe that she has misidentified the class of cases and misanalyzed the examples. First, I think the cases are all those cases that can be interpreted propositionally, not the ones headed by action nouns—*accusation* is more of an action noun than *connection*, but only the latter hosts the NPI. This is significant, for it suggests the following analysis: where *any* can be given scope subordinate to the governing verb, it can be licensed; but where its scope must be higher than the governing verb, it will not be licensed by that verb. This is just what we would expect, given our analysis of the semantics of negation in chapter 5: *any* is licensed in exactly those elements that negation can attach to, namely, propositions and predicates.

Now, suppose that when an NP is interpreted propositionally, it can serve as a locus of quantifier scope, but not otherwise. Then exactly the pattern in (93) would result.

Laka's proposal that the *any* in (93f–g) is "free choice" *any* actually undermines the rest of her predictions. She identifies "free choice" *any* as a universal quantifier, paraphrasable by *all*. But actually, all of the cases in (93), including (93d), have a "free choice" *any* interpretation. The stars in (93) pertain to the clearly distinguishable NPI readings.

Under the view I am suggesting here, then, the Leftness Condition is a special case of the general condition on anaphora (i.e., the antecedent must precede); it is even subject to the same exceptions to this condition that definite anaphora is subject to.

In effect, under the view presented here (88) is classified as a WCO case, governed by the Leftness Condition, even though it contains no quantifier. But (88) has in fact been analyzed as a WCO violation as far back as Chomsky 1972, but for a different reason than the one given here. Chomsky supposed that there was a Focus rule, which, like *wh*-movement and QR, moved a (focused) NP to the left, leaving a variable, so that the structure of (88) was as follows:

(94) John$_i$ his$_i$ boss saw t$_i$.

For Chomsky, the special feature of (94) is the presence of the variable (*t*). In fact, though, I think that the effect that (88) illustrates arises independently of special focus—namely, it arises whenever the putative antecedent is not specifically destressed. Naturally, a sentence-final argument will receive the main sentence stress, even when the sentence receives noncontrastive "nuclear" stress. Consider the various possible responses of B to A in the following exchange:

(95) A: Well, no Democratic administration has ever been embarrassed while it still held power.

   *B1: Are you kidding? His children forced Jacob Lewis to resign as Secretary of Defense in 1948 by their misdeeds.

   B2: Are you kidding? Jacob Lewis's children forced him to resign as Secretary of Defense in 1948 by their misdeeds.

   B3: Are you kidding? After his children exposed him in the papers, Jacob Lewis was forced to resign as Secretary of Defense in 1948.

These sentences exhibit no special contrastive stress or focusing—just the normal stress that occurs on a sentence when it is all "new information."

Only B1 is odd—odd because the pronoun occurs before its only possible antecedent. In B2 the pronoun follows the antecedent, and in B3 it precedes it, but in an embedded clause.

There is a way to distinguish between Chomsky's view and the one presented here. Suppose that we have an NP that is truly contrastively stressed—that is, not because it is new, but rather as a consequence of being put in opposition to something else. In that case the result is grammatical:

(96) John is such a fool. He thinks his children hate him. But in fact his children don't hate JOHN, they hate HIS NEW WIFE.

Under the usual view, (96) should be ungrammatical, since the focused element, *John*, is to the right of a dependent pronoun. But under the view I am suggesting here, (96) should be acceptable, since the pronoun does have a preceding antecedent: the instance of *John* in the first sentence.

The discussion so far rests on a somewhat subtle distinction. In the basic example (97),

(97) His mother loves John.

we are not saying that *his* and *John* cannot be coreferential; rather, *his* cannot depend on *John* for its reference. That is a different matter from coreference. However, in other circumstances we are not interested in dependence, but in absolute equality of reference:

(98) He thinks that John is sick.

It is not enough to say of (98) that *he* cannot depend on *John* for reference; rather, *he* cannot corefer with *John*, no matter what. Hence, Condition C is a condition on coreference, whereas the condition that governs WCO is a condition on dependence.

Why distinguish equality and dependence? The most important reason is that (as we will see) they are correlated with different structural conditions: equality may be regulated by a pure c-command condition (or if I am right, a th-command condition), whereas dependence is regulated by the Leftness Condition. Furthermore, it is possible to have equality without dependence, and dependence without equality.

Equality without dependence occurs when two noun phrases happen to share reference, but neither is dependent on the other for its reference. This can arise, for example, when each of them is dependent on a third:

(99) His mother doesn't like John.

Our earlier discussion of such examples indicated that coreference is possible here only in the case that *his* and *John* are each anaphoric to an antecedent in previous discourse—that is why *John* must be destressed. In this case, then, we do not have dependence, but we do have coreference, between the two.

Dependence without coreference can occur in a number of ways. In the following kind of sentence, studied by Mitchell (1986), the referent of *nearby bar* varies with the referent of the subject, even though there is no pronoun in the object bound to the subject:

(100) Everybody went to a nearby bar.

We might be tempted to supply a covert *him* to (100), and read it as either (101a) or (101b),

(101) a. *Everybody went to a [nearby him] bar.
       b. ?Everybody went to a bar nearby him.

which gets the meaning right if not the syntax. We might do this to reduce all cases of dependence to equality of reference: the object in (100) is dependent on the subject exactly because it contains a (covert) pronoun equal in reference to the subject. Or we could imagine that the quantifier is binding the unexpressed (implicit) second argument of *nearby* (the y argument of "x is nearby y," where x is bound to *bar*), with equivalent result.

But dependence cannot be eliminated in favor of either equality of reference or pronoun (or implicit argument) binding, for two reasons. First, in the general case, illustrated in (102), there will not be a position in which a pronoun can appear:

(102) Every surgeon hates the hospital administrator.

Here, what must be supplied is not just a pronoun, but something like *the hospital administrator [of the hospital where he_i works]*. It is not plausible to reduce this sort of dependence to pronoun binding—clearly, the phrase *of the hospital where he works* is a good guess, but one that depends on practical experience, not grammar. The use of *the* in (102) means that there will be an obvious function, a Skolem function, whereby the hearer, for each value of the subject, can identify the hospital administrator referred to. The function is not given; it is simply implied to be obvious to the hearer.

If this is correct, then this sort of referential dependence does not reduce to variable binding, even if (101) does. However, we might attempt to effect such a reduction for (102) by appeal to a covert or deleted possessive pronoun in the object. Thus, (102) would be equivalent to (103),

(103) Every surgeon hates his hospital administrator.

where *his* is bound to the subject. I think this solution is implausible for this case; but it works, simply because the possessive is a two-place relation ("*x* is to *y*") that is sufficiently vague in its applicability to encompass most of the relations we can think of. Under this analysis, either (102) could be derived from (103) by deleting the possessive bound pronoun, or (102) could be understood as involving the binding of an implicit argument of an implicit possessive.

However, I think even this will not work for cases like the following:

(104) a. Every surgeon hates the head of pharmacy.
      b. Every surgeon hates the assistant to the head of pharmacy.

Here, putting in a pronoun does not get the right meaning. *His head of pharmacy* implies a narrower set of relations than (104a) does; it implies, for example, that the head of pharmacy is institutionally subordinate to the surgeon, not simply that he is at the same hospital as the surgeon. And in (104b) the possibility becomes even more remote: *his assistant to the head of pharmacy*, if it has a meaning at all, has nothing in common with the designation in (104b).

It seems to me inescapable that dependence is primitive here, and not reducible either to pronoun binding or to the binding of implicit arguments.

If we substitute the indefinite for the definite article in (102), we still have referential dependence, but with no obvious function for picking out the referent:

(105) Every surgeon hates a hospital administrator.

Here, there is a possibly different referent for the object for every value of the subject, but it is implied that there is no "obvious" function for choosing the value for the object. This perhaps encapsulates the difference between *the* and *a* in these contexts, and perhaps in general: *the* implies an obvious function, *a* implies no obvious function. (That is, in the case of the indefinite there is some sort of function, which is only to say that each choice of subject maps into some value for the object; but there is no obvious function). Even more than in (102), there is no reason to reduce (105) to a case of variable binding.

In fact, perhaps the right strategy is not to reduce dependence to pronoun binding, but to reduce pronoun binding to dependence; that is, in (106)

(106) Every surgeon$_i$ thinks he$_i$ is the best.

he is dependent on *every surgeon*, and the use of the pronoun *he* signals that there is an "obvious" function for picking the referent of the embedded subject position—namely, the identity function.

The second reason why dependence cannot be eliminated in favor of either equality of reference or pronoun binding is that even in (101), there is reason to distinguish these phenomena.

In an example like (101b) the object is clearly dependent on the subject for reference: for each choice of an individual as subject, we get a possibly different bar in object position. This variation is an obvious consequence of the equality of reference of the subject and the pronoun *him*.

Now, in the typical WCO sentence, a dependent NP precedes the NP it is dependent on:

(107) a. His mother likes everyone.
      b. His mother likes John.

Recall that we determined earlier that it is not the coreference that is disallowed in these sentences, but the dependence.

But dependence of what on what? We spoke earlier about the dependence of *his* on *everyone*; but perhaps what is disallowed is instead the dependence of *his mother* on *everyone*. The following examples support the notion that this is the relevant dependence:

(108) a. The hospital adminstrator hates every surgeon.
      b. A nearby bar attracted everybody.

These are ungrammatical on readings where the subject is dependent on the object. There is a clear relation between (107) and (108), and clearly (108) shares features of the WCO phenomenon.

But in (108) there is no pronoun on which the dependence can be pinned; the dependence is primitive, not derivative. But if we can block dependence here, then we can block it in (107), without targeting the pronoun directly, since the pronoun is apparently not an essential component of the WCO phenomenon.

"Donkey" pronoun sentences exhibit the same dependence:

(109) a. Every farmer who owns a donkey beats it.
      b. It is beaten by every farmer who owns a donkey.

    c. Anyone who has ever had an operation owes a lot to the hospital administrator.

    d. The hospital administrator is owed a lot by anyone who has ever had an operation.

    e. The hospital administrator is owed a lot by anyone who has ever been operated on.

(109a) is the typical "donkey" sentence, and (109b) shows that the anaphora exhibited in (109a) is subject to the Leftness Condition. What dependence is being blocked in (109b)? One possibility is that it is the dependence of *it* not on *a donkey*, but on *every farmer who owns a donkey*, an NP it is not bound by, but is nevertheless dependent on.

(109b) confirms that this is so, and shows again that what is primitive here is the dependence, not binding. In (109c) there is no sense in which *the hospital administrator*, in its varying reading, is bound by *an operation*. Rather, it is dependent on the subject NP, and there is some "obvious" referent-picking function that, given a person who has had an operation, yields a hospital administrator. The function goes from the fact of an operation, to the inference that it took place in a hospital, to the fact that hospitals have administrators. (109e) completely eliminates the possibility that this is a case of binding, since it does not even contain an NP *an operation*.

In chapter 5 we observed a similar phenomenon in the analysis of Superiority, which we may now understand to be treated by the Leftness Condition. There we saw that when two *wh*-phrases are in a dependency relation, the dependent one must follow the independent one. We did not discuss the issue then, but I think the same considerations just brought to bear on (102) would suggest that in Superiority cases as well, the dependency cannot be reduced to a case of pronoun binding. Thus, in (110)

(110) Who bought what?

what is dependent on *who* in the way mentioned there, but there is no sensible way to include a pronoun coreferential with *who* in the NP *what*.

Leftness then is a general condition blocking dependence: if X precedes Y, then X cannot depend on Y, even though X and Y may corefer. On the other hand, c-command (or, if I am right, th-command) is a general condition on equality of reference: if X c-commands Y, then X and Y must be disjoint in reference, even though neither depends on the other.

Properly speaking, it is two theta roles that do or do not corefer, not two NPs. Furthermore, th-command is defined directly as a relation among theta roles. Leftness, on the other hand, must hold of the syntactic realization of theta roles—that is, of the NPs that theta roles are assigned to:

(111) *Weak Crossover Condition*
      Role A cannot depend on role B for its reference if the position to which A is assigned precedes the position to which B is assigned.

An immediate consequence of (111) is that WCO, or bound anaphora in general, will exhibit "reconstruction" effects:

(112) Which of her pictures does every painter like t best?

Here, *which of her pictures* is dependent on *every painter* and seems to precede it. However, in fact the relation is between the subject and object arguments of *like* (*liker* and *likee*), and the likee theta role is assigned to a position that follows the position to which the liker role is assigned.

Now, (112) actually exhibits two dependencies: *her*, as well as *which of her pictures*, is dependent on *every painter*. The theta position of one of these, *which of her pictures*, does follow *every painter* (it is the trace position), but the theta position of the other, *her*, does not. Why then does (112) not violate the WCO Condition, as stated in (111)? I think the answer is a sort of A-over-A effect: when two NPs are dependent, one inside the other, and the containing one is dependent *because of* the contained one, then only the containing one counts. In a sense, the dependence of the contained one is parasitic on the dependence of its parent. We might revise the WCO Condition to read as follows:

(113) *Leftness Condition*
      If A th-commands B, role A cannot depend on role B if the position to which A is assigned precedes the position to which B is assigned.

Recall that Condition C bars equality of reference, whereas this condition bars dependence of reference. However, this condition bars dependence in a narrower set of circumstances: only if the expression of the dependent role precedes the expression of the independent role.

Under this formulation, the Leftness Condition simply does not hold between *his* and *everyone* in (107a) directly. Rather, *his* makes *his mother* depend on *everyone*, and the WCO Condition bars this dependence. So this is why bound anaphora can hold in (112): the theta position of *which of her pictures* does follow *every painter*, and so may depend on it, consistent with (113); and the relation between *her* and *every painter* is not ruled out by (113) because *her* does not th-command *every painter*.

At least part of the embedding effects discussed earlier can be accounted for in these terms. Consider again (92b–c), repeated here:

(114) a. That he might someday meet the Queen inspired every British soldier.
     b. *The girl that he met in front of him in the registration line married every incoming student.

Apparently, only NP dependencies are barred by the WCO Condition. In (114b) the pronoun *he*, if bound to *every incoming student*, renders the subject (*the girl that he met in front of him in the registration line*) dependent, and hence ungrammatical. But the *he* in the sentential subject in (114a) has no such effect, since no NP is rendered dependent by the pronoun. One must ask, of course, why the sentential subject is not itself barred from being made dependent on the quantified object—that is, why the Leftness Condition applies only to NPs. Moreover, the cases where a pronoun occurs in a preceding conjoined clause are still not accounted for (see (92c)).

Further corroboration comes from the interaction of adverbs, modals, and quantified nouns. In general, there is no requirement that a quantified NP in the scope of a modal or adverb appear to right of that modal or adverb:

(115) a. Someone usually came early.
     b. John bought something pretty usually.
     c. Someone must be here when the gates open.

In each of these cases the indefinite NP can be very naturally interpreted as inside the scope of the modal or adverb in the sentence. Hence, the Leftness Condition is truly limited to NP-to-NP dependencies.

The separation of dependence (governed by Leftness) from coreference (governed by the binding theory) distinguishes the proposal made here from that of Higginbotham (1983), which sought to reduce the binding theory to conditions on antecedence.

If this line of reasoning is correct, then the Leftness Condition introduces a new semantic element, dependence, not found in Conditions A, B, C; it is not simply a further structural term compounded with th-command.

The Leftness Condition differs from the other conditions of the binding theory in two interesting ways. First, it is stated in terms of precedence, whereas the binding conditions are stated in terms of th-command. For Conditions A, B, C, leftness plays no role. For example, in the following sentences *John* and *him* or *he* cannot be coreferential (regardless of course of whether there is a preceding discourse antecedent):

(116) a. John likes him.
      b. He likes John.

This is because Conditions B and C are indifferent to precedence.

The second way that the binding conditions differ from the Leftness Condition is that the binding theory holds whether or not the theta roles are actually expressed. This is illustrated in the following sentences, from Ross 1969 (see also section 6.1.1):

(117) a. The realization that John had won surprised him.
      b. The realization that the Queen was dead inspired every British soldier.

In (117a) *John* is understood to be distinct from the *realizer* role of *realization*, and this follows if the coreferential possibilities of implicit, unexpressed roles are regulated by the binding theory. On the other hand, (117b) permits the *realizer* role of *realization* to be bound by the quantifier in object position; this shows that the Leftness Condition does not hold of unrealized theta roles, just of their realizations.

I think these two features of the binding theory are connected, and that they distinguish it from the Leftness Condition: the binding theory holds of theta roles, whereas the Leftness Condition holds of expressions of theta roles. This difference may be connected as well to the fact that the binding theory regulates coreference, whereas the Leftness Condition regulates dependence. Coreference is a relation among arguments, whereas dependence is a relation among realizations of arguments.

That the Leftness Condition does not govern patterns of coreference, but only patterns of dependence, can be argued for in several other ways.

We saw in chapter 5 that Superiority obeys the Leftness Condition, in that the unmoved *wh*-phrase is dependent on the moved *wh*-phrase. We saw further that some locally ungrammatical cases become grammatical when embedded in the right matrix:

(118) a. *Where did who go?
      b. Who knows where who went?

In (118a) *who* is dependent on *where*, but precedes its trace, so ungrammaticality results. In (118b), on the other hand, although *who* precedes the trace of *where*, the sentence is nevertheless grammatical, since *who* need not depend on *where*, but may instead depend on *who*, whose trace it follows. This shows that it is not the configuration that is being ruled out, as certain accounts of superiority might suggest (accounts based on the ECP, for example), but rather dependence.

V. Déprez (personal communication) notes that the same point can be made with respect to a variety of cases that have been treated under the rubric of "weakest crossover" by Lasnik and Stowell (L&S) (1991). A "standard" or ECP account of weak crossover would deem all of these cases ill formed, but they are not; the Leftness Condition construed as a condition on dependence does not rule them out. For example, L&S consider the case of a pronoun preceding a parasitic gap, as in the following, like their (23):

(119) What book did the police confiscate t before its author renounced t?

Here the local configuration of t and *its* in the *before* clause should be enough to prevent binding, but it does not. L&S solve this dilemma by positing that there is a different sort of operator binding the t, and that this operator (or its trace) is not subject to Leftness. This is a poor solution on general grounds, and it suffers empirically as well. In the following example the two traces are surely equivalent, since the structure is a coordinate structure, and therefore are bound by one and the same *wh*-phrase in Comp:

(120) What book did the police confiscate t and its author renounce t?

These two cases are surely the same. If Leftness blocks not coreference but dependence, then in both of these cases we can plausibly say that the pronoun is dependent on the trace in the first clause, not on the trace that follows it, and so Leftness is not violated.

Another sort of case in which Leftness may be invoked is inalienable possession constructions. In these constructions the possessor must precede the inalienable possessed thing:

(121) a. I gave John a headache.
      b. *I gave a headache to John.

Perhaps this is because an inalienably possessed thing exists only in connection with its possessor (this could be what the term means); in that case the referent of an NP denoting an inalienably possessed thing would be dependent on the NP denoting its possessor, and Leftness would demand that one precede the other. I think that this view can shed light on the following examples:

(122) a. *I gave a headache to John.   [not my headache]
    b. I gave John a headache.
    c. I gave John a cold.   [not my cold]
    d. I gave a cold to John.   [my cold]
    e. I gave an idea to John.   [my idea]
    f. I gave John an idea.   [not my idea]
    g. J'ai   (un) mal à la tête.   [no article means dependent]
       I have (a) headache
    h. J'ai donné un mal à la tête à Pierre.
       I gave   a headache   to Pierre
    i. *J'ai donné mal à la tête à Pierre.
       I gave   headache   to Pierre
    j. Je lui   ai donné mal à la tête.
       I   him gave   headache

A cold differs from a headache in that it can exist independently of the person who has it; that is, someone else can have it and can transmit it. Thus, the reference of an NP denoting a cold is not dependent on the possessor; hence the possibility of (122c). Ideas are ambiguously like colds or headaches, with the result that (122e) and (122f) have different presuppositions: (122e) carries a presupposition that I had the idea that I gave John, but (122f) does not have this presupposition. Again, if an idea is had by more than one, then it is an entity that exists independently of the person who has it.

Similar facts hold in French (V. Déprez, personal communication), where article-less NPs denote inalienably possessed items; interestingly, clitic movement is sufficient to satisfy the Leftness Condition (122j) where the possessed item is inalienable.

6.4.3 Weak Crossover and Quantifier Scope Interactions
In this last section we explore a tentative extension of the coverage of the Leftness Condition, which unites WCO phenomena with known asymmetries in quantifier interpretation. If correct, the extension suggests again the great dissimilarity between the Leftness Condition and the binding theory.

We have formulated the Leftness Condition in terms of "referential dependence." In a sentence with two quantified NPs, one universal and the other existential, the latter can be understood to be "referentially dependent" on the former, in that for each choice of an element in the domain of the universal, a possibly different element in the domain of the existential is referred to. So, in (123),

(123) Every boy likes some girl.

for each boy, a possibly different girl makes it true that that boy likes that girl. On this reading, (123) conforms to the Leftness Condition, since the dependent NP follows the one it depends on. In general, a narrow scope quantifier will depend on higher scoped quantifiers for its reference, and therefore must follow them, by the Leftness Condition.

In fact, though, (123) has an opposite reading, where *some girl* is given wide scope, and one might wonder why the proposed extension of the Leftness Condition does not rule it out. It would, except that on that reading, the NP *every boy* is in fact not dependent on the existential—it has the same value, no matter what value is assigned to *some girl*. In general, a universal is not dependent on an existential whose scope it is in, the way an existential is dependent on a universal whose scope it is in.

When we look at the converse of (123), we find the interpretations more restricted:

(124) some girl likes every boy.
      *Every boy x (Some girl $y(x$ likes $y))$

The overwhelming interpretation of (123) is the one in which *some girl* has wide scope and *every boy* has narrow scope. The other interpretation, the wide universal reading, is gotten only with great difficulty. This is because on that reading, the subject is dependent on the universal for its interpretation, but precedes it. The Leftness Condition thus successfully distinguishes these two cases, (123) and (124), and explains why one has a narrower set of readings than the other.

In the face of this asymmetry, it has been supposed (e.g., by Fodor and Sag (1982)), that the indefinite NP is ambiguous. On the one hand, it is an item with scope, and on the other hand, it is a "referential" item; and the very wide scope usage is really the latter.

However, an examination of sentences with two indefinites gives a different picture. With two plural indefinites, there is detectable dependency no matter which has wide scope. The notion that the indefinite is ambiguous is not consistent with the fact that the preferred reading for (125a) is the ridiculous "polyglot" interpretation, and the other reading (the preferred reading for (125b)) is essentially not available:

(125) a. Less than 1000 people know 1500 languages.
      b. 1500 languages are known by less than 1000 people.
         1000 languages (1500 people $(\dots))$

    c. These languages are said to be dying out, because less than
       1000 people know them.
    d. These men have two wives.

Since (125a) and (125b) have two indefinite NPs, if the indefinite were
ambiguous, we might expect all readings to be possible. In fact, though,
we find exactly the same sort of restriction we found before: a dependent
NP must follow the NP it is dependent on, giving a single dominant
reading for each of (125a) and (125b).

The proponent of ambiguity must explain why (125a), for example,
cannot have the interpretation in (126),

(126) [Less than 1000 people]$_i$ [t$_i$ know [1500 languages]$_{ref}$]$_s$.

where *1500 languages* is taken as referential, and *less than 1000 people* as
scopal. (125d) is an uncontroversial example of exactly this sort, and it
shows that in such a case the scopal NP can receive a nonspecific interpretation—*two wives* need not refer to a single pair of women. This would
give us the reading for (126) where there were 1500 fixed languages, and a
different 1000 people for each, a reading (125a) does not have. I conclude
from this that the indefinite does not have a "referential" interpretation
different from its quantified interpretation.

I concur with the arguments of Kripke (1977), who points out that
(127) is three-ways ambiguous,

(127) Hoover charged that the Berrigans plotted to kidnap a high
      American official.

depending on whether the embedded object takes scope under *plotted*,
scope under *charged*, or matrix scope, and so a two-way distinction will
not suffice. I do not think that scope gives the full story on how definite
descriptions interact with intensional contexts. Consider the following
sentences, for example:

(128) a. John thinks a Belgian jazzist committed a murder.
      b. Someone on the 4th floor committed a murder, but I don't
         know which one.

Consider the situation in which no one committed any murder, and where
John has uttered (128b). If I happen to know, but John does not, that the
4th floor residents are all Belgian jazzists, I can report his belief with
(128a), even though this would not be his way of putting it. I take respon-
sibility for the form of the description (RFD). So, although the description is the speaker's, the scope of the quantifier is beneath *think*. RFD is

distinct from scope. RFD is assigned logophorically, to agents of saying or thinking. RFD can be assigned only at the same level or higher, not to an agent lower than the scope of the quantifier. RFD extends to elements of the sentence other than NPs as well, elements that do not undergo QR at all (see Williams, in preparation).

I think that examples like (126) also rule against the theory proposed by Heim (1982), where multiple existentials can be bound by a single covert existential quantifier. If this is possible, then why are (125a) and (125b) not both freely ambiguous? In my view, an existential may be unselectively bound by an overt NP quantifier (and when it is, it is subject to Leftness, since it shows weak crossover effects; see section 2.5.2); or it can generate its own quantifier.

In fact, singular indefinites take wide scope more easily than universals because they "complicate" the interpretation less in their wide scope readings; items falling in their scope do not become dependent on them for their reference, the way items in the scope of a universal or plural indefinite do. This "pragmatic" account perhaps fully explains the observed asymmetries between indefinite NPs and universals.

Wide scope for universals in object position is difficult to get, but not impossible. This is what we might expect if it were governed by the Leftness Condition—after all, the effect of its prohibitions are weak (hence the term *weak crossover*). Consider the following examples:

(129) a. Less than 1000 people know 1500 LANGUAGES.
         1500 languages (1000 people (p know l))
      b. Less than 1000 people know that language.
      c. His mother likes John.

To my ear, (129a) is grammatical under the indicated interpretation only when *1500 languages* receives heavy stress. This interpretation violates Leftness, so we expect the reading not to be normally available; but why should heavy stress make such a difference?

In parallel cases involving definite pronoun anaphora, already discussed but repeated in (129c), we saw that the coreference was permitted so long as *his* was dependent not on *John*, but on some previous occurrence in discourse of an antecedent for *his*. But of course in the case of a quantified NP like *1000 people* in its narrow scope usage, there can be no such thing as a previous antecedent to which it is coreferential. Nevertheless, I think something quite similar is going on here.

The reason heavy stress on *1500 languages* makes (129a) so acceptable is not so much the heavy stress itself, but the consequent lack of stress on the rest of the sentence. In (129a), under the intended interpretation, the destressed material constitutes a property, as in (130),

(130) λx(Less than 1000 people know x)

and this property is presupposed to have occurred, or be under discussion, in previous discourse; (129a) asserts that 1500 languages have this property. An utterance of something like (129b) would be sufficient to give rise to this presupposition, to put the property in the air; the destressing then signals this presupposition. In a sense, then, *1000 people* is not dependent on *1500 languages* here, but rather on the discourse antecedent for the property, of which it is a part. In this way, this example closely resembles the previously discussed cases of Leftness with pronouns and definite antecedents: certain meanings are not absolutely barred, but make strong presuppositions about the preceding discourse.

We are supposing here that quantifier scope interactions and WCO phenomena are governed by the same law, Leftness, a law forbidding backward dependencies. We may base a sort of argument for this identification on parallel behavior of the two phenomena across a variety of constructions. For example, the double object construction in English is particularly resistant to backward dependencies, at least compared to the dative "NP *to* NP" construction. When we examine both quantifier scope interactions and pronominal binding in this context, we find parallel behavior:

(131) *WCO*
  a. *I assigned her daughter every congresswoman.   every$_i$ ... her$_i$
  b. ?I assigned her daughter to every congresswoman.   every$_i$ ... her$_i$

(132) *Quantifier scope interaction*
  a. *I assigned a reporter every congresswoman.   every (... a ...)
  b. ?I assigned a reporter to every congresswoman.   every (... a ...)

In both cases the (a) sentence (the double object case) is quite incapable of having the meaning that would necessitate a backward dependency, whereas the (b) sentence ("NP *to* NP") allows it, at least marginally.

References

Aoun, J., N. Hornstein, and D. Sportiche. 1981. Some aspects of wide scope quantification. *Journal of Linguistic Research* 1:69–95.

Baker, M. 1983. Noun incorporation in Iroquoian. Ms., MIT.

Barss, A., and H. Lasnik. 1986. A note on anaphora and double objects. *Linguistic Inquiry* 17:347–54.

Belletti, A. 1988. The Case of unaccusatives. *Linguistic Inquiry* 19:1–34.

Belletti, A., and L. Rizzi. 1988. Psych verbs and theta theory. *Natural Language & Linguistic Theory* 6:291–352.

Besten, H. den. 1982. Some remarks on the ergative hypothesis. In *Groninger Arbeiten zur germanistischen Linguistik 21*, 61–81. University of Groningen.

Bloomfield, L. 1911. A set of postulates for the science of language. In *Readings in linguistics I*, ed. M. Joos, 26–31. Chicago: University of Chicago Press.

Borer, H. 1984. The Projection Principle and rules of morphology. In *Proceedings of NELS 14*. GLSA, University of Massachusetts, Amherst.

Bresnan, J. 1972. Theory of complementation in English syntax. Doctoral dissertation, MIT.

Browning, M. A. 1987. Null operator constructions. Doctoral dissertation, MIT.

Browning, M. A., and E. Karimi. 1990. Scrambling to object position in Persian. Ms., Princeton University.

Burton, S., and J. Grimshaw. 1992. Coordination and VP-internal subjects. *Linguistic Inquiry* 23:305–13.

Burzio, L. 1986. *Italian syntax: A Government and Binding approach*. Dordrecht: Reidel.

Chierchia, G. 1984. Topics in the syntax and semantics of infinitives and gerunds. Doctoral dissertation, University of Massachusetts, Amherst.

Chierchia, G. 1992. Functional *wh* and weak crossover. In *The proceedings of the Tenth West Coast Conference on Formal Linguistics*, 75–90. Stanford Linguistics Association, Stanford.

Chomsky, N. 1955. *The logical structure of linguistic theory*. Ms., Harvard University. (Published by Plenum, New York, 1975; University of Chicago Press, Chicago, 1985.)

Chomsky, N. 1957. *Syntactic structures*. The Hague: Mouton.

Chomsky, N. 1970. Remarks on nominalization. In *Readings in English transformational grammar*, ed. R. A. Jacobs and P. S. Rosenbaum. Waltham, Mass.: Ginn.

Chomsky, N. 1972. *Studies on semantics in generative grammar*. The Hague: Mouton.

Chomsky, N. 1973. Conditions on transformations. In *A festschrift for Morris Halle*, ed. S. Anderson and P. Kiparsky, 232–86. New York: Holt, Rinehart and Winston.

Chomsky, N. 1981. *Lectures on government and binding*. Dordrecht: Foris.

Chomsky, N. 1986. *Barriers*. Cambridge, Mass.: MIT Press.

Chomsky, N. 1991. Some notes on economy of derivation and representation. In *Principles and parameters in comparative grammar*, ed. R. Freidin, 417–54. Cambridge, Mass.: MIT Press.

Cinque, G. 1990. *Types of Ā-dependencies*. Cambridge, Mass.: MIT Press.

Davidson, D. 1967. The logical form of action sentences. In *The logic of action and decision*, ed. N. Rescher. Pittsburgh: Pittsburgh University Press.

Déprez, V. 1988. Raising in Haitian Creole: A case of NP movement. Ms., MIT.

Déprez, V. 1990a. On the typology of syntactic positions and the nature of chains. Doctoral dissertation, MIT.

Déprez, V. 1990b. On two ways of moving the verb in French. In *Papers on wh-movement*, 47–85. (MIT Working Papers in Linguistics 13.) Department of Linguistics and Philosophy, MIT.

Diesing, M. 1990. Verb movement and the subject position in Yiddish. *Natural Language & Linguistic Theory* 8:41–79.

Di Sciullo, A. M., and E. Williams. 1986. *On the definition of word*. Cambridge, Mass.: MIT Press.

Dowty, D., R. Wall, and S. Peters. 1981. *Introduction to Montague semantics*. Dordrecht: Reidel.

Emonds, J. 1976. *A transformational approach to English syntax*. New York: Academic Press.

Emonds, J. 1978. The verbal complex V'-V in French. *Linguistic Inquiry* 9:151–75.

Emonds, J. 1985. *A unified theory of syntactic categories*. Dordrecht: Foris.

Fiengo, R. 1974. Semantic conditions on surface structure. Doctoral dissertation, MIT.

Fodor, J. D. 1978. Parsing strategies and constraints on transformations. *Linguistic Inquiry* 9:427–73.

Fodor, J. D., and I. Sag. 1982. Referential and quantificational indefinites. *Linguistics and Philosophy* 5:355–98.

Freidin, R. 1978. Cyclicity and the theory of grammar. *Linguistic Inquiry* 9:519–49.

Gazdar, G. 1982. Phrase Structure Grammar. In *The nature of syntactic representation*, ed. P. Jacobson and G. K. Pullum, 131–86. Dordrecht: Reidel.

Geis, M. 1970. Adverbial subordinate clauses in English. Doctoral dissertation, MIT.

Grimshaw, J. 1990. *Argument structure*. Cambridge, Mass.: MIT Press.

Haïk, I. 1985. The syntax of operators. Doctoral dissertation, MIT.

Heim, I. 1982. The semantics of definite and indefinite noun phrases. Doctoral dissertation, University of Massachusetts, Amherst.

Higginbotham, J. 1983. Logical Form, binding, and nominals. *Linguistic Inquiry* 14:395–420.

Higginbotham, J. 1985. On semantics. *Linguistic Inquiry* 16:547–93.

Higginbotham, J. 1986. Elucidations of meaning. Ms., MIT.

Higgins, F. R. 1972. The pseudocleft construction in English. Doctoral dissertation, MIT.

Holmberg, A. 1986. Word order and syntactic features. Doctoral dissertation, University of Stockholm.

Hornstein, N., and A. Weinberg. 1981. Case theory and preposition stranding. *Linguistic Inquiry* 12:55–91.

Huang, C.-T. J. 1982. Logical relations in Chinese and the theory of grammar. Doctoral dissertation, MIT.

Jackendoff, R. 1972. *Semantic interpretation in generative grammar*. Cambridge, Mass.: MIT Press.

Jaeggli, O. 1980. On some phonologically-null elements in syntax. Doctoral dissertation, MIT.

Jaeggli, O. 1986. Passive. *Linguistic Inquiry* 17:587–622.

Jenkins, L. 1975. *The English existential*. Tübingen: Niemeyer.

Jespersen, O. 1924. *The philosophy of grammar*. New York: Henry Holt and Co.

Johnson, K. 1988. Clausal gerunds, the ECP, and government. *Linguistic Inquiry* 19:583–609.

Kayne, R. 1975. *French syntax*. Cambridge, Mass.: MIT Press.

Kayne, R. 1984. *Connectedness and binary branching*. Dordrecht: Foris.

Klima, E. 1964. Negation in English. In *The structure of language: Readings in the philosophy of language*, ed. J. A. Fodor and J. J. Katz, 246–323. Englewood Cliffs, N.J.: Prentice-Hall.

Koopman, H. 1984. *The syntax of verbs*. Dordrecht: Foris.

Koopman, H., and D. Sportiche. 1982. Variables and the Bijection Principle. *The Linguistic Review* 2:139–60.

Koopman, H., and D. Sportiche. 1988. Subjects. Ms., UCLA.

Koster, J. 1986. The relation between pro-drop, scrambling, and verb movement. Ms., University of Groningen.

Koster, J. 1987. *Domains and dynasties*. Dordrecht: Foris.

Kratzer, A. 1989. Stage-level and individual-level predicates. Ms., University of Massachusetts, Amherst.

Kripke, S. 1977. Speaker's reference and semantic reference. In *The philosophy of language*, ed. A. P. Martinich, 249–67. Oxford: Oxford University Press.

Kroch, A. 1989. Amount quantification, referentiality, and long movement. Ms., University of Pennsylvania.

Kuno, S. 1976. Gapping: A functional analysis. *Linguistic Inquiry* 7:300–318.

Laka, I. 1990. Negation in syntax: On the nature of functional categories and projections. Doctoral dissertation, MIT.

Larson, R. 1988. On the double object construction. *Linguistic Inquiry* 19:335–91.

Lasnik, H., and M. Saito. 1992. *Move α*. Cambridge, Mass.: MIT Press.

Lasnik, H., and T. Stowell. 1991. Weakest crossover. *Linguistic Inquiry* 22:687–720.

Lewis, D. 1975. Adverbs of quantification. In *Formal semantics in natural language*, ed. E. Keenan, 3–15. Cambridge: Cambridge University Press.

Longobardi, G. 1985. Connectedness, scope, and c-command. *Linguistic Inquiry* 16:163–92.

Manzini, M. R. 1992. *Locality: A theory and some of its empirical consequences*. Cambridge, Mass.: MIT Press.

May, R. 1977. The grammar of quantification. Doctoral dissertation, MIT.

May, R. 1985. *Logical Form: Its structure and derivation*. Cambridge, Mass.: MIT Press.

Milsark, G. 1974. Existential sentences in English. Doctoral dissertation, MIT.

Mitchell, J. 1986. The formal semantics of point of view. Doctoral dissertation, University of Massachusetts, Amherst.

Mithun, M. 1983. The evolution of noun incorporation. *Language* 60:847–94.

Moltmann, F. 1990. Scrambling in German and the definiteness/specificity effect. Ms., MIT.

Moortgat, M. 1984. A Fregean restriction on metarules. In *Proceedings of NELS 14*, 303–24. GLSA, University of Massachusetts, Amherst.

Moro, A. 1991. *There* as a raised predicate. Ms., University of Venice.

Neeleman, A. 1992. The VP puzzle revisited: Complex predicates in Dutch and English. Ms., University of Utrecht.

Obenauer, H.-G. 1985. On the identification of empty categories. *The Linguistic Review* 4:153–202.

Pesetsky, D. 1982. Paths and categories. Doctoral dissertation, MIT.

Pesetsky, D. 1987. *Wh*-in-situ: Movement and unselective binding. In *The representation of (in)definiteness*, ed. E. Reuland and A. G. B. Ter Meulen, 98–129. Cambridge, Mass.: MIT Press.

Pollock, J.-Y. 1989. Verb movement, Universal Grammar, and the structure of IP. *Linguistic Inquiry* 20:365–424.

Postal, P. 1971. *Crossover phenomena*. New York: Holt, Rinehart and Winston.

Pustejovsky, J. 1984. Studies in generalized binding. Doctoral dissertation, University of Massachusetts, Amherst.

Reinhart, T. 1983. *Anaphora and semantic interpretation*. London: Croom Helm.

Reinhart, T., and E. Reuland. 1991. Anaphoric territories. Ms., University of Tel Aviv and University of Groningen.

Riemsdijk, H. van. 1978. *A case study in syntactic markedness*. Leiden: Peter de Ridder Press.

Riemsdijk, H. van, and E. Williams. 1981. NP-Structure. *The Linguistic Review* 1:171–217.

Rizzi, L. 1982. *Issues in Italian syntax*. Dordrecht: Foris.

Roeper, T. 1987. Implicit arguments and the head-complement relation. *Linguistic Inquiry* 18:267–310.

Ross, J. R. 1967. Constraints on variables in syntax. Doctoral dissertation, MIT.

Ross, J. R. 1969. On the cyclic nature of English pronominalization. In *Modern studies in English*, ed. D. A. Reibel and S. A. Schane. Englewood Cliffs, N.J.: Prentice-Hall.

Selkirk, E. 1972. The phrase phonology of English and French. Doctoral dissertation, MIT.

Sells, P. 1987. Aspects of logophoricity. *Linguistic Inquiry* 18:445–79.

Sengupta, G. 1990. Binding and scrambling in Bangla. Doctoral dissertation, University of Massachusetts, Amherst.

Solan, L. 1978. Anaphora in child language. Doctoral dissertation, University of Massachusetts, Amherst.

Speas, M. 1986. Adjunctions and projections in syntax. Doctoral dissertation, MIT.

Sportiche, D. 1988. A theory of floating quantifiers and its corollaries for constituent structure. *Linguistic Inquiry* 19:425–49.

Stowell, T. 1983. Subjects across categories. *The Linguistic Review* 2:285–312.

Talmy, L. 1985. Lexicalization patterns. In *Language typology and syntactic description*, ed. T. Shopen, 57–149. Cambridge: Cambridge University Press.

Travis, L. 1984. Parameters and effects of word order variation. Doctoral dissertation, MIT.

Vikner, S. 1990. Verb movement and the licensing of NP positions in the Germanic languages. Doctoral dissertation, University of Geneva.

Wasow, T. 1972. Anaphoric relations in English. Doctoral dissertation, MIT.

Webelhuth, G. 1989. Syntactic saturation phenomena and the modern Germanic languages. Doctoral dissertation, University of Massachusetts, Amherst.

Williams, E. 1971. Small clauses in English. Ms., MIT.

Williams, E. 1974. Rule ordering in syntax. Doctoral dissertation, MIT.

Williams, E. 1977. Discourse and Logical Form. *Linguistic Inquiry* 8:101–39.

Williams, E. 1978a. Across-the-board rule application. *Linguistic Inquiry* 9:31–43.

Williams, E. 1978b. Notes on lexical theory. Ms., University of Massachusetts, Amherst.

Williams, E. 1979. The French causative construction. Ms., University of Massachusetts, Amherst.

Williams, E. 1980. Predication. *Linguistic Inquiry* 11:208–38.

Williams, E. 1981a. Argument structure and morphology. *The Linguistic Review* 1:81–114.

Williams, E. 1981b. Language acquisition, markedness, and phrase structure. In *Language acquisition and linguistic theory*, ed. S. Tavakolian. Cambridge, Mass.: MIT Press.

Williams, E. 1981c. On the notions "lexically related" and "head of a word." *Linguistic Inquiry* 12:245–74.

Williams, E. 1982a. Another argument that passive is transformational. *Linguistic Inquiry* 13:160–63.

Williams, E. 1982b. The NP cycle. *Linguistic Inquiry* 13:277–95.

Williams, E. 1983. Against small clauses. *Linguistic Inquiry* 14:287–308.

Williams, E. 1984. *There*-insertion. *Linguistic Inquiry* 15:131–53.

Williams, E. 1985a. NP trace in theta theory. Ms., University of Massachusetts, Amherst.

Williams, E. 1985b. PRO in NP. *Natural Language & Linguistic Theory* 3:277–95.

Williams, E. 1986a. NP trace in theta theory. *Linguistics and Philosophy* 4:433–47.

Williams, E. 1986b. A reassignment of the functions of LF. *Linguistic Inquiry* 17:265–99.

Williams, E. 1987. Implicit arguments, the binding theory, and control. *Natural Language & Linguistic Theory* 5:151–80.

Williams, E. 1989. The anaphoric nature of θ-roles. *Linguistic Inquiry* 20:425–56.

Williams, E. Forthcoming a. Bach's generalization and Rizzi's pro. *Canadian Journal of Linguistics*.

Williams, E. Forthcoming b. The clause as a coordinate structure. To appear in *Proceedings of GLOW 1990*.

Williams, E. In preparation. Why crossover? Ms., Princeton University.

Wyngaert, G. vanden. 1989. Object shift as an A-movement rule. In *MIT working papers in linguistics* 11. Department of Linguistics and Philosophy, MIT.

Zanuttini, R. 1990. On the relevance of tense for sentential negation. Ms., University of Pennsylvania and University of Geneva.

Zubizarreta, M. L. 1985. The relation between morphophonology and morphosyntax: The case of Romance causatives. *Linguistic Inquiry* 16:247–89.

Index